AUSTRALIA'S GAME

Stories, Essays, Verse & Drama
Inspired by the Australian Game of Football

The Slattery Media Group Pty Ltd
1 Albert St, Richmond
Victoria, Australia, 3121

National Library of Australia Cataloguing-in-Publication entry
Title: Australia's Game: stories, essays, verse & drama inspired by the Australian game
            of football game of Australian football / edited by Ross Fitzgerald and Ken Spillman.
ISBN: 9780987500205 (paperback)
Subjects: Australian football–Anecdotes.
            Australian football–Biography.
            Australian wit and humor.
            Essays
Other Authors/Contributors:
            Fitzgerald, Ross, 1944- editor

            Spillman, Ken, 1959- editor.

Dewey Number: 796.336

Group Publisher: Geoff Slattery
Editorial Manager: Bronwyn Wilkie
Creative Director: Guy Shield
Cover Design: Kate Slattery

Printed and bound in Australia by Griffin

slatterymedia.com

AUSTRALIA'S GAME

Stories, Essays, Verse & Drama
Inspired by the Australian Game of Football

visit *slatterymedia.com*

About the Editors

Ross Fitzgerald was born in Melbourne on Christmas Day, 1944. Emeritus Professor in History and Politics at Griffith University, he is well known as a historian, biographer and social and political commentator.

He is the author of five satirical novels and has worked as script editor, historical adviser and co-producer of documentary television and film, including ABC TV's *Red Ted and the Great Depression* (1995) and *The Legend of Fred Paterson* (1996). Recent books include his memoir *My Name is Ross: An Alcoholic's Journey* and two co-authored biographies, *Alan ("The Red Fox") Reid*, which was short-listed for the 2011 National Biography Award, and *Austen Tayshus: Merchant of Menace*.

Fitzgerald writes for *The Weekend Australian*, *The Canberra Times* and *The Sydney Morning Herald* and regularly appears on radio and television. Ross Fitzgerald and his wife, artist Lyndal Moor, now live in Redfern, Sydney.

Ken Spillman is the author of around 35 books and editor or co-editor of many others. His work spans the areas of fiction, history, poetry and criticism. In the 20th century he was a prolific author of local and sporting histories, but the Y2K bug caused a regression and he now works primarily in the area of books for young people.

Spillman's illustrated *Jake* series for young readers appears in more than a dozen countries, with translations into such diverse languages as French, Farsi, Serbian and Vietnamese. The popularity of *Jake* in India has led Spillman to write a number of acclaimed books with Indian characters and settings. He chairs the judging panel for Singapore's inaugural award for children's books and is featured in the major US reference publication, *Contemporary Authors*.

Ken still enjoys kick-to-kick with his sons and his former English teacher. He lives in Girrawheen, Western Australia.

For Bill ('Long Tom') Fitzgerald and Zak Spillman,
with thanks to our contributors—living and dead—and
their families, whose generosity made this book possible.

CONTENTS

About the cover artist

Michael Leunig painted the artwork which has been used as the cover for this book on commission by the AFL for the 1995 *Grand Final Record*. Born in East Melbourne in 1945, he grew up in Footscray and went to Maribyrnong High School before tertiary study at Monash University and Swinburne Film and Television School. A cartoonist, writer, painter and philosopher, his commentary on political, cultural and emotional life now spans more than forty years, often exploring the idea of an innocent and sacred personal world. His newspaper work appears regularly in the *The Age* and *The Sydney Morning Herald*. Well known works include *The Adventures of Vasco Pyjama* and the *Curly Flats* series. He was declared an Australian Living Treasure by the National Trust of Australia in 1999. There has also been a Leunig Melbourne tram.

Introduction

The Things That Matter

Twenty-five years ago, we compiled *The Greatest Game*. It was the kind of book we'd most like to have found on the shelves of our local bookstore—a collection of fine writing about Aussie Rules football. It was the first such book ever published.

Each year, we knew, millions of Australians attended or watched the footy. They argued about it, revelled in it, despaired of it, or even made vain attempts to ignore it. But while the news kept us informed about who had been dropped, traded, injured or suspended, and which teams were winning, losing or facing the prospect of a merger, the bigger picture was hidden away. We asked:

> *What about the things that really matter? What about the heart that aches and the memories that linger? The sleepless nights and the rainy afternoons? What about grandmother's stories and our own hopeless dreams? The ecstasy and the grim despair? Most of all, the sense of loss, and the betrayal of tribes? How often do we turn to the sports pages and read about our own injured and depleted spirit? How often do we read the back page first for hope and confirmation of our fragile identity, for a sense of mythic self? This is the abiding reality of football, the life beyond the transitory, manufactured image.*

The Greatest Game canvassed all this. It was akin to a manifesto. *Yes*, it said—it's okay for footy folk to be cerebral and creative, and for thinking Australians to be footy folk. *Yes*, it said—it's fine to express deep feelings that begin with a game but ultimately transcend it. *Yes*, we said—let's celebrate Aussie Rules as a form of art through our nation's greatest exponents of literature. Reprinted many times, *The Greatest Game* came to be regarded as a classic, influencing a generation of football writers.

In this new volume, we continue to celebrate our Australian game and honour those who have observed it, reflected on it and written about it with a sense of its pervasiveness and grandeur. *Australia's Game* retains the best of *The Greatest Game*, with pieces from many who are now iconic cultural figures—the likes of historian Manning Clark, playwright David Williamson, broadcaster Andrea Stretton and poet Bruce Dawe. Sadly, some contributors are no longer with us—but their work kicks on. In footy tradition the collection also needed some 'ins' to replace pieces omitted. Among the authors running through the banner this time are our finest crime writer, Peter Corris; songwriter Paul Kelly; comedian Peter Helliar; and another of our leading historians, Stuart Macintyre. These days in Australia, it's not just cricket that has a fine literary edge.

Some contributors express a sense of nostalgia about 'the old football'—a kind of yearning for simpler times. Glad for what football has given them—confirmation, hope, a sense of meaning, participation even—they are anxious about what lies ahead. Others are much more positive. We are grateful for all their contributions.

For us, ageing on opposite sides of this vast and still mysterious continent, the compilation of this book—a new edition of an old friend—has been a joy. As writing and football united us in friendship and in work, we again bring our twin passions together for the pleasure of other readers.

Ross Fitzgerald and Ken Spillman
2013

DON WATSON

Lingering Memories of Monster Kicks at Loch

Don Watson was born in 1949 and raised on a dairy farm in the hills of South Gippsland. He played football for Loch (now defunct) in the Bass Valley and Wonthaggi District Football League (also defunct). After undergraduate study at La Trobe University he took a PhD at Monash. He wrote books on Australian history before turning his hand to satire, speeches, films, essays, literary non-fiction and articles for newspapers and journals. For several years he combined writing political satire for the actor Max Gillies with political speeches for the Premier of Victoria, John Cain. In 1992 he became Prime Minister Paul Keating's speech-writer and adviser and his account of those years, *Recollections of a Bleeding Heart: A Portrait of Paul Keating PM*, won a swag of awards including *The Age* Book of the Year, the *Courier-Mail* Book of the Year and the National Biography Award. Among the feature films he has written are *The Man Who Sued God*, starring Billy Connolly and Judy Davis, and *Passion*, a film about Percy Grainger. This essay first appeared in the *Times on Sunday*, 10 May 1987.

T he pundits of the big smoke, the legends, the tyros with moustaches who chose careers in television instead of boundary umpiring, can say that football is on the decline. They can say it until we all abandon the habit of a lifetime and begin reading the front pages first.

Today's decline of League football is nothing. It is a mild dip, at worst. In time it will be seen to have left a small vacuum where a portion of the heart used to be. But it is nothing compared with a broken love affair, or even a punt on the neddies gone astray. It is easy to see why the crowds have fallen off—easier than seeing why everyone feels compelled to write about it. The fifteen-metre penalty, for instance, is a farce, and the change to metrics is only partly responsible. The game is played like a relay race for greyhounds; coaches have the charisma of commissars; Waverley is an historic boil on the nose of Victorian society; and the ABC recruits too many moralisers who judge a footballer not by the length of his kick but by his attitude to life.

It is true that the great players have gone. Not all of them, but far too many. Last year I saw Carlton run on the ground without Rod Ashman, and felt sick. Ashman, who for years brought a Methodist revival to the team's last quarter. Ashman, the only man in memory to forge a path through Mick Nolan's legs, baulking his left by selling the dummy to the Gasometer's mother in the crowd on the right. Ashman was smart—chapel smart. No Ashman, no Barry Gill, no Robertson, Crane and Quirk.

It is like imagining Geelong without Hovey, Gazzard and Renfrey; no Haygarth, Walker and Devine, Norm Sharpe, and many more. All of them wool classers, hence hands as quick as a concert pianist's, their refusal to work with wet balls, and their decisiveness—go for it or no, the judgement was breakfast to them.

Forget Geelong. I did when I saw Jesaulenko play. And Robertson. Robertson never received the acclaim he deserved. Ian Robertson was the longest kick in history. I once saw him put a ball through from the centre of Princes Park. It went through goalpost high and lace up. (The demise of the torp is another blot on the game.) Robertson had a broken finger when he kicked that goal. Next week he lined up with Footscray and, soon after that, with Oakleigh. I have seen Robertson bring Francis Bourke to his knees—to bring him any further would have required an elephant gun or the sudden appearance over Richmond of the Blessed Virgin.

Robbo came from Dalyston, a bleak village frequented by sheep farmers, garfisherfolk and mulleteers near the Borough of Wonthaggi. When the ANZ bank transferred him across the hills to Loch, Robbo signed up with us. We needed him at Loch. The permit player had not put in all year. His credit had run out at the pub, and there were unpleasant murmurings around the hotdog stand on the wing. Those old permit players were brave men; Pud Kees, Ray Poulter, Ron Caruthers, Don Scott (the first) came up our way for about ten quid a match. They stood in the goal square and were murmured at by dairy farmers from one week to the next.

Robertson was heaven sent. He brought not only a reputation for scrupulous and convivial telling, but he could kick. Although he came from sandy country, he revelled in our mud. We trained with him in the pre-season and thought the flag was ours. I remember the night the smoke went up from behind the showers on the Thursday before the first match. There were grins on all our faces.

I suppose the kick-to-kick sessions should have sounded the warning. Robbo ruined them. The ground was not long. We spent all night retrieving balls. In the interest of engaging others in the marking contests, he was asked just to stab pass or handball.

Came the day of the first match. I think it was Glen Alvie we were drawn against. Glen Alvie was a tough side and, like Footscray, master of its own terrain—a hillside. The lambing season made the Glen Alvie players virtually unbeatable; no one could match their skills in the after-birth. But we were drawn at home.

Our selectors had a problem with Robertson. Where to play him? Kicking towards Tuckfields Hill, centre half-back was reckoned most expedient. A deal was done with the proprietor; to have Ian's torps returned by the son, who looked like being an achiever. The southern end presented a greater problem. It was farcical to play your best goal-kicker at full back, but beyond the boundary at that end swirled Alsop's Creek. From any closer than the last line of defence Robertson's spiral punts would have ended up in Bass, and we had no desire to donate our balls to that mob. By mid-winter, when the creek ran a banker, our prize recruit would be a curse. The selectors envisaged matches going on until ten, while teams of urchins with Aladdin lamps retrieved the pill in tin canoes.

In the end there was no alternative. On the Tuesday, Robbo was put on the train with a letter of recommendation from our president to

Carlton's. Saturday night we saw him on *Pelaco Inquest*. Best on ground. No transfer fee.

Our club did not go into mourning, although there was plenty of regret. He was one of nature's gentlemen. Just kicked too far. In a way we were proud. With Richmond wizard Donny Davenport, he was our most celebrated export, although we always reckoned Willy Paterson was as good as any of them, if too light. Not that we got any credit for Robertson. It was always said he came from Dalyston, but we knew that it was Loch he left.

Still, Robbo's sudden and unforeseen departure coincided with a decline in fortune at the club; that and the premature retirement of Ray Humphrey, a peerless centreman in the mould of Whitten. At forty, or so, Ray hung up his boots, and I never saw a better footballer. His mother also was a lion of the club, and his father, with Lyle Davenport, breathed the life of yesteryear into the Loch Football Club. We might have won a string of premierships if the ground had been longer. But it's been a battle ever since. It's true what they say—things are never the same again.

It's the same all over the countryside, I hear. Not so long ago a Swan Hill man, passing through Maldon near midday on a Saturday, thought it wise to catch the butcher there so he might provide his family of five with sausages for tea. At twenty past the hour he found himself unfogging his spectacles in the back pocket for the seconds.

It's an extended season of nostalgia we are going through, I know. It's the long post-urban and industrial disquiet in our hearts. There was nothing like the smell of saveloys wafting from the kero tin at three-quarter time in the thirds. There was nothing like the toot of horns when a goal was scored.

Perhaps our judgement is distorted. Perhaps country football is still the same. Perhaps Loch will rise again, or is, at this very moment, rising. But when I hear my almost teammate, Ian Robertson, broadcasting from the Gold Coast, I think not. When I see the sign outside Victoria Park, saying 'Collingwood v. Bris Bears', I can hardly think at all.

I wonder about country football; all kinds of non-League football.

Are they playing the modern game? It doesn't matter really. It's other things that count. Mighty goals and missed ones, the failures of nerve and confidence, the grubbed pass in the last seconds of cliff-hanging preliminary finals linger as long in our memories as they do in Swan McKay's. Only when one no longer hears the expression, 'the psychological moment', will the game really be in decline.

BARRY OAKLEY

McCarthy's Debut

Barry Oakley was born in Melbourne in 1931. His extraordinary literary output has included plays, novels, short stories, children's books and essays. Oakley shared the Captain Cook Bicentenary Award with Thomas Kenneally and, in 1988, won an Awgie for *The Feet of Daniel Mannix*. He is the author of the classic Australian Rules football novel, *A Salute to the Great McCarthy* (1970) from which this piece is extracted. He explains his otherwise inexplicable allegiance to the Melbourne football team thus: 'When I was very young, support for the Demons sank into my being, leaving a red and navy blue stain that neither age not intelligence would expunge'.

Saturday, and the city invaded. A medieval plague, a hysteria that holds its fever down till the crowds get to the arenas. Five thousand people are homeless in a flood in India: an inch on page nine, never mind, IT'S ON AGAIN—the front page of the *Sun* is all football. In Martin Street, the kids are out early in their team jumpers, their ball thumps the road all morning, thud thud, a muffled drum on this clear sunny day like the beginning of the world.

Before the match, a players' lunch. The chosen, twenty men at a long table, surrounded by the high priests—club president, coach, committeemen. The president, Les Ware, a Khrushchev in a fawn suit, natty polkadot about to pop at the neck, slow moving, with weeping red eyes, cuts his steak with surprisingly deft movements, little finger out at an elegant angle, at his right wrist the gold peep of a watch. He rises, so fat he must have a pillow stuffed under his belt, welcomes us hoarsely, congratulates us all, then presents the jumpers; it's a rite, a lodge, each of us going up in turn to receive his holy robe.

At 1.45 we rise from our seats and sing the team song, then cross a passage to the dressing room. Above us, the noise of feet in the grandstand, thumps and shuffles that beat into my head. I slip ashamed into the can, let my insides drop with a splatter, and come out light as paper. The property stewards have laid out our garments on the trestle tables; crimson jumper, white stripes, and on the back a big 35. My shorts a virgin white, socks a rich burgundy, bright boots freshly studded.

I lie on the table for a rub-down. Charlie the trainer works on me, his broken nose close to my flesh. The smell of liniment pierces me, wakes hidden feelings, stirs my country-town days. My body is stroked and smoothed; I feel a kinship with the essence of football, a crystallised thing of leather and oil; I come to life.

On with the jumper and become 35—a new man, a new number, one of three greenhorns in the side. I watch the other guys changing with the line of summer brown still above their white behinds. I see them sexual and male, all hair and organs, now being pouched in Sumo-wrestlers' straps. Try your best to be normal, like the others, playing it cool and chewing the gum. We're quiet, exchanging only brief words, the bang of locker doors loud as small explosions, the crowd-noise mounting, lapping at the two opaque windows at the far end of the room. The fleet little wingmen showing their sparrow bodies, the big ruckmen proud of their great shoulders. Each of us stripping down to the real man, each in his own world in those last moments before the coach, the great, the irritable, the mean-eyed Twentyman, tries to hammer you into a team. McCarthy? Number 35? Who's he? I sit there waiting while thirty thousand fingers glide over my statistics in the *Football Record*, my bowels cleaned, throat dry, listening to the lions roaring out there and ready to give up the faith.

A bell goes. Right, says Twentyman. Clear the room. Everyone out. The reporters, the hangers-on who know somebody, the pot-bellied ex-players hoping to be noticed, all go. Only the trainers and players are left, a small group in the big room. Twentyman, gloomy and ginger in a long grey overcoat, goes over to a pitted blackboard propped against a wall. Sour and pinched, with a complex roadmap of tiny red veins on each cheek.

'Now listen to me, ready? This is a new year, a new season. Last year? Never mind. Past. Forgotten. This year, we start level with the other mobs. We start level—and we start winning. I want you to think win, eat win, talk win (smacking his fist each time). From now. From the word go. Right?' We nod agreement, mumble yair, yair, hypnotised in thirty seconds flat. 'Our first game? Like hell. We've been playing together for weeks, and now? We're run in, we're ticking over smooth. We know each other—where to look, where to kick. We got youth, right? We got experience, right? We got skill and we got muscle. We're going to bowl 'em over from the word go, knock 'em off balance. The Bears! (He shouts it, with his eyes shut, this is some mad revivalist meeting.) The Bears! The Bears!'

Yair! Carn! Grrr! We're aroused, we make wild animal noises, snort and paw the ground, jump about, smack the fist. He holds out a restraining hand. Right, easy; we got to talk tactics. He works right down the ground, pointer poking away at the abstraction on the blackboard, and in front of goals (four white strokes of chalk) he comes to me.

'And up front? We got McCarthy. Look for him. Feed him. He'll be up against Moose Tucker, one of the greatest animals ever to put on a boot. But McCarthy, you don't have to worry, McCarthy's okay, because you got Fred Yates right up there with you. Right Fred?'

All eyes turn to Fred, fifteen stone of bone and muscle, a wharf labourer, all chin, with LEST WE FORGET tattooed on each bicep.

'S'right,' says Fred. 'I'll watch ya, kid.'

On the clock over the door, the red second hand's going round like a propeller, my guts are potato crisps, at the windows the carnivores bellow for blood. One minute forty seconds to go.

'Listen,' says Twentyman, lean and tall, obsessed. 'It's time to think win. For the next sixty seconds I want every one of you to concentrate, focus your mind on three little letters, W-I-N. Come on. Write it there inside you. And keep your mind fixed on it, right?' (We are in a strange ship, twenty crew in crazy uniforms, outside a tornado, together we pray.) The silence goes on for an age, I hear the spiral twirling of a nervous gut, no thoughts come before me, 'win' is a meaningless word, when suddenly there is this awesome explosion—the other mob's out, I see them prance round in the TV of my mind, slow and stately from a distance, their bare arms oiled and glistening, gazelles in black and white.

Righto, boys. All stand, the big gate pulls back, I mechanically follow the others, boot-stops clattering on the concrete race. Lord have mercy and big Fred keep close, my big-chinned guardian angel and Captain America.

A great space opens up, then closes in with noise. There they are, the enemy, not the other mob, but the watchers, the thirty thousand with violence in their hearts, tiny smoke-puffs everywhere. The captains toss a coin, we lose, I'm pleased—we start against the wind, the ball won't come my way too often. Now we break formation, tail off into our positions. The crowd! I walk towards them, I am an inch high, the fullback's standing up ahead waiting, hands on hips. At first almost invisible against the grey mob, he gradually emerges, grows tall, against all those faces flapping in and out like scenery. I introduce myself to Tucker the Moose, our extended hands brush limply—last vestige of the gentlemanly days, the opposite pole to the bullock charges to come later.

We turn to face the play. *Mama mia!* The umpire, a small man in white, another species, a brain, a whistle with no body, holds up the ball for all to see, then bounces it down hard. The tall ruckmen spring straight up, the roar holds them suspended, then click! The movie comes to life, flicks over at super speed, a dart here, a flurry there, and the ball rockets down the other end. I have a blank watcher feeling, this has nothing to do with me—until the Moose reminds me, his hips against mine, niggling, worrying; I am soon to die.

But Fred Yates is watching, about twenty yards to my right, in the pocket. 'Hey,' he says, 'Hey Moose. You lay a finger on that kid, and I punch you up the throat.'

'Shut up Flintstone,' says Tucker. 'I can take the fucking pair of you. Any place. Any time.'

Wake up! Over in the centre Snowy Adams has the ball, our greyhound wingman. He's bumped, sails high, comes down in a heap, the whistle blows, he's helped to his feet, totters back on white stick legs for his free kick.

Ian Garrett our centre half's in action, races forward, grabs the ball, turns, kicks—towards me! Tucker alongside, I, he, we, race for the ball in mindless madness, I stoop, get one hand to it (that first warm touch of leather!) and am run over by a General Grant. It reminds me of surfing: first you're hit by the board, then these great waves roll over your head as the crowd protests.

I look up to see Tucker and Yates, two monsters, exchanging dinosaur blows, with the umpire yelling breakitup. Incident, incident! Photographers hopping round like sparrows on the side of the field, cameras going peckpeck, with McCarthy the unfortunate victim now registering on the brute public mind. Free kick to that man! Number 35! Who? McCarthy? New recruit, country boy, smart mover, the typewriters going tap tap in the press box. McCarthy kicks, all eyes on him, TV screens in half a million houses show him grubbing the ball off the side of the boot. What a beginning! And the ball's swept up the other end.

'Ya sore, boy? That's just a taste. Today, I flatten you out like you was a tack.'

'I hear ya, Moose,' says Fred. 'Y'got a big boil on the back of yer neck. I'll make it pop like it was a volcano.'

But Moose is out, lumbering, this fine invective is lost, the ball's coming—the way I like it, high, spinning slowly, taking its time. I let him toil on ahead, then put a foot in his back, climb, and pull it down about a mile over his head. The kid! McCarthee! Do I hear the name?

Hold it, freeze it there, cut to Monday morning's paper, where it's in the middle pages. Spectacular Debut. Recruit Notches Six Goals. On the bus, half a hundred commuters have me opened or rolled. With McCarthy anxious to give them a fast nudge and announce that he is the man, here among them, in person. I have the pic even now in my cutting book, the first yellow already on it, Tucker (now running a pub in Brunswick) pushed forward, head down, one pole arm extended, and with a foot in his kidneys, poised up there and comfortable, Orville

Wright McCarthy, taking his first public flight. There was grace and style in that pic, and at work I was a new man. Office boys, executives, typists, tea lady, Ackermann, all reaching out for my hand, how's it Macka, you were great!

PETER CORRIS

Barracking for the Bombers

Peter Corris was born in Stawell, Victoria in 1942. After taking a Master's degree at Monash University and a PhD at the Australian National University, he worked as an academic historian until 1975 when he gave up academia for journalism. He was literary editor of *The National Times* at the time his first novel was published in 1980 and two years later became a full-time fiction writer. Corris is credited with reviving the Australian crime novel with local settings and reference points, and with a series character firmly rooted in Australian culture—Cliff Hardy. In 1999, he received a Lifetime Achievement award at the Ned Kelly Awards for Crime Writing. This essay first appeared in *Best on Ground* by Peter Corris and John Dale (eds., Viking, 2010).

In 1947, when I was five years old, my parents moved from Stawell in the Wimmera to Melbourne. I already had a sense of what sport was all about from having been taken to the major annual event in Stawell—the Stawell Gift, a high-stakes professional footrace. Do I remember the runners, in floppy shorts and black shoes, lined up on their staggered marks, flashing down the grass track and bursting through the tape strung across the finishing posts for each lane? I think so, or I choose to think so.

In Melbourne, for the next seven years I lived in Yarraville, a suburb within the Footscray council area to the west of the city. Yarraville—like the adjacent suburbs Kingsville and Seddon—was an intensely working-class area, and here my support for the Essendon Football Club was irrevocably forged. My street ran from Somerville Road, a major artery, down to acres of waste ground around Stony Creek. It was a short street with perhaps thirty houses on each side, and residents mostly knew each other, although there were two divides—sectarian, between Protestants and Catholics, and according to which of two football clubs, Footscray or Essendon, a household supported. Indifference to football was not unknown, but it was rare.

When I began writing this piece I wondered why I had chosen Essendon, which was not geographically close to Yarraville though still a western suburb, and had rejected Footscray. Essendon was known by the abbreviation the 'Dons', or as the 'Bombers' because their home ground was close to Essendon Airport, where military aircraft had been based in the Second World War. The name Dons meant nothing to me then, although I later associated it with the Spanish Armada:

> *If the Dons sight Devon*
> *I'll quit the port o' Heaven,*
> *An' drum them up the channel*
> *As we drummed them long ago*
> —Henry Newbolt, 'Drake's Drum'

Or it could refer to academics:

> *There was a young man from St John's*
> *Who attempted to bugger the swans,*
> *When up came a porter saying 'Sir, take my daughter,*
> *The swans are reserved for the dons.'*

Nor was I romantically attached to aircraft as I hadn't yet encountered Major James Bigglesworth.

I had to check with my sister, three years older, as to why we opted for Essendon. 'For the basest of reasons,' she said. 'Essendon was doing well at the time and Footscray wasn't. We went for the winners.' If calculated, it was nevertheless a wise decision. In the period of my support to date, the Bombers have carried off eight VFL/AFL premierships and Footscray/Western Bulldogs only one. Eight flags in sixty-two years doesn't seem like a lot but, as everyone knows, they're hard to win.

My parents were utterly uninterested in sport of any kind, but other family members were in the swim. An uncle who had played for Essendon reserves before the war took us to matches at the MCG, and another uncle, who incidentally had run a two-up game in Tobruk and sent enough money home for a deposit on a house, barracked for St Kilda and took us to games at the Junction Oval. With our bachelor uncle, a Footscray supporter who lived with our paternal grandmother two doors away, we went to games at the Western Oval.

In those days, children were admitted to football grounds at half-time without having to pay (or it may have been three-quarter time). My sister remembers us going to the Western Oval after matinees at the Footscray picture theatres—the Sun and the St George. I remember the matinees—the serials and cartoons, and some of the films, the westerns and *Tarzan of the Apes*. I don't remember the games. They must have been Footscray games, but our faith never wavered.

Our support for Essendon was consolidated in 1949 by the arrival and fluorescence of John Coleman, goal kicker extraordinaire. Coleman had kicked 160 goals in his last season of country football and he kicked twelve on debut with Essendon in 1949, and a hundred in the season to become the only first-year player to top the list. Essendon won the premiership that year and the next. Our opportunistic choice was validated, and the team continued to give satisfaction into the 1950s, my school years, without winning premierships. It mostly figured in the finals and won more home-and-away matches than it lost. Just as well, because, like most of the kids I knew, a loss on Saturday gave me the blues until into the middle of the week.

Essendon, and Coleman in particular, provided drama. When Coleman was suspended for striking in retaliation in the last match before the 1951 finals, he pushed through the crowd, stumbled, hit his head and wept. My father called him a 'sook' and added to the ongoing friction between us. Like most Essendon followers, I clung to the belief that the suspension had been a put-up job—that an inducement had been offered to bait Coleman into retaliation and so cripple my team's chances for the flag. No evidence, but none needed. It was obvious. In

1954, Coleman injured his knee and his career was over. I may have wept myself at that.

For decades afterwards, Essendon was in search of a full-forward to duplicate Coleman's charisma. Me too. Ron Evans won the league's goal kicking in 1959 and 1960, but his tallies were less than 100 and he lacked glamour. In the 1960s, hopes were entertained for Ted Fordham. Coached and instructed by Coleman, Fordham—similarly dark-haired and high-flying—topped the list in 1966 with 76 goals, but his performances were erratic in following years. Alan Noonan headed the Bombers' goal-kicking list seven times in the sixties and seventies and wore Coleman's number ten on his back, but never quite captured the magic of the original wearer. Geoff Blethyn was the first Essendon player after Coleman to kick more than 100 goals. He scored 107 in 1972 but was topped by Collingwood's Peter McKenna with 130.

Remembering Blethyn today provides a reminder of the way football was to change. He wore glasses—unthinkable and probably illegal in the modern hard-tackling, blood-conscious game. Both Blethyn and Coleman were slim. Coleman stood at 185 centimetres and only weighed around eighty kilos. Prefigured by Doug Wade in the 1970s, by the 1980s the day of the big 'power forward' had arrived with the likes of Jason Dunstall and Tony Lockett, the latter who eventually kicked more goals in his career than any other player. In the late nineties Essendon found their power forward in Matthew Lloyd, who headed the list in 2000-01 and 2003, and had something of Coleman's magnetism with his high marking and accurate kicking.

But the player I saw who came closest to Coleman in style and performance wasn't a professional footballer at all, but an amateur. The same uncle who'd played for Essendon seconds became an umpire in the Melbourne amateur competition. He regularly took me to games, where I watched with interest, mooched around the dressing sheds and drank Tarax lemonade. Duncan Anderson was full-forward for the University Blues, and I often saw him kick twelve goals in a match, sometimes fourteen. He was tall and lean like Coleman, with a shock of dark hair, and took a towering mark. In the days before the drop punt, Anderson kicked high flat punts that crossed the goal line well above posts, which were much shorter then than they are now. I had the impression that the goal umpires sometimes gave him the benefit of the doubt in recognition of his brilliance.

Many years later I wrote about Anderson in *The National Times*. He wrote to me, thanking me for the tribute. He said that he'd been approached by two VFL clubs at the time, but that he'd opted for a Rhodes Scholarship to Oxford and the diplomatic service. As it happened, his sister and mine were school friends and I knew something of his distinguished career. There was another sad parallel with Coleman—like him, Duncan Anderson died young.

When I reached high school it was gratifying to see John Coleman's name in the record book for the interschool athletics. His record for the triple jump—then called the hop, step and jump—when at University High School had lasted for more than ten years.

At school the best footballers were notables, and at both primary and secondary level there were boys I knew who went on to make names for themselves in senior ranks. At Kingsville Primary, the star players were Mervyn Hobbs and Ian Bryant. Outstanding cricketers and sprinters, they were captains of the house teams and I have a faded fourth-grade photograph with Hobbs and Bryant looking the part, exhibiting better posture than most of the rest of us. I knew Bryant slightly because he was an Essendon supporter. Both went on to play for Footscray, and Bryant also played for Victoria in interstate matches. Hobbs figured in a famous VFL photograph, sailing over the head of a lofty Melbourne ruckman.

Hobbs and Bryant—Anglo names. Other names I remember from our street were Barnes, Hardiman, Jones, Curwood and Ogilvie, but the refugees from Europe had arrived and at school I befriended Hendrik Kip, who was Dutch. The fourth grade photograph shows others whose names I've forgotten, but their clothes were distinctive—scarves and jackets not of a local style. For some reason I recall that one of the boys was Lithuanian. There was no forgetting another of the arrivals—Rita Torrielli, who glowed. Several times I caught a bus not going my way just to watch her. We called them 'Balts', no matter where they came from, and accepted them, but whatever games they had played in Europe took no hold. They played Australian Rules and cricket, and before long their exotic names began to figure in the sporting press.

The outstanding footballer at Gardenvale Central School was Peter Walker. Playing as a ruckman or forward, he dominated the school matches. Playing kick-to-kick in the schoolyard I once marked one of his short passes and thought I'd broken all my fingers. Walker played many seasons for Geelong and was regarded as one of the best centre half-backs of his time.

At Melbourne High School, science teacher Kevin 'Skeeter' Coghlan, formerly a Collingwood and Hawthorn rover, was held in great respect by staff and students alike. Did he play a role in getting David Parkin, a Melbourne High boy, to Hawthorn? I don't know. But I remember sitting in the library high above the school football ground and seeing Parkin, then a student, play in an interschool match. The ball appeared to follow him around the ground. He went on to captain a premiership team and coached Hawthorn and Carlton to premierships. I never spoke to him, though—I was a 'swot', not a sport. I was no footballer, never played for a school team and was lucky to be selected for the house thirds. Being tall, I could take an occasional good mark and deliver a respectable flat punt in the kick-to-kick games we played in the paddocks that were then still part of the suburban landscape. But the timing needed for the drop kick and stab pass—a required skill at the time—was beyond me.

The names, nicknames and characteristics of the Essendon players of that period are still fresh in my memory. Saturnine Dick 'King Richard' Reynolds, triple Brownlow Medallist; red-faced Bill Hutchison, dual Brownlow Medallist; diminutive Syd 'Spudda' (for obvious reasons) Tate; beefy ruckman Wally May, one of the few at that time to play in bare arms. Two others were of particular interest to me—Aboriginal half-back Norm McDonald (the first in a long line of Indigenous players nurtured at Essendon), and wingman Lance Mann. Mann won the Stawell Gift in 1952 with McDonald as runner-up.

To my distress, my family moved to the dreary southeastern suburbs in the mid-fifties. Bentleigh was then so dull it was where ASIO chose to place the defecting Petrovs, presumably on the assumption that no one would imagine them in such a social and cultural graveyard. The suburb was also St Kilda territory. The nearby Moorabbin Oval became St Kilda's venue in the 1960s but the idea of changing teams never occurred to me. The tribal/geographic basis of club support was breaking up under the influence of the car and suburban sprawl, but team loyalties remained intact.

My interest in football waned through the later years of secondary school when I concentrated on my studies, determined to escape the prospect of work in a shop or office. At university I studied through the weekends, never went to the football and only occasionally listened to games on the radio, saw a match on television or watched the only program dedicated to the game—*Pelaco Inquest*. Football was not part of the discourse for honours students at Melbourne University, but had I been asked who I barracked for the answer would have been automatic and emphatic.

I married initially into a football family. My first wife, Margaret, was raised in Seddon, part of the Footscray heartland. Her entire family barracked for the Bulldogs and regularly attended the team's home-and-away matches. Margaret's cousin on her mother's side was Jack Collins, full-forward for Footscray in the 1950s. Collins played in Footscray's only premiership in 1954, kicking 84 goals for the season. His brothers Alan and Bob had played for Footscray earlier, and their father had played for Essendon. I met Jack Collins once or twice and remember his handshake as I do Greg Norman's and John Newcombe's. These men appear to be made from a different, stronger material than most of us.

Margaret and I parted amicably and still stay in touch, with football figuring occasionally in our emails. Her brothers inherited the Collins ability and she told me her father announced that the day his youngest son ran out to play for Footscray seniors was 'the proudest day of his life', obviously eclipsing her honours degree and other successes.

In the 1970s, with postgraduate work and travel behind me, my interest in football revived, although it was a lean time for the Bombers. I've never known a supporter to abandon a club in its down times. I maintained my support for Essendon through their struggles, even though moving to Sydney in 1976 meant restricted television and print coverage. My partner, Jean Bedford, was a Richmond supporter, so there was a shared interest and a shared indifference towards soccer and both codes of rugby.

Considering myself a naturalised New South Welshman after a few years in Sydney, I attended a couple of rugby union matches with filmmaker Stephen Wallace to see if I could develop an interest in this puzzling throwing, tackling, mauling game. I couldn't, and the indifference remains. 'I can't get excited about Australian Rules,' Fred Hollows once told me. 'Fred,' I said, 'I feel the same about rugby.' A fellow Victorian and now Sydney resident, playwright Louis Nowra, nailed it when he described rugby as 'wrestling on the run'. The hands-off nature of soccer, as well as the low scoring and use of the head have always seemed ludicrous to me. And gridiron is even more so. David Parkin neatly caught the Australian football fan's attitude to American gridiron: 'When the team that has the ball loses it, they don't even trust the players who lost it to get it back. They send out a whole new group of players to win the ball back. When they win it back, they don't trust them to play with it. They send out the same bunch of blokes who lost it.'

With the transformation of South Melbourne into the Sydney Swans and the move north in 1982, interest in AFL in Sydney increased, although the Swans languished for many years. Television and newspaper coverage grew, and it became possible for a naturalised New South Welshman to follow the game more closely. Nice timing, because Essendon won back-to-back premierships in 1984-85 under charismatic coach Kevin Sheedy, and the 'Baby Bombers' won again in 1993, ushering in one of the best players the game has seen—James Hird.

A legend similar to that about Coleman surrounds Hird. Someone— I've forgotten who—told me that an opposition coach instructed his players to stand on Hird's feet whenever possible. It may be true. Hird missed many matches through injuries to his feet. In an earlier era, referring to Melbourne's Don Cordner, an opposition coach advised players to 'go for his hands. It's how he makes his living.' The coach was under the mistaken impression that Cordner, a GP, was a surgeon. Football is a rough business.

Many football teams have had legendary coaches—Phonse Kyne at Collingwood, Reg Hickey at Geelong, Norm Smith at Melbourne. Among them must be named Kevin Sheedy, Essendon coach from 1981 to 2007. Sheedy played 251 games with Richmond, and his style could best be described as hard at the ball and the man. Many times as a barracker I groaned when he turned back an Essendon attack with a clearing kick, a bump, a tackle or all three. In 1965, Ron Barassi broke the mould by coaching a team he hadn't played for. Melbourne was stunned, but by 1981 Sheedy's move to Essendon was no longer controversial; in any case, he had barracked for the Bombers as a kid. Sheedy stamped his personality on the club and lifted it to great heights on and off the field. He was a good media performer. He wore a military helmet to publicise the Anzac Day Essendon-Collingwood match, and his famous jacket-waving after Essendon got up off the deck to beat West Coast became a feature of crowd involvement in subsequent games.

Footballers' autobiographies are some of the worst books ever published, but Kevin Sheedy's *Stand Your Ground* (2008) is a notable exception. Sheedy's account of his own career as a player and coach, of the role of football in society and the economics and politics of the sport has depth and perception. A photograph shows him in his library in front of well-stocked shelves. Significantly, the shelves are not particularly tidy, an indication that the books are being used. The photo makes a strong contrast to statements like that of star North Melbourne winger Keith Greig who, when asked what books he'd read that year, admitted he hadn't read any. Famously, Peter Daicos, the 'Macedonian Marvel', said when his ghost-written autobiography was published: 'I've now written one more book than I've read.' Actor Bill Hunter was an Essendon supporter and a friend of Sheedy's. In an interview he told me that Sheedy, a teetotaller in his playing days, had become fond of red wine but never drinks during the season. I am well aware of the discipline involved in that.

I know supporters of less successful clubs who view their life-long allegiances almost as a burden, as if they have to pay a penance, match by match, year by year. Their lows are deep and their occasional highs are ecstatic. It's not so with the Bombers. No club has won more premierships—but it's more than that. There has been a stability, almost a decorum, about Essendon in my time. The stability is partly due to Sheedy's twenty-seven years as a coach, but also to the class of the captains, from 'King Richard' Reynolds through Bill Hutchison and Jack Clarke to James 'Gentleman Jim' Hird. Statistics are not available, but tribunal appearances for leading Essendon players are relatively few, except in the case of Dustin Fletcher, whose misdemeanours have included 'shaking the goal posts'. When Kevin Sheedy was asked to run his mind back over all the players he'd dealt with, the most critical thing he could say of any of them was that John Barnes could be 'a pest' and was once put off the team bus when it was still an hour away from Melbourne. If a pest is the worst you have, things can't be too bad.

In 2000, succumbing to the lure of pay television, I was able to watch most of the matches Essendon played in that triumphal year. The team lost only once—to my long-ago alternate choice Footscray, now called the Western Bulldogs. There has been no comparable success since, but every season brings new hope. Although I always want them to win, I confess that I sometimes desert Essendon in the tipping competition. But as a similarly pragmatic (and competitive) friend rightly says, 'You tip with your head, not with your heart.'

My heart stays where it has always been.

JON DOUST

The Last Game

Jon Doust was always listed as best player against his school's Catholic nemesis and graduated to amateur colts in Perth before reaching the pinnacle of his football career in three league games for regional legends, the Deanmill Hawks. He co-authored the successful Serventy Kids books and has written two adult novels. *Boy on a Wire* was long-listed for the 2010 Miles Franklin Award and *To the Highlands* was published in 2012. Doust now lives in Albany, Western Australia, where he writes in a smart house, runs, surfs, grows vegetables and agonises over the future of everything. 'The Last Game' appears for the first time in this collection.

Footy season deep in the south west of Western Australia. I'd played a few big games in my time but this one beat the lot. Deanmill Hawks against the mighty Pemberton Southerners, 1971.

A lot of people who know me say, come on Dousty, what about the game you played on the Guildford mudflat in the middle of the big flood of sixty-three? Can't forget that! That was the day Brett Jones kicked ten goals under water. Just before the whistle for the big break, Jonesy swam the full length of the oval without coming up for air, ball constantly in touch with the long reeds and, thus, technically, the ground. When he put through his ninth, the ump stopped the game and called for registration papers. Tried to have Jonesy banned on the grounds he was a freak, claiming the strange markings behind his ears were gills. Once all the paper work had been seen to, the game went on. The ump was right about Jonesy being a freak—but he was a registered freak.

You may not have heard of Deanmill, but you should have. John Todd, a Sandover Medallist at seventeen years of age and one of the greatest players ever never to have played in Victoria, grew up in the mill town. There aren't many on the western side of the continent who could claim to be bigger legends of the game.

The Millers were tough. In the old days, if a bloke got an itchy back he'd pull the cord on a chainsaw, sling it over his shoulder and let the blades run rampant over his naked flesh until the irritation eased. John Peos, perhaps the toughest man ever never to have played in the West Australian Football League, once ran thirty-seven kilometres home at half-time to help his dad bring the cows in for the final milk. He ran back for the last quarter and kicked a goal from a half-back flank. On his wrong foot.

The day I can't forget began as usual with me waking up bang smack in the middle of Manjimup Imperials country, just around the corner from their home ground. Two slouching, early morning walkers acknowledged me with g'days but nothing more as I loaded my gear and got ready to drive deeper into timber country. The locals tried hard to ignore me on game day because they feared anyone who played for the Millers, and more than anything wanted The Mill to lose. This was because The Mill was not *meant* to have a champion team—it wasn't even a proper town. There was no doctor, no shop, no service station. Just a mill and a workers' club. Life for Deanmill folk revolved around The Mill, The Club, and The Team. To be valued as a member of the human race you had to engage in at least two of the three. I belonged to The Club and The Team.

It's not a long drive to the other mill town, Pemberton, but if you're playing the Southerners the nerves start jingling about the time you pass through the potato fields and think of the massive hands belonging to Big Johnny Turner and Flick Moltoni. Flick's were big, but Big Johnny's were bigger. If Flick's were the size of baseball mitts, Big Johnny's could cover an average beer garden table.

I wasn't meant to play that day. When the lists went up in the clubrooms on Thursday night after training, I was down for the seconds. But someone got hurt after training. One of the youngbloods mistimed his chainsaw throw over the shoulder, caught a rib, ripped it out and the coach told him he'd better sit on the bench for the first half.

The game started as usual with Big Johnny grabbing the ball and running it straight down the ground to Bubba Roach, who kicked it through. It went on like that until half way through the second quarter. About then, I got my first look at the ball on the half forward flank. Only trouble was, Big Johnny was getting his fifty-third look and it was a look I didn't like the look of.

Here's what happened

Big Johnny is running at it. I'm running at it. We're both running at it. I'm not a big bloke and if I'm standing on the boundary and watching me and Big Johnny running at it at the same time I'm holding my breath because I'm concerned for my safety. But since this is my best chance of a ball-get, I don't stop running at it. And Big Johnny doesn't stop running at it because it's the only way he knows how to play the game and, up until now, he's never let another human being stop him running at it. Big Johnny gets there first, snatches it out of the sky with one hand, turns and kicks. Bubba grabs it, kicks, and it's another goal to Pemberton. That's when Peter Fontanini, my best mate, yells out: 'Where's Dousty? Where's he gone?' All the Millers join in. 'Dousty! Dousty! Where are you, Dousty?'

No sign of me. Anywhere.

The ump calls a halt to the game and all agree I've left the field. No one knows where I am but because I'm not there they decide to bring on the rib-less youth.

At half-time, Big Johnny complains of an itchy palm. Old George Germantse, the Southerners' trainer for eighty-four years, lets out a cry as he prises me out from Big Johnny's hand, right out of his life-line, where I'd fallen unconscious when Big Johnny took the mark.

Everyone reckons it's a helluva joke, but Old George hasn't finished and keeps working the barbecue tongs to bring forth the entire Northcliffe Salvation Army Band, the Lower South West Hide and Seek Champion of 1967 and a bloke who looked a lot like Lord Lucan.

The game got interesting after half-time.

About five minutes into the third quarter, Flick Moltoni caught his leg in a pothole, left it there, ran all the way to the goal mouth, swerved past the waiting Bubba, raised his remaining leg, hung in mid-air for what seemed like an eternity, brought it through to connect with the ball in a perfect meeting of opposing forces, sent the ball bang between the big ones, and fell flat on his backside.

The game went on.

Just before three-quarter time, the ump, a blow-in from a soft-hand town further north, called a halt. It had nothing to do with the commotion started by the Pemberton supporter who claimed there was a rule about the required number of ribs per player, or the Mill runner who tripped on Flick's loose leg and broke his ankle. But it was about Flick.

Flick was hopping towards the ball on his good leg when the toughest Miller of them all, Harvey Giblett, brother of Ray, the only bloke ever to call Mal Brown's sexuality into question and cop a wink, gave the flick to Flick. Flick was tough, no doubt about that, but anybody bumped fair and square by Harvey Giblett was going somewhere other than the immediate vicinity. Flick found himself crashing through the fence and when he came out the other side he got his arm caught in a roo-bar.

If the loss of a leg didn't stop Flick playing on, you can sure as hell imagine that a ute hanging off his arm wouldn't make much impact. But the ump blew his whistle so hard that a flock of cockatoos five hundred kilometres away rose in the air expecting a goshawk to drop from the sky and rip their hollow tree out by its roots. When everyone had finished blowing their noses and slapping their heads in attempts to re-align their ears, the ump explained Rule 67c, which stated clearly: 'No player engaged in a game in progress shall be allowed to continue his involvement in the current passage of play whilst waving a utility attached to a limb, and, or, limbs.'

The two blokes in the front seat of the ute looked a bit peeved. They hadn't had so much fun since the time they were swept all the way to Kojonup in the Donnelly River backwash of sixty-six. It took three weeks to untangle the ute from Flick's right arm—but that didn't stop him from attending training, milking his cows, or putting up a new shed.

Pemberton won 21.16 (142) to 11.12 (78). It was the last game of football I ever played.

GEOFFREY BLAINEY

Football the Way it Was

Geoffrey Blainey was born in Melbourne in 1930, and raised in a series of Victorian country towns. An Emeritus Professor of the University of Melbourne, he is Australia's most prolific historian and has been an influential social commentator for more than forty years. Some of Blainey's many publications are *The Rush That Never Ended* (1963), *Tyranny of Distance* (1966), *The Causes of War* (1973), *Triumph of the Nomads* (1975), *A Land Half Won* (1980), *A Shorter History of Australia* (1990), *A Short History of the World* (2000), *A History of Victoria* (2006) and *A Short History of Christianity* (2011). His ten-part series on Australian history, *The Blainey View*, appeared on ABC TV in 1982-83, while his richly illustrated book *A Game of Our Own* (1990) explored the origins of Australian football. This essay first appeared in Melbourne's *The Herald*, 16 August 1984.

My father first took me to VFL football when I was seven. We had just moved to Geelong, and I remember walking up the muddy earthen mound behind the goals and suddenly seeing a green oval sprinkled with players in vivid colours. I have never forgotten the scene. The red and white of South Melbourne was especially eye-catching. But that day Geelong won, and I have followed them since. For years I could remember the final scores of every game in which Geelong played between 1937 and 1941. But that information has slipped from my memory, to be replaced, no doubt, by less useful facts.

The next year, my Dad bought a member's ticket, and that entitled him to take a child or two into the grandstand, and from that enormous height we looked down on the oval and saw patterns of play that we had never seen from the outer. In those days Corio Oval was Geelong's ground, and in the distance you could see the marshes, and in memory I even seem to smell the sea. From chinks in the wooden floor of the grandstand came up the smell of eucalyptus oil, straight from the players' well-rubbed limbs. From the fires that cooked the saveloys came the scent of wood smoke, and it mingled with the tobacco smoke and beer. Far more people smoked than drank at the football in those days, and on a still afternoon you could see a wreath of smoke hovering just above the crowd. As eucalyptus in those days was considered to be wholesome, and smoking and drinking were deemed to be evil, it was as if the angels and the devil were besieging the grandstand from different angles.

Most footballers came to the oval on foot, carrying their gear in a gladstone bag and often wearing their Sunday best. Footballers travelled to Melbourne matches on the train, and the ability to go on such long journeys was imagined by us as one of the advantages of being a League footballer. A stir was caused on the eve of the last match of one season when Richmond, eager to make the final four, travelled to Geelong on the Friday night so that they would be doubly fresh for the next day's match. I can still recall—or I think I can—the Richmond captain, Percy Bentley, taking his kick after the final bell and kicking the ball a prodigious distance from the half-forward flank. His kick made no difference because Geelong was far in front, but the grandeur of his gesture and the time he took to aim for the goals made him memorable in defeat.

A boy who lived next door to us played for Geelong. His name was Jimmy Knight, and this small, blond unassuming rover assumed a hero's height in our eyes when he walked past our house. He once got me the autographs of the whole Geelong team, and it was remarkable to see the handwriting—the grand flourishes, the sweeping strokes underlying the signatures, the grand curl at the end of some surnames. Of course, there were also neat spartan signatures, the product of some patient teaching in those country schools where most players had learned to read and write.

Many players in those days had no teeth, and that gave them an old man appearance as they grinned through their gums. Geelong had a ruckman named George Dougherty, and we saw him one summer day at Barwon Heads fishing from the rocks. He looked quite young, away from the football ground, and we stared at him in puzzlement: 'Are you George Dougherty?' He gave us some fish he had caught. No fish ever tasted so sweet.

The game, in every generation, gains something and loses something. Position play was more important in the late 1930s than it is today, and players did not wander far from their set place. Most players could do a stab kick and drop kick, and it was something special to watch a drop kick for goal from an acute angle. There was symmetry in the way the ball spun, and a sense of illusion that the kicker still controlled the ball long after it had left his boot. The kicking is what I remember: Old Reg Hickey kicking in from full back, a drop kick, of course—or Jack Collins so elegant at centre half-forward. In those days the play-on game still lay in the future, and venerable players walked back to take their kick with the slow dignity of an undertaker.

Wingmen were entrancing, for they stood in a sea of space, waiting in their long sleeves for the ball to come their way. They were also nearest to the grandstand, and the small champions from opposing teams like Smallhorn and Doug Nicholls of Fitzroy and the chubby Carney of Carlton were inspected closely before being hissed. Some had great skill in picking up the ball on the run, extending one arm along the ground in such a way that the ball ran up it like a mechanical toy.

There was less talk about football in the media and rumour and word of mouth seemed to busy itself in the absence of reliable news. A half-forward had been kicked by a horse at work and might not be playing. A ruckman had fallen from his bike yesterday and might not last the match. Rumours multiplied at the start of the season. I once rode a bike to Corio Oval, on the Saturday before the season opened, and rested the bike against the fence and stood on the seat to watch a training match. A drover came along with his horse and covered cart and a few hundred sheep, and asked who was playing. He was a master of the rumour and told me, on the most reliable authority, that North Melbourne—a pitifully weak team in those days—would be premiers that year. 'Don't tell a soul,' he said. Of course, I told everybody. My reputation sank as the season progressed.

It is curious to think of the nicknames of teams at the time. Many have vanished. Hawthorn was called the Mayblooms—I assumed they won a few matches in May, which in those days was early in the season. Melbourne was often called the Fuchsias, Geelong was called the Pivotonians, and Footscray the Tricolours. A nickname did not yet have to signify ferocity.

During the war, Geelong dropped out of the league for a few years. Jimmy Knight from next door was killed in New Guinea, and when Geelong returned to the league it played no more games at Corio Oval. These thoughts came rolling back recently. I normally stand in the outer, but the Geelong president invited me to lunch, and afterwards I sat in the front row of the grandstand: the first time I had sat in a grandstand at Geelong for more than forty years. There was not a whiff of eucalyptus oil, and no smell of wood smoke came from the saveloy pot, and South Melbourne had the same colours though not the old name.

But the umpy was said to be as blind as ever. Nobody could remember worse umpiring. In that, at least, I thought, not much had changed after all those years.

B.A. SANTAMARIA

The Agony and the Ecstasy

B.A. Santamaria (1915–1998) was born in Melbourne and finished his schooldays as dux of St Kevin's College, East Melbourne. He later graduated in Arts and Law from the University of Melbourne. He founded and edited several newspapers and became a major influence on Australian thought and politics from the 1940s to the 1990s through the organisations he founded, the National Civic Council, the Australian Family Association and the Thomas More Centre, and through his regular newspaper columns and television appearances. In his later years, he became increasingly disillusioned with the corporatisation of football. This essay is an edited extract from his book, *Australia at the Crossroads: Reflections of an Outsider* (Melbourne University Press, 1987).

With me, supporting Carlton was initially a matter of local patriotism, as it once was for so many supporters of all league clubs. When marriage took me away from Brunswick to Kew, my whole environment might have changed, but changes in environment make no difference to a man's major loyalties.

I was born in Sydney Road, Brunswick, a few doors from the Sarah Sands Hotel, almost in the shadow of the Carlton grandstand. My father took me to my first game in 1921. Holding a membership ticket since the mid-1920s, I have watched Carlton teams, good and bad, brilliant and awful, generally from the outer, on practically every Saturday in every football season ever since, which is over sixty years.

Irving Stone once wrote a novel called *The Agony and the Ecstasy*. Like all Carlton supporters, I have experienced both. Who will ever forget the 1970 Grand Final when, down eight goals at half-time, Hopkins kicked the miraculous three and Jezza took that long shot half over his shoulder from over sixty yards out, which bounced three times before it went through? Who will forget Kevin Hall's magnificent dash from nowhere to take that incredible mark out of Peter McKenna's hands and play on down the field to decide the issue? That was the end of Collingwood in that final.

I remember the 1968 Grand Final, in which we beat Essendon by three points. It was won, of course, by the whole team: but if one player can claim to have turned the game, it was Wes Lofts. When Geoff Blethyn flew for the mark only a few yards from the goal, Wes Lofts gave him a gentle push in the back, which unbalanced him. It should have been a free kick: but the umpire was in front of Blethyn and he missed it. I cannot condone illegality, but there are occasions when one may justifiably follow Nelson's example and turn his blind eye to the telescope.

On the other hand, I remember another type of Grand Final in the 1930s, this time against Richmond, who then had the habit of administering regular thrashings to the Blues. Carlton was seven points ahead, with five minutes to go. Ron Cooper, perhaps the best long-distance pass I have ever seen, took the mark on the half-forward boundary. Micky Crisp was in the goal square with no Richmond backman within thirty yards. That goal would certainly have sealed the match. It was the only time I ever saw Ron Cooper miskick, but he did. It went out of bounds. A Richmond player named O'Halloran ran on to the field and kicked two quick goals which sealed the game for Richmond. We were out of it, once again. I saw my father repeat the annual ritual of tearing up his season ticket, throwing it on to the asphalt, walking on it, and swearing that that was the last time he would ever follow Carlton. And he always kept his word—until the first game of the following season.

If there was tragedy, there was also farce. There was the game against Essendon at Windy Hill, which I missed because of illness, but my father's testimony is reliable. The umpire had butchered Carlton.

The Carlton supporters were apoplectic. At that time a well-known Methodist minister was running a mission—of the kind with which Billy Graham was later to travel the world. It had been an overwhelming success in Sydney, but was a bit of a 'fizzer' in Melbourne. The Essendon President was a convinced Methodist, so Essendon gave him the opportunity to advertise the mission at half-time. From the centre of the ground, holding the microphone in his hand, he addressed the startled fans: 'Ladies and gentlemen, we are all Christians together.' Dead silence, which after ten seconds was broken by the anguished cry of a Carlton barracker which reverberated across the ground, 'Wot about the bloody umpire?'

With highs and lows like these, it was impossible for one born in the shadow of Princes Park not to love the game. And although we hated the Magpies, the Tigers, and the Dons with a mighty hatred, we accepted the fact that their supporters—although barely qualifying for the species *homo sapiens*—also knew what life was all about.

BRUCE DAWE

Life-Cycle

(for Big Jim Phelan)

Bruce Dawe was born in Fitzroy, Victoria in 1930. He left Northcote High School at the age of sixteen and worked in a variety of jobs including labourer, sales assistant, office boy and farmhand. Dawe joined the RAAF in 1959 and was still serving at the time his first volumes of poetry appeared. After leaving the Air Force, he became a teacher and then a lecturer at the Darling Downs Institute of Advanced Education. He served that institution after its re-badging as the University of Southern Queensland, and was appointed USQ's first Honorary Professor upon his retirement in 1993. *Sometimes Gladness* (1978) is perhaps Australia's most read volume of poems. His awards include the Grace Leven Prize (1978), the Patrick White Literary Award (1980), the Christopher Brennan Award (1984), and the Australia Council's Emeritus Writers Award (2000). 'Life-Cycle' first appeared in *Sometimes Gladness*, while 'The High Mark' appeared in *The Age*, 17 July 1987.

When children are born in Victoria
they are wrapped in the club colours, laid in beribboned cots,
having already begun a lifetime's barracking.

Carn, they cry, Carn... feebly at first
while parents playfully tussle with them
for possession of a rusk: Ah, he's a little Tiger! (And they are...)

Hoisted shoulder-high at their first League game
they are like innocent monsters who have been years swimming
towards the daylight's roaring empyrean

Until, now, hearts shrapnelled with rapture,
they break surface and are forever lost,
their minds rippling out like streamers

In the pure flood of sound, they are scarfed with light, a voice
like the voice of God booms from the stands
Ooohh, you bludger, and the covenant is sealed.

Hot pies and potato-crisps they will eat,
they will forswear the Demons, cling to the Saints
and behold their team going up the ladder into Heaven,

And the times of life will be the tides of the home-team's fortunes—
the reckless proposal after the one-point win,
the wedding and honeymoon after the grand-final...

They will not grow old as those from more northern states grow old,
for them it will always be three-quarter time
with the scores level and the wind advantage in the final term,

That passion persisting, like a race-memory, through the welter of seasons,
enabling old-timers by boundary-fences to dream of resurgent lions
and centaur-figures from the past to replenish continually the present,

So that mythology may be perpetually renewed
and Chicken Smallhorn return like the maize-god
in a thousand shapes, the dancers changing

But the dance forever the same—the elderly still
loyally crying Carn... Carn... (if feebly) unto the very end,
having seen in the six-foot recruit from Eaglehawk their hope of salvation.

The High Mark

(for Nick Lynch)

begins with the nod of head
or flicker-signal of fingers
and a run that gathers in
the green day and the
grey crowd that rolls on its
great humble tides
and the run is a thinking
to the ball's end-over-end parabola
that has sinews tough
—tensioning for the upward
leap,
   hands now
        eagle claws,
god's hooks, hungering
for the leather dove, the run
among mere mortal men
in time, in place, become
the leap into heaven,
into fame, into legend
—then the fall back to earth
(guernseyed Icarus)
to the whistle's shrill tweet.

KATE ELTHAM

Nothing Like a Convert

Kate Eltham is the Festival Director of Brisbane Writers Festival. For six years she was CEO of Queensland Writers Centre, where she supported emerging writers to establish successful careers, and established if:book Australia, a think tank exploring digital futures for writing and publishing. Kate has published numerous pieces of journalism and short fiction in Australian publications. She grew up in an AFL household in a rugby league town. From her grandmother, Kate learned how to make perfect scones and the term 'Chewy on yer boot'. Her favourite player will forever be the Brisbane Lions' No. 33, Darryl 'Inspector Gadget' White. 'Nothing like a Convert' first appeared in *Best on Ground* by Peter Corris and John Dale (eds., Viking, 2010).

I love Sundays the best. They play Powderfinger over the Gabba loudspeakers. An easterly breeze floats the chorus of 'My Happiness' towards the crowds approaching from Vulture Street. On the southern side of the ground, the Thai Rose does a brisk pre-game trade in satay sticks. If you linger at the traffic lights opposite Gate 2, the smell of peanut oil will settle into your hair.

Lions fans are mellow on Sundays. There is time for a pre-game lunch at the Pineapple Hotel—a beer perhaps and a steak bigger than your head. The afternoon sun is menacing, but only until quarter-time when it passes behind the stands and we all take our sunnies off. It's too hot for footy scarves. We are fond of caps and polo shirts in Brisbane. Perhaps a guernsey, but not the wool variety.

In Section 69, Ron greets us with a smile and an update.

'Craig McRae's out.'

'He's out, is he?' says Dad.

'Injured.' Ron knows McRae's father. He has an inside line.

It's only twenty minutes to the first bounce but Ron and wife Lyn have been here for hours. Every home game, for more than ten years, they've caught the ferry from Stradbroke Island, stowed their gear at their friend Lorna's place and walked over to the Gabba in time for the reserves game before the main event.

'How long?' says Dad.

'Two weeks.'

Dad nods and props the footy backpack on one of the seats. He slides out four square, flat cushions with Brisbane Lions logos on them, balances his cushion on the plastic seat and keeps it in place by weighing it down with a copy of the *Football Record* and the *Australian Financial Review*.

'Right, I'm off for a coffee,' he says, and disappears to go stand in a queue. Later in the season, if our performance is a bit loose or if he's brought a mate to the game, he might have a plastic cup of mid-strength or two. But for now, it's a weak flat white.

Mum settles herself and begins catching up on the news from Ron and Lyn and Lorna. I open the *Record*. I check the match-ups first and then turn to the Pocket Profiles. *The Shawshank Redemption* is Tim Notting's favourite movie. If he could invite anyone to dinner, it would be Jennifer Hawkins.

Wally's son, daughter-in-law and grandkids arrive. This is my favourite pre-game moment. I've been watching these kids come to the footy since they were barely old enough to see over the seats, and I don't even know their names. By now they're probably nine or ten, and nearly every Gabba game they come with Mum and Dad and eat home-brand chips and lollies from a bag. The girl usually wears a Lions guernsey. She might even brave a bit of face paint if she's feeling game. And the thing that's always amused me is that half the time they don't even seem that engaged by the play on the field. They probably missed that crazy banana kick from Akermanis. They weren't looking when Jonathan Brown booted it from beyond the fifty-metre line.

But they wouldn't miss *this*. They wouldn't dream of being anywhere else, because this is what families do when the Lions are entertaining a home crowd.

You can tell, when Wally looks at those kids, he's seeing the future of Australian Rules in a heartland town of rugby league supporters.

The Lions trot down the race. Mum claps and yells along with 30,000 others.

'Here we go, here we go!' says Dad, coming back with his coffee.

As the umpire raises his arms for the bounce, with cries of 'Go Lions!' echoing around the ground, one shout is louder than the others. It is just over my right shoulder. Ben—late as always—slides into the seat beside me, beer in hand.

'Hey, sis.' He gives me a friendly bump with his shoulder.

And I wouldn't dream of being anywhere else either, because this is what you do with your family when the Lions are entertaining a home crowd.

The birth of my interest in AFL coincided with the birth of the Brisbane Lions, when the Bears merged with Fitzroy in late 1996. I was there for the club's awkward adolescence—the frequent drubbings from North Melbourne, West Coast and the Doggies, culminating in a wooden spoon in 1998—but only arrived at full-on footy mania just as the Lions were cranking up to be a 'dynasty' team.

Until then, I'd been to a few games with my parents and my biggest obstacle was always vocabulary. I just didn't speak the language.

'He can push out to the fat side of the ground. He's got plenty of acceleration when he wants to,' says the man in the row behind me one chilly August night.

'But not the consistency!' says his mate.

'Good grabs, though. What about that screamer at the top of the square?'

'Yeah, that was good.'

'Was it ever.'

'G&D, that's old Whitey. G&D.'

I squint at the players running all over the field, wondering who Whitey is. I lean over to whisper to my father. 'Dad, what's Gee and Dee?'

'Hmm?'

'Guts and determination,' chips in my brother on the other side.

I look down the list of players in the *Record* and locate Daryl White. Number 33. I take out a pen and write *Whitey* next to his name. I pause for a moment and then next to that I write *G&D*.

Players all seem to have nicknames. I begin writing them next to their name in the *Record* to keep track.

'What's he called?' I point to number 20.

'Blacky.' I write Blacky next to the name Simon. I also add, *Nice bum.*

Johnno (cute, but short) goes next to Chris Johnson, followed by *Braddy* (widow's peak), *Lukey* and *Aker*.

'What about him, number 44? What's his nickname?' The *Record* identifies him as Nigel Lappin.

'Lappin,' says Dad. Lappin. Of course.

Referees get nicknames too. But I don't write those down.

White indeed performs some great grabs in this game, his wiry body almost horizontal in the air as he plucks the ball one-handed from its mid-arc flight.

'Inspector Gadget!' yell the punters behind me. (More scribbling in the *Record*.)

It's a tight game. Our conversion rate is terrible, racking up thirty-two kicks for goal but only twelve majors. But heading into the fourth quarter we're ahead by a goal, and Bradshaw and Boyd are really firing.

Ashcroft is everywhere. He marks the ball on the goal line. He doesn't wheel around and line up, he plays the advantage and boots it toward the goals. It arcs around and Ashcroft bends too. He's willing the ball to curve but it passes behind.

'That's all right, that's all right,' says Dad. He shifts around in his seat and rubs his palms on his legs. It's how I can tell he's excited. 'That's all right,' he says again, 'we've got plenty of momentum.'

His blue eyes are bright, and I smile. He shoots back his silly grin, the one that's all teeth and eyebrows. I can't remember this before, this feeling of connection to my father about something we're both excited over. I used to tell him about writing and music and doing well at school, and he was always encouraging, always proud. But this isn't those things. This is something shared.

Ashcroft gets another kick and this time he slots it. He and Bradshaw end up hauling in more than half the goal tally between them.

That was Round 22 at the Gabba in 1998. We finished the season wooden spooners but won that nail-biter against St Kilda by just one point.

I spent half the summer on the Lions website. For the first time ever, I tuned into the sports pages of the paper, and I watched the finals.

By the time St Kilda showed up at the Gabba for a pasting in round 1 the following year, I knew every guernsey number and every player's name.

'Nothing like a convert,' said my mother.

◆•◆◆•◆

There are things I remember about being a kid in Brisbane in the 1980s. I remember lining up on the road outside my kindergarten to wave at Robert de Castella leading the marathon in the 1982 Commonwealth Games. I remember eating sherbet at the Red Hill Skate Arena, watching girls older than me circle the rink as effortlessly as Olivia Newton-John in *Xanadu*. And I remember Mum and Dad watching Saturday afternoon VFL, sitting in their armchairs with their matching tracksuit pants and cups of tea, Mum shrieking loud enough for the Hams in number 28 to hear.

The only other time she would scream like that was when she was very, very angry with me or Ben. She was angry watching the football too—angry at dropped passes, dodgy bounces and misapplied free kicks. But what that really meant was she was thrilled to be so engaged, launching out of her chair and shrieking, 'It's a goal!' or 'That is a *disgusting* call, umpire!'

I would feel a little thrill in my belly, even though I didn't know who had kicked the goal or which team they were barracking for or why they looked so wistful about the miserable Melbourne weather misting the television screen. But football had never been part of my life the way it had been for my parents.

Mum and Dad grew up in Melbourne. My father was a Geelong supporter from a young age. 'My early memories of games were of standing on the terraces in the outer,' he tells me, 'trying to get a glimpse of the game over the shoulders of adults, the mud everywhere, the roar of the crowd when someone got biffed, the crush of people as we left the grounds, the long queues of trams lined up at the end of the game to take people away. I can remember going to Geelong games at Kardinia Park when the great Polly Farmer was playing, and marvelling at how far and accurately he could send handpasses flying to teammates. He absolutely revolutionised the game at that time.'

Mum, an Essendon supporter, would also go to games regularly with her father Bob, often to the MCG where he had a casual job in the bar. Bob was a mad-keen Collingwood supporter, much to the chagrin of my grandmother, Dot, who preferred Essendon—probably on principle because they weren't Collingwood.

My parents moved to Queensland just days before the 1977 VFL Grand Final. They brought me—less than a month old—and their footy passions with them. But their new homeland was a rugby league stronghold. Barely a few thousand locals could be mustered to watch the Queensland Australian Rules state team. By contrast, 108,224 people packed into the MCG for the Grand Final that year. Even after the game ended in a draw and had to be replayed the next weekend, more than 90,000 people turned up. The attendance at both finals was more than two-fifths of Brisbane's population at the time.

My parents started following the Brisbane Bears when the team was established in 1987. Ben had begun playing footy with Wests juniors. Dad umpired occasionally and Mum coached the Indooroopilly State School Aussie Rules team. They went to a few games at Carrara on the Gold Coast, in the days before the M1 was upgraded and going to the Gold Coast was a real day trip. But they didn't become club members until Fitzroy merged with the club in 1996 to form the Brisbane Lions.

'Of course,' says Dad, 'you never really completely lose your original alliances.'

The floodlights illuminate the streets of Dutton Park as we walk towards the Gabba. It is Round 3 of 1999 and there are only two things anyone wants to talk about: Leigh Matthews and Michael Voss.

'Vossy's first game back at the Gabba tonight,' I say knowingly to Dad, as if I understand how significant that is, even though I've never seen Michael Voss play. I've been reading up about young Voss, about how he was a Brownlow Medallist in 1996 and a burgeoning star in the AFL before shattering his leg at Subiaco in 1998.

'What was it like when he broke his leg?' I ask Mum. She has told me before but I like hearing her tell the story. These days I scoop up pieces of trivia about the Lions like a crumbing forward.

'Oh God, that was terrible,' she says, scrunching her shoulders against a shudder. 'Remember, Timmy? When Vossy did his leg?'

Dad shakes his head. 'Terrible.'

'We saw it on television. You could tell right away he'd shattered it. It kind of flopped around above the ankle. He was in agony. I was in agony.'

I experience a strange stab in the gut. Jealousy? Voyeuristic curiosity? I want to be a witness to that too, to be able to say I was watching when the great Michael Voss broke his leg. I want to know what that fear and anxiety for your team feels like.

'Tonight will be good,' I say confidently.

I am dyed in the wool these days. A bona fide Loyal Lion. To show my allegiance I wear a brand-new Lions scarf and new Revlon lipstick in 'Red Currant' to match. One man keeps nodding and smiling at me as we wait at the traffic lights across from the Gabba. He is wearing a number 3 Lions guernsey. It is worn around the sleeves, sagging at the armpits where sweat stains have turned the gold trim into baby-poo brown. His cap has loads of signatures on it, the names of football players from across the years. He raises one eyebrow and nods again. I keep nodding and smiling back. Eventually he says, 'You forgot to take the tag off.' I look down to see the price tag hanging off the end of the scarf. Brilliant.

At the half-time mark the Power has twenty points on us and all around me people are tucking into Four'N Twenties and chips. I take a packet of sushi from my bag, which elicits a snicker from the gallery of hardcore fans behind me. Mum hugs me in sympathy and hands over a cup of sweet milky coffee from the thermos.

'Your grandmother Dot used to bring a whole cooked chook and a fruitcake,' she says.

Voss gets a few touches, but overall we are pretty flat. The Lions trail Port Adelaide at every break and lose by 23 points. Ben is not here to commiserate with me, to give me post-game analysis and tell me what to think about Matthews' coaching tactics. He is overseas, somewhere on an island in the Caribbean. I think about him a lot as the season unfolds. I imagine him folding his thin body into a plastic seat at the Gabba, eyes intent on the play. I imagine his commentary: 'Come on, Lambert, hold your body together for one more game', or 'It was very smart of Matthews to move Leppitsch to defence, you know.'

Despite the loss, the Lions went on to play their best season of footy to date, including a 100-point shellacking of West Coast and a record 21-goal first-half haul against Freo. I just wish Ben had been there to share it. He'd have loved it.

———◆·❉·◆———

In the last few months of 1999 and the first half of 2000, I was living in San Francisco and working in a dotcom just before the first great Tech Wreck. When you're alone, living on the other side of the world, a lot of things come into sharp focus: the importance of family and friendships, a quixotic fascination with things that remind you of home and the undeniable ecstasy of a third-quarter fight-back.

I became more obsessed with the Brisbane Lions in those months than I'd ever been at home. I would scour the web for every nugget of information: the sputtering return to form of Alastair Lynch after chronic fatigue syndrome; Adam Heuskes' parade of bizarre hairstyles; the rise and rise of the Lions' midfield. I would stay in on Friday nights to listen to Saturday night games streamed live over the AFL website.

But when I really thought about it, the thing that I missed most about the footy wasn't so much the game itself, but the ritual of loving the game and having informed sympathisers to share it with. I missed the post-game analysis with family (and complete strangers) on the bus home from the Gabba. I missed the bull-headed arguments I'd pick with Ben about the strength of our back line just so I could impress him with words like 'hospital pass'. I missed the anticipation of climbing the Gate 2 steps and pausing, breathless, to appreciate the brilliance of the ground laid out before me, to hear Ben murmur, 'Magnificent!', to receive the welcoming smiles of Ron and Lyn and everyone else who shared our section.

'You just don't understand how good you've got it,' a work colleague said with some bitterness after Brisbane easily accounted for the Western Bulldogs in the qualifying final of 2000. I'd got excited as I recounted the game on Monday morning and said some unkind things about Doggies supporters.

'You're a Johnny-come-lately to a team that hoovered up all of Fitzroy's best players and a coach who was the greatest player the game has ever seen,' he said. 'You've never endured the wilderness years. You've never had multiple generations of the one family follow a team that's never taken a flag. Do you know how long my father has been waiting for St Kilda to win a premiership? Since before I was born! You don't know what it means to love footy until it has broken your heart.'

<hr />

On Grand Final day in 2001 we aren't together. Mum and Dad are in Melbourne for the game. Ben is at This Is Not Art festival in Newcastle. I am at home in Brisbane. The only thing we share is perfect weather. It's a great day for a Grand Final, and a great day for watching one.

I have invited a bunch of people over to watch the game. Few are footy fans. The pre-game entertainment thunders from the TV as I heat up Four'N Twenty pies and party sausage rolls. I have drawn a B and L on my face in maroon lipstick, one for each cheek, only I forgot about the reversing effect of the mirror so the letters are backwards. A steady stream of guests arrives during warm-up. On TV Leigh Matthews and Kevin Sheedy strut like roosters, their barrel chests out. Julie Anthony sings the national anthem. And Michael Voss wins the toss.

It's time. The siren sounds, the umpire lines up for the first bounce, and I am watching the Lions' first ever Grand Final appearance in a room full of people who couldn't care less.

Barnes takes the first bounce out of the air, but the ball is locked up and we have a second go. Moorcroft gets a behind and the Bombers are on the board first.

There's a beautiful passage of play when Caracella grabs the pill and passes to Solomon. Solomon, on hands and knees, handballs to Jacobs but tiny little Shaun Hart surges through the middle and crumbs the ball. He dobs to the top of the goal square. But what's this? Fletcher, knees and elbows flying, has floored Lynch. Lynch holds the mark, but the kick is off and Brisbane have missed their first shot at a Grand Final goal. One behind a piece. Lappin gets the ball and kicks a cloud-seeder. As it comes down to a contest Lynch sails over the top and grabs it. This time he doesn't miss.

Akermanis is everywhere. Hart and Black are racking up disposals like it's a Thursday night training session. Luke Power snatches the ball from the pressure zone and kicks true for our second goal. Bruce McAvaney is calling it a break, not huge, but a break. With eight minutes left in the opening stanza, Scott Lucas nails the Bombers' first goal and at least 70,000 of the 100,000-strong crowd erupt.

Matthew Lloyd's been hanging back, desperate to get into the contest, and right at the end of the quarter he gets his chance. He tosses his blade of grass, not once but twice. He slams the ball through the sticks. Essendon hits the front. That feels like a turning point—Essendon have asserted their strength and will go into the second quarter with the lead, which everyone feels is how it should be. The Lions have had plenty of opportunities but haven't converted them, and this is an upstart young team after all, playing against the minor premiers and reigning champions. This is where it will start to open up, and it will be my turn, like my colleague said, to have my heart broken.

But suddenly Jacobs is down, Pike gets the ball and sends it deep into the forward pocket. Lynch is there, Voss is there, but it's Akermanis in the box seat. He scoops the ball from the deck and snaps it off the left boot for a freakish checkside goal. Brilliant.

At half-time people shift from couch to floor to armchair, trying to find a good vantage point. Beers and Cokes are distributed. A flurry of texts is exchanged with Ben in Newcastle and Mum and Dad in Melbourne. Sandy Roberts says it's very much a game of chance. Bruce McAvaney says it's very much a match to be won. But that's okay, because Brisbane's got legs. We like a warm, sunny day and we'll run 'em out in the end. At least that's what Ben will be saying in a pub on Darby Street somewhere in Newcastle.

The premiership quarter begins and a magnificent passage of play unfolds. Hart smashes the ball clear and Whitey's there. Handpasses to Crackers. Back to White. Voss grabs it at the same time he's charged by Caracella, but somehow manages to keep hold of the cherry behind Caracella's head, like they're dancing or embracing. But before Blake can steal a kiss Voss has passed it to Notting, then it's White, Black and back to Notting again, and though the mighty James Hird is on his heels, Possum kicks it inside fifty. It bounces too high for Lynch but not for Brown, who goes down, thanks to Fletcher, but not before he passes to Power, who slots the goal.

We're even-stevens again.

The Lions open up full throttle and by the end of the third quarter, Brisbane is sixteen points in front. There's a sense of disbelief from the Essendon players. Marching down the steps ahead of the siren, Leigh Matthews looks like a five-star general. The champions are in trouble. You can smell it. Ben calls me but I can hardly hear him for the background noise. The texts from Mum and Dad have stopped.

'It's the start of the last quarter in so many ways,' says Bruce.

The commentators are already talking about Brisbane's first premiership, and the Lions' first since 1944. Like it's a done deal. I can't let myself believe it.

Halfway through the term Lloyd takes a mark, misses, takes another, kicks a goal. The lead is only ten points and all of a sudden it doesn't feel quite so safe. Jonathan Brown takes a mark inside fifty. He walks it back, and back, and back. He takes his long run-up. It looks a chance.

Brown bends his body back, wincing, elbow cocked. He wants it. But it clips the post and Brown slumps in disappointment. Two minutes later Akermanis kicks another poster. It hits the stick so hard you can hear the reverberation.

But the momentum is with the Lions. Has been for nearly two quarters. The commentators have already started their round-up of congratulations, naming the players who have been key to this historic win: Akermanis and Ashcroft; Johnson and the Scotts; Shaun Hart.

With eight minutes still to go Michael Voss slams a six-pointer to seal Essendon's fate. The fans are in raptures. We're home.

The next day I take the bus in to the Gabba to welcome the triumphant Lions home. The tiers are empty. I stand on the grass of the oval and watch Vossy hoist the premiership trophy. I wait for bleary-eyed players to make their way down the line of fans, shaking hands, signing caps and premiership posters. I collect signatures for Ben's guernsey from Whitey, Leppa, Power and Black.

I linger at the edge of the crowd as the afternoon meanders toward dusk. I feel hollow. I'm sharing this moment with hundreds of other Lions fans. But there's nobody here I know.

<hr />

In Round 10 of the 2008 season I've brought my stepdaughter, Imogen, six years old, with me to Section 69 at the Gabba. Mum and Dad and the usual suspects are here, Wally and the grandkids, Ron and Lyn and Lorna, but not Ben, who now lives in Melbourne.

Imogen was impressed by the Auskick demonstration at half-time. She has been doing Auskick at school with her prep class. I thought she'd be bored by now, but she is intent on the game. Going into the final quarter we are leading North Melbourne by thirty-two points. She gets excited as the umpire steps up for the bounce.

'Come on Brisbane, you can still win this!' she cries.

And we do.

LAURIE CLANCY

The Coach

Laurie Clancy was born in 1942 and educated at Christian Brothers College, St Kilda, and Melbourne University. He was a prolific and acclaimed writer of short stories and also penned four novels, including the award-winning *A Collapsible Man* (1975) and *A Perfect Love* (1983). As an English lecturer at La Trobe University for three decades, and later as a lecturer in Creative Writing at RMIT, he influenced many young writers and students of literature. He also made a significant contribution to literary criticism as the author of *A Reader's Guide to Australian Fiction*. As a young man, Clancy played almost 200 games of junior football. He later reflected that he could not recall receiving a cut or a graze, let alone missing a game through injury. With the self-deprecating wit for which he was well known, Clancy mused this was not so much because he was a skilful player as because he was 'an arrant coward'. He passed away from cancer in 2010. 'The Coach' was first published in *The Greatest Game* by Ross Fitzgerald and Ken Spillman (eds., 1988).

Waht did I do in the football season, son? Oh, I played a lot of football, first with Melbourne University, then with La Trobe. But at a very junior level.

—What? No, I didn't go on TV. That's the League, the VFL. Then there's the next best, the Association, the VFA. Then the amateurs, the VAFA. I played with the amateurs. Now think of A-grade, B-grade and, so on, all the way down to E-grade. Well, I played in E-grade. But only a few games when the team was short. Usually I played in E-grade reserves.

It was good fun, though, and you played with some very interesting people. We had a couple of speedy conscientious objectors on the half-back line, who used to keep fit by running away from the cops, a full back who went on to become a very successful writer of adolescent fiction, and the rover I used to ruck to was Gary Weaven. One match Gary was really burning. As we stumbled off the ground at half-time for a beer, I said, with just a touch of complacency, 'You seem to be picking up a few kicks, Gus.'

'Yeah,' he replied. 'I worked out that the opposition ruckman was winning every knock and just roved to him.'

It took Gary a while to develop the diplomatic and negotiating skills that took him into the top echelon of the ACTU.

Then, let me see, there was Jamie Grant, the poet, who played on the wing. Jamie was so light opponents didn't have to bump him, they just blew him over. There was Don Watson, the comic writer for the premier John Cain. And there was David Morgan. I played a few games with Dave, mainly college and social games. I even had the privilege of hand balling to him for one of his goals. He thanked me afterwards personally.

—What's that, who's David Morgan? He wouldn't like to hear you say that, son. Dave was a very good footballer. Almost as good as he thought he was. One year he kicked 150 goals at La Trobe uni. Then he went to Canberra the next year and did the same thing, in a pretty good comp. He could have made it with Richmond. I saw him once in a full-scale practice game against Carlton, the last week before the start of the season when everyone was pretty serious. He came on after half-time and kicked three goals. He got a free kick in the goal square and went down holding his groin.

'He's gone,' said my mate next to me.

'You watch,' I said.

He got up, limped back to the mark, and kicked faultlessly.

He didn't want to embarrass the umpire so he limped out to the half-forward flank but within thirty seconds he forgot and started to chase the ball again. Yeah, Dave could have made it at Richmond but much to the amazement of all of us at uni he went to London instead and did a PhD in economics. Then he became John Stone's protégé and later he designed Keating's Option C and let the Prime Minister beat him at tennis. Pity. There was a real career wasted there.

—Highlights? Well, one day I kicked five goals. Mind you, it took me two matches. I played in the reserves and kicked three, but the seniors were short of players, and I had to stay on the field. I was stuffed, of course, but I got two kicks. One was a free down field when our centre half-forward was knocked unconscious, and the other was a wild miskick that hit me on the chest, and I held onto it as I fell over.

—Those trophies and awards? Yes, that's always surprised me too. I did have some ability as a cricketer but only won one award, and I had none at all as a footballer and won three or four. Take that tankard, for example. Yes, the one with the dint in it. We were celebrating after the award night, and it got a bit of a battering. See what it says? Melbourne University Reds, E Grade Reserves Best and Fairest 1963. I played every game that season. No spectators were ever at the game to watch us, so they decided to give the best on the field the umpire's votes.

Now, if you're tall and thin, and you let blokes jump over you all day, occasionally the umpire will get sorry for you and give you a vote. I got six that year—all ones for third best. There was another bloke called Dick Wilcox. He had a few games with South Melbourne later but, even so, he wasn't a bad player. He'd broken his collarbone and wanted to try himself out in the reserves for a couple of games to make sure it was okay. He got about fifty or sixty kicks in both games (we didn't call them possessions in those days), and the umpire gave him best on the ground both times, so he and I were tied on six votes each. The committee gave the award to me on the basis that I had more games up. It was a very democratic football club, Melbourne Uni.

—La Trobe? Yeah, I had some good times there, too. It was a very rough comp we were in called the Panton Hill League, filled with blokes who'd spent the week biting the balls off sheep and who were desperate for a game on Saturday. They really loved to beat up uni students. They regarded us with a mixture of loathing and fascinated envy and used to make frequent insulting speculations on what they considered was our ambiguous sexual identity.

—What? Oh, I meant they called us poofters, son. Anyway, I wasn't much of a footballer, as I say, but in my last year I became playing coach and achieved a legendary reputation, particularly for my pre-match addresses. Our fellows weren't into this 'incentivation' stuff, it was no use trying that on them, so I made the best of a bad job and tried to make the pre-match talks as witty and informative as possible, lots of one-liners in among the erudition. My account of existentialism just before the Mernda game is still spoken of with awe in the district while I understand my Religion and the Rise of Capitalism address to the lads went down well at St Andrew's.

Opposition coaches would stop their thundering abuse of players in the adjacent room and listen in amazement through the wooden walls or sneak their teams around the back to listen . They loved it when I used words like *weltanschauung* and *zeitgeist*.

'A lot of ethnics in the side,' I heard one veteran explain to his baffled players as they slunk away.

We had a very weak, undermanned side, and my real triumph as a coach that year was that we managed to win two games through the sheer brilliant conception and ruthless execution of a master plan, which I improvised on the spot.

The first was when we played a team that had a wide, almost rectangular ground, rather like the Western Oval. A gale force wind blew diagonally down the ground into the south-eastern pocket. The opposing captain, the umpire and I met just before the start of the game.

'We'll have to keep the fucking ball over in this fucking side of the ground if we're going to get any sort of fucking game on a fuck of a day like this,' my opposite number opined as he massaged his tattoos.

'Quite so,' I said cordially, with rather less venereal emphasis.

I won the toss, and we kicked with the wind. Innocent players who had been abused for short passing on the back line suddenly found themselves kicking fifty metres. We slammed on eight goals to none in the first quarter.

At quarter-time we regrouped.

'Now, whatever you do, kick it over towards that side of the ground,' I said, pointing east. 'Even if you have to kick straight across the ground.' The wind over there was so strong that sometimes, when the boundary umpire threw the ball into play, it would blow straight back and hit him on the back of the head.

The lads responded to my instructions magnificently. We never came near kicking another goal but, by bottling up play entirely, finished up winning, eight goals to seven. I didn't see much of the last three quarters, because I was being chased up and down the ground by the outraged Tattoo.

The other game we won was against Kinglake, in a match we played in a passing cloud. No, son, not a heavy fog. Kinglake is two thousand feet above sea level (we didn't have metres in those days), and this was quite literally a cloud. After a stirring run-down on the thinking of Kierkegaard, we took the field, shivering (all except for one player who, I later discovered, returned to the bus and emerged only in the last five minutes to take the field and kick the winning goal).

We couldn't see a thing. Play proceeded entirely by sound. We guessed where the ball was, roughly, by the yelps and curses in the area. It was rather like being a blind man on a fox hunt. The field umpire carried a sopping bit of paper on which he recorded the scores. When a goal or a behind was scored, he would run the length of the ground to inform the other goal umpire. There was no point in waving flags.

I could see a more flexible strategy was necessary. At quarter-time, I gathered the players together, those of them I could still find. 'Listen, lads,' I said. 'I want you to kick the ball low, along the ground if necessary. I don't want anyone hurt by being hit on the head. And when you're certain one of our chaps has the ball I want the rest of the team to take off in the opposite direction, yelling as loud as you can. That way we draw them off in a feint, and the chap with the ball should be able to run it down to the goal line, dodging any enemy patrols he meets on the way.'

It worked. We kicked three goals like that before they woke up to it. It wasn't much but that, and the surprise appearance of our eighteenth man at the end, was just enough to win the game.

—Yes, you're right, son. As a player I wasn't much but, as a thinking coach, I was years before my time.

PETER HELLIAR & PAUL CALLEJA

Strauchanie
Gives Back

Peter Helliar was born in Melbourne in 1975 and is a comedian, actor, media personality and writer. He attracted attention as a stand-up comedian in the mid 1990s and, in 1998, became a regular guest on ABC's Triple J. After teaming with Rove McManus on Melbourne community television, Helliar co-starred with McManus on the popular national television talk show, *Rove*. He has hosted numerous radio shows and also wrote the screenplay for a romantic comedy film, *I Love You Too* (2010). Helliar's bogan alter ego, Strauchanie, made his television debut on *Before the Game* in 2005. Strauchanie was the last pick in the 2004 national draft and is yet to play an AFL game, but has unshakeable belief in his destiny as a superstar. 'Strauchanie Gives Back' is an edited extract from Peter Helliar and Paul Calleja, *Bryan Strauchan—My Story: The rise and rise of a genuine superstar of Australian Sport* (Allen and Unwin, 2007).

Lachlan Quigley. Heard of him? Anybody? Didn't think so. He's not a household name. He should be though. If Strauchanie had his way, he would be. If Strauchanie had his way, fish and chip shops would develop a hybrid delicacy combining dim sim and a potato cake, but Strauchanie doesn't always get his way. That's why I'm taking this opportunity to let everyone know about a 13-year-old boy called Lachlan Quigley. Not any ordinary 13-year-old boy I might add—a special boy. Lachlan Quigley mightn't go down in history books like Burke and Wills did for discovering Tasmania, or Ned Kelly, or Swans player Paul Kelly, or Collingwood hard man Craig Kelly, or Dame Kelly Melba, or any other member of the Kelly Gang for that matter, but that's fine. He's still a hero to me. Let me take you back to when Strauchanie first met him.

Being born with amazing natural footballing ability is not something I take for granted. As an AFL player I have certain privileges and responsibilities. So, when I get an opportunity to give something back to the community, I'm more than happy to allow Strauchanie to involve himself in a bit of charity work and hospital visits, providing I'm not too busy making paid appearances. One day I happened to be walking into a hospital because I had parked across the road to buy a coffee scroll and didn't have enough coins for the parking meter.

As I entered the lobby I stumbled upon an attractive, thirty-something brunette woman, looking a bit distraught. Unable to assist me with my request for some spare change, she ran off crying into her hands. Concerned about her well-being, and still interested in her general hotness, I chased her down the hallway and into the lift. When the lift doors closed she turned around, screamed, threw her handbag at me and said: 'Just take what you want, but please don't hurt me!' Twenty minutes later I'd managed to convince her, and hospital security staff, that all was above board (quite surprised none of them recognised me, actually). I spent the next half-hour sitting with her as she told me the story of her son.

It was a heart-wrenching story. A story of pain. A story of struggle against the odds. But also a story of hope. Strauchanie could only listen and try to comfort her by holding her hand and rubbing that soft part of the inside of her leg, just above the knee. In circumstances like these, you think to yourself, *there must be something I can do.*

'Does your son follow footy?' I asked.

'He absolutely lives for it,' she replied through her tears. 'He's Essendon through and through and has pictures of Matthew Lloyd all over his bedroom wall.'

I moved in a little closer and put my arm around her as I prepared to tell her something that would change their lives forever. 'So he loves his footy does he? Maybe I can help?'

Her eyes popped wide open and sparkled in anticipation. 'Do you know Matthew Lloyd?'

'No, well, I have met him, but it's not often that you can get two superstars in the one room at the same time. It's not like we have a Superstars Club and gather on a regular basis.' (Although Strauchanie must admit he does think the idea has merit.)

You could feel the air shoot out of her lungs as she sighed. 'Oh, well. Never mind.'

'There is something I can do,' I said. 'I can pay your son a visit.'

Her response was not as enthusiastic as I expected. 'That's okay, thanks anyway but, as I said, he's Essendon mad and...'

I was insistent. 'Leave it to me. Strauchanie has universal appeal. Just tell me what room he's in and I'll surprise him.'

Hospitals have a certain smell about them. Just as football change rooms do, and just as a two-week old souvlaki that has been sitting on the floor of your car does. But the smell of hospitals makes me feel really uneasy. This can be attributed to the many operations I've had over the years, beginning with my appendix being removed when I was ten. Something I'll never forget—especially the moment when I awoke from the anaesthetic, pulled the appendix out of a jar next to my bed and took a bite out of it, thinking it was a pickled gherkin. But who am I to complain? Young Lachlan Quigley has been in and out of hospitals his entire childhood.

As I approached Lachlan's room, a number of thoughts began rushing through my head. Firstly, how lucky am I? Not only being in perfect health, but also in peak physical condition. Secondly, why are only some of us chosen to achieve greatness? And thirdly, I wonder does this hospital have a McDonalds?

Before I knew it, I was standing outside Lachlan's room. Room number 59. How weird's that? Strauchanie's jumper number—59. A friendship that was meant to be. This called for a grand entrance. I took a deep breath and then, in typical Strauchanie fashion, jumped around the corner and into the room with my hands in the air yelling, 'Strauchanie!'

I was in the wrong room. There was an old bloke in there getting a catheter removed. I quickly pulled out a texta, signed the obvious and left. Turns out that Lachlan was in room 49. I should've been paying attention to what his mum, in the tight skirt and revealing top, was saying earlier. Couldn't really remember what illness Lachlan was suffering from either, but, by all accounts, it was a pretty nasty one.

I finally arrived at Lachlan's room. A skinny, grey-haired nurse was just leaving. She put her finger to her mouth and whispered that he was asleep. I put my foot in the door as she tried to close it. I explained who I was, but I could tell from the expression on her already wrinkly face that she wasn't going to let me in. A minor scuffle developed. We both got in a few jumper punches before I was left with no choice but to put her in a Brendan Fevola-style headlock. She managed to release herself by biting me on the tummy. She then grabbed my arm, twisted it behind my back and forced me against the wall. A crowd began to gather. Then, just as I was about to unleash some patented Strauchanie judo moves, a couple of interns pulled Strauchanie off her. While they were holding me back she got in a couple of cheap shots and then disappeared. Feeling a bit sore and sorry, I comforted myself with the knowledge that I would be storing that incident in my memory for when the opportunity came for a payback.

The sleeping Lachlan looked so calm and peaceful. With his dark hair and olive complexion, he looked like a young, weedier version of Paul Licuria. Lachlan should be happy with that. The ladies think that Lica's a bit of all right. Not that I'd know. I wouldn't know which players were good looking or what order of good-lookingness they'd be in. Although, if you were below Heath Shaw on the list, you'd be worried.

I got to thinking, if Lachlan knew that Strauchanie had been there and he'd slept through it, he'd understandably be a very disappointed young man. So, what better way to wake him up than to break into a gut-busting rendition of 'Good Old Collingwood Forever'? The Strauchanie version, that is. I counted myself in... a one, a two, a one, two, three, four.... five, six, seven... *Good Old Strauchanie Forever*... Bang! Lachlan sits bolt upright, looking like you do when you've had an afternoon nap, your alarm goes off and you've got no idea what day or time it is. I grabbed the red-and-black footy from the cabinet beside his bed, called 'heads up' and handballed it in his general direction. With his hand-eye co-ordination not at its best, owing to him being heavily sedated, the ball smacked Lachlan fair in the face. A few seconds passed before a wide robotic smile appeared. He fell back onto his pillow and slowly drifted off into a deep sleep again. I thought, well, I've done all I can for today.

I left my number with his mum, so that we could arrange the next visit. I asked for hers, but she couldn't find her phone and was having a mental blank about her number. I told her that it wasn't a problem and that I would pop in to see Lachlan next week. I could pick her up if she liked. Even make a day of it. Start with a bit of lunch, visit Lachlan, maybe catch a movie and then who knows where the night will take us from there? Unfortunately, before we could organise anything, she had to rush off because she was worried she'd left the iron on.

As I was walking down the corridor, who did I see coming towards Strauchanie? None other than Essendon champion Matthew Lloyd. I greeted Lloydy with a handshake. There's a special bond between AFL footballers. Unless you've experienced the intensity, the pressure and the demands of a professional sport at an elite level, then you wouldn't understand. It's something people who have been to war can relate to, and similar to the experience of those who, along with Strauchanie, queued up for days waiting for the first Krispy Kreme doughnut franchise to open in Australia.

'What are you doing here, Lloydy?'

'I've heard about Lachlan's plight,' he replied, 'and was coming to personally deliver a signed Bombers jumper.'

'I've got Lachlan covered thanks, Lloydy. Go find your own kid. It's a big hospital, full of sick kiddies and you're trying to move in on mine.'

Lloydy was a bit affronted. 'But Lachlan's an Essendon supporter. I'm sure he'd be happy to receive this.'

'All right, all right, leave the jumper with me and I'll pass it on. There's no point seeing Lachlan anyway—he's asleep.'

Lloydy stuck his head in the door, saw for himself that Lachlan was asleep and handed over the jumper. 'Don't forget to give it to him.'

With a wry grin on his face, Lloydy shook his head at me and then left. It was as if we were in a game, I'd kept him goalless and he'd been dragged. I couldn't believe the nerve of Lloydy, trying to trump me by offering Lachlan a signed Essendon jumper. Fortunately, I was able to offload the jumper on eBay.

I eventually did get back to see Lachlan. It was a couple of weeks later and I'd decided to give him a pair of Strauchanie's footy boots from last year's Round 2 victory in which I probably would've kicked five, had I been playing. As I approached Lachlan's room something didn't feel quite right. I hesitantly walked in, only to find that his bed was empty and freshly made. I grabbed a passing nurse and asked where Lachlan was. She put a supportive hand on my shoulder and said, 'I'm afraid he's gone.'

I felt numb. My heart sank as I slowly sat down on the chair and put my boots on the bed.

'Gone?'

'Yeah, to Queensland. The whole family moved up there for his dad's work.'

Tears welled in Strauchanie's eyes, 'Is Lachlan going to be all right?'

'I think so. Tonsillitis usually takes about two weeks to recover from.'

Strauchanie slept well that night. There's a lot to be said for giving back.

MARTIN FLANAGAN

Tomorrow We're Playing Away

Martin Flanagan was born in 1955 and played 120 games in the Southern Tasmanian B-division amateurs with the Tasmanian University Football Club. He still remembers the grand final they lost in 1978 and thinks, 'If only...' A storyteller, journalist, poet, author and speaker, he has written thirteen books including *1970: & other stories of the Australian Game* (1999), which was listed by the Victorian State Library as being one of the top 150 books in Victoria's history. Other titles include *The Game in Time of War* (2004) and a biography of Matthew Richardson titled *Richo* (2011). He has also co-authored a play titled *The Call* (2004) based on his imaginative retelling of the life of Tom Wills, codifier of Australian football. For all this Flanagan is probably best known as author of the most respected weekly sports column in Australia, which appears in *The Age*. 'Tomorrow We're Playing Away' was first published in *The Greatest Game* by Ross Fitzgerald and Ken Spillman (eds., 1988).

My grandfather could write no more than his name, but he read the *Sporting Globe*. His father, a farm labourer, had emigrated from sad Ireland to escape the unimaginable misery of the potato famine. Nothing else is known of John Flanagan, not even where he is buried, so that is where it starts, the memory of the race, as it were, in the limpid stillness and broad plains of central Tasmania, among the silent towering gums of Epping Forest, in a random collection of houses called Cleveland.

In those few years that lingered like a wistful reflection between the end of World War I and the start of the Great Depression, football matches and the occasional dance in Joe Pike's woolshed completed Cleveland's social round. (Who can forget the mournful utterance of the British television commentator at a European Cup final in Brussels— 'Sport used to be something which brought people together'—remote in his electronic eyrie, witnessing panic, chaos and death on the terraces?)

Cleveland was mindful of its football tradition because Cleveland had produced George Challis, and George Challis had played VFL football for Carlton. Batman had founded Melbourne from Tasmania, then Van Diemen's Land, but the metropolis had long since grown ashamed of its island parent with the ugly past that no one in the wider world wanted to recall. It is said of writer C.J. Koch that he sees Tasmania as a metaphor for Australia. It is, which is why there is a certain type of Australian who doesn't like it. But, to those brought up in the unmoving air of the island state, Melbourne represented the outside world in all its dazzling diversity, all its promise and hope. George Challis had been listed in Carlton's best in the finals of 1914 and again in 1915. Then he'd come home in the uniform of a soldier and gone to the small school and told them he'd be back after the war to show them the finer points of the game. But in the 1916 Grand Final, Carlton wore black armbands for Sergeant George Challis, killed in action in France.

Home matches at Cleveland were played on a fallow paddock, and the bell was borrowed from the school. My grandfather stood at one end with two white handkerchiefs while a visiting potentate performed the same function at the other. These were pre-elastic days, and the more flamboyant players might choose to support their trousers with a tie knotted around their midriffs. When it came to away games, they each tossed in a bob and travelled in the back of a truck.

Both Patrick Flanagan, railway ganger, and my maternal grandfather, Jack Leary, Melrose farmer, played the odd game for the Latrobe Football Club. In 1924, Patrick Flanagan caught the rattler and travelled to Hobart to see LaTrobe's great champion Ivor Warne-Smith, later to win a Brownlow Medal with Melbourne, lead the North-West Coast in yet another of its quixotic tilts against the hated imperialists from the South. The cause of the two northern leagues for equal status with the south is like the claim of the Stuarts to the throne of the United Kingdom, doomed and glorious, its victories similarly few but celebrated.

In time, the family moved to the big city of Launceston, but the sun of the twenties was setting, and the winter of the thirties was closing in. There would soon be thirty per cent unemployment, and in the street there would be the lost, desolate faces which, a generation before, had haunted Henry Lawson. The working people, who suffered most, as they always do, turned their lonely eyes to the performances of a horse, Phar Lap, and a cricketer, Don Bradman. For my father, then an adolescent, the source of wonderment in an otherwise bleak and unpromising world was a diamond of a young footballer named Laurie Nash, who played in the local league for the City club. In just a couple of years, Laurie Nash would go from opening the bowling for Parattah, a house and a pub in central Tasmania, to opening the bowling for Australia. South Melbourne would win its last VFL premiership (1933), with Laurie Nash at centre half-forward. Nash said they would have won another had they only left him there.

In 1984, Laurie Nash returned to Launceston for a sporting memorabilia exhibition at which he was the chief exhibit. The body that had once been taut and compact, that could release itself like an arrow from a bow and gloried in the freedom of its flights, had billowed and blown; his jowls hung like sacks of flesh. But the spirit was still intact. Nash was introduced to his fellow guest of honour, lawn bowler Glyn Bosisto. 'We've met,' said Nash. 'I beat you once at bowls.' There was an eruption of mirth; this, it was felt, was vintage Nash, but beneath the noise Nash was earnestly explaining that Bosisto had given him a handicap start. L.J. Nash was doubly different. He was a sporting genius who saw no reason to deny it.

Longford won the NTFA premiership in 1956, the state premiership in 1958. This must be declared, just as financial interests must be declared on government committees, because I was born in Longford. Our family of eight (nine with Grannie) dutifully packed a varnished pew at church each Sunday morning, but Saturday was always my holy day, the baked dinner with gravy thick as Guinness, the entry to the ground past the Old Men's Home where the veterans sat dozing in the sun, the dizzy greenness of the oval, the bright light bouncing off car bonnets and windscreens. Here, life had the sharp aromatic edge of liniment and a forbidden language that was savage and muscular. And in the course of the afternoon the effects would change and with them the game: the light would lengthen and mellow and reach through the tall gums on the west of the ground, the insolent tooting of the horns would give way to the sound and fury of the three-quarter time address. It was part passion play, part rite of nature.

VFL football can be a wonderful spectacle, but it can also be dramatic; like all top-level sport, it reduces an aspect of life to single elements and pursues them to the point of excellence. It risks absurdity, but anyone who journeys towards abstract pinnacles within themselves can tell you much from what they learn along the way. It is not, however, the same as Tasmanian football, or, at least, what Tasmanian football means to me.

When the Fitzroy Football Club was in danger of passing away in 1986, former Richmond rover Kevin Bartlett said that, should it occur, it would mean Victoria losing one of its eleven Michelangelos. His statement is as expressive to those born within the culture of Australian sport as it is preposterous to those who stand outside it. Sport was one of the few decorations in the bare room of pre-affluent working-class Australia. It was the repository of the popular imagination, and such myths and local heroes as we possessed were contained within its purple glow. It would take Elvis to change all that...

The myth of football required a brother, as myths so often do. Being older, my brother got to cast the roles. He was Longford and Barry Lawrence; I was North Launceston and the feared, reviled Porky Withers. Twenty-five years later, it is still part of us. It's not a question of choice, it's a question of where the pre-pubescent male mind, ardent for life, first encounters the archetype of the hero. Once that fusion occurs, its subjects can deride the myth, ridicule and belittle it, but they can never wholly escape it. I have written newspaper articles on my brother's post-adolescent reaction to football, chronicling how he incorporated the ritual and mannerisms of football into a theatre of the imagination, how he endeavoured to become the sport's first Marcel Marceau. It made for a splendid silliness, part of a larger joke whose theme is that life is a ball, but when we are together on a Saturday, we still choose to go to the footy, not necessarily to watch the game, but because it is part of the rhythm of our lives and closer to the reflections of light and shade that are our true communion.

When I was eight, my father, a schoolteacher, was transferred to Rosebery on Tasmania's dank, mountainous west coast. Longford had been a tranquil village with a bluestone church and huge English trees whose foliage, come each autumn, departed with the lingering glory of sunsets. Rosebery was a mining town. The poet Graeme Hetherington, who also lived in Rosebery as a child, has written of the smell of carbide, the drunks stumbling through the air like trees and King Billy, the Aborigine who fought for the shillings they threw at the Community Hall and whose only friend was his shadow on the floor. But there was also something of the Decameron about Rosebery, a vitality that was raw, earthy and vivid. My father-in-law played most of his football there. He played in one Grand Final where the weather was so arctic the umpire officiated in a greatcoat, and the Williamsford officials passed scalding tea among their players during the interval but could not revive them sufficiently to have them re-take the field after half-time. It is remembered as the premiership Rosebery won by a half and seven points. It was fourteen-a-side football with games played on Sundays because the mines worked a six-day week. Once, at Zeehan, the fourteenth man for the home side lined up on a half-back flank in a blue pinstriped suit with a white chrysanthemum in the lapel. It was Mothers' Day.

When Rosebery travelled to play Tullah, which meant traversing Mount Black, most of the journey was courtesy of a steam engine on a two foot gauge that belonged to the mining company and was named the Wee Georgie Wood. The Wee Georgie would be met by representatives of the Tullah Football Club who would inquire solicitously whether the Rosebery policeman had made the trip. If he hadn't, the news would be telegraphed back to Tullah, and the pub would re-open.

The 'oval' at Tullah was an area of clay carved out of the wet, dark scrub. Officials were always in short supply and, on one occasion, a passing boy scout was co-opted into acting as boundary umpire. Early in the game, the ball went past the lad and into the scrub. When he failed to blow his whistle, the miners continued to make the ball their object. Soon ball and men were lost from sight and the progress of the game could be discerned by the crashing and falling of tea-trees. 'D'you think she's out,' asked the central umpire of his minor official. 'Dunno,' said the boy. The Australian Solomon considered. 'Think I'll ball her up,' he said. Every family has its folklore, and so does every community.

In the forties and fifties, Tasmanian club sides performed creditably against their VFL counterparts. There were historic victories over South and Western Australia and, in 1961, a Tasmanian representative side defeated Victoria at York Park (I know, I was there), which was Gallipoli and Bannockburn and the Boston Tea Party all rolled into one. But once football began its passionate affair with business, time was running against Tasmania. The talent scouts went over the island like combine harvesters. Tasmania's outstanding product of the sixties, Darrel Baldock, played football in his home state until he was twenty-four; Steve MacPherson, who played with Footscray, left when he was in his mid-teens. And in former times, the traffic was not all one-way. In 1930, Collingwood champion Albert Collier was lured to Hobart to captain-coach Cananore at the age of twenty-one, and the year after he had won the Brownlow Medal! Collier's 1985 equivalent, Brad Hardie, went to Brisbane and the vision of the future—a national competition and football as a television product. Tasmania is now like Great Britain, roaming the world of second-grade football powers in search of its Falkland Islands. The latest crusade is for a place in the national league, which will presumably entail a synthetically coloured uniform, a suitably clichéd name like the Tassie Devils, and such other design touches deemed necessary by the wizards of the entertainment industry.

Peter Hay is a Tasmanian poet, publisher, political scientist and folk culture enthusiast who is thought, in his intemperate youth, to have been an accessory to the scandalous uprooting of the goalposts in the 1967 State final at Burnie's West Park oval. One of his poems, published in the December 1986 edition of *Overland* and entitled 'An Oral History Interview with Alf Frimley, 97', is about Wynyard, his home town on the far Tasmanian north-west coast. Part of it goes:

> *Frimley sporting prowess was a legend in the town.*
> *It has new Legends now,*
> *Raised from the shallow loam of its memory:*
> *'The War' marks the nether of that—*
> *A sea-wall dividing tangible past*
> *From the ocean of a history without shape...*

It concludes:

> *Over tea my thoughts turn to place.*
> *Its speech, the fleeting sadness of it,*
> *The regretfulness in the river-flow of its leaving...*
> *Outside the wind is up. Tomorrow?*
> *Tomorrow we're playing away.*

SERGE LIBERMAN

The Man Who Hated Football

Serge Liberman was born in Russia in 1942 and came to Australia in 1951, where he now works as a medical practitioner. He has been editor of the *Melbourne Chronicle*, associate editor of *Outrider: a Journal of Multicultural Literature in Australia*, and literary editor of *Australian Jewish News*. Liberman has contributed writing and translations to many other journals, and has been included in anthologies in Australia and overseas. As author of six short story collections— *On Firmer Shores*, *A Universe of Clowns*, *The Life That I Have Led*, *The Battered and the Redeemed*, *Voices from the Corner* and *Where I Stand*—he has three times been awarded the Alan Marshall Award for fiction and also won a NSW Premier's Award for Ethnic Writing. In 2011, the definitive third edition of his *The Bibliography of Australasian Judaica* was published. Several of his works have been set as study texts in Australian and overseas high schools and universities. 'The Man Who Hated Football' was first published in *The Life That I Have Led* (1986).

'Peasants!'

He loved Man, but not men—Mr Cleanslate, the recluse sequestered in the dust-laden greyness of his house with his *Newsweek*, *Bulletin* and *Time*, in which he read with contempt of prime ministers and presidents and scorned those ambassadors, businessmen and movie stars who luxuriated arrogantly in the crystal of elegance and basked unabashed in the shimmer of fame.

'Sheep!'

He loved Man, but not men—the retired schoolmaster sitting on a Saturday afternoon under the cobwebs of his verandah, scowling with char-black odium at the current of legs that streamed towards Princes Park a block away to waste precious hours in the delirium and frenzy of a football match.

'Animals!'

He loved Man, but not men—the widower peering out through curtainless windows, before which he gritted his teeth with stifling distemper as young fellows and girls idled on the nature strip or splayed themselves out under the elms or clung or petted or giggled in distracted amusement.

He loved Man, but not men—and yet, and yet, Mr Cleanslate, he loved me.

Gnarled tubers were those fingers that probed through my hair, wrinkled hide the hand against my cheek, and bursting blasts the breath that pelted my face.

'Listen, just listen,' he said, touching my arm. 'Shut your eyes, let yourself go, and listen.'

Mother, pitying, concerned, had sent me in with soup, stewed fruit and cake for our neighbour. My trouble he rewarded with music.

Ever obedient, I listened; to the sound that cascaded along the murky shafts of mote-laden light; to the resonance that dispelled the muteness of the shadowed corners; to the reverberations that danced about the grubby globe that hung orphaned from the ceiling.

Himself leaning back, chin on chest, he sat, his thin lips flaccid, his eyes lidded caskets recessed in the scalloped hollows above his cheeks.

'Shh, don't breathe,' he said. 'Open your ears, and hear, hear with your soul the splendour created by Man.'

I listened, though I could not help but breathe, and heard with what I understood to be my soul the splendour that had been created by Man. First Mozart, then Schubert, then Bach, and Beethoven, Mendelssohn and Brahms. Each day another name, each day another feast offered in exchange for Mother's meagre morsels.

'Learn music,' he said, turning over the record, his emery eyes the while probing mine. 'Learn. And keep on learning. The mind of a child is a fertile plain. Feed it. Nourish it. Don't let it fall fallow like the minds of those unthinking creatures outside.'

He reached out. My cheeks felt both the warmth and the quiver of his hand.

'Men are a rabble, a mob, ignorant as beasts. But Man, Man has the capacity to be a god.'

Long after I left him, the words reverberated. *To be a god... To be a god...* With Beethoven, Mozart, Bach. With Schubert, Mendelssohn, Brahms...

Fired, influenced, I prevailed upon my parents to have me taught music.

I continued to deliver meals. Mr Cleanslate seemed to await my visits.

The morning had been dew-laden, the afternoon splendid, the evening cool once more. Scarcely had I set down the tray upon his table before he thrust a weathered book into my hand.

'Here, read this,' he said, with the tip of his index finger rapping at a chosen page. 'The universe is contained in every word, in every line eternity, infinity, perfection.'

He straightened and raised his face in impenetrable reverie. His lips, thin and ridged and drily liverish twitched in readiness for oration. His fingers manipulated air.

> *To be or not to be—that is the question:*
> *Whether 'tis nobler in the mind to suffer*
> *The slings and arrows of outrageous fortune,*
> *Or to take up arms against a sea of troubles,*
> *And by opposing end them?*

I marvelled. Not a mistake, no hesitation or fumbling. Mr Cleanslate, the teacher turned actor, held me. More than the words, whose meaning eluded my comprehension, the rhythm of the phrases and the flowing-ebbing tide of the old man's tremulous voice burrowed a shivering core down my spine and stirred nests of goose-pimples to bristling. I scarcely breathed.

'Who would fardels bear,' he continued, his voice pitched to graver intimacy,

To grunt and sweat under a weary life,
But that the dread of something after death,
The undiscover'd country, from whose bourn
No traveller returns, puzzles the will,
And makes us rather bear those ills we have,
Than fly to others that we know not of?

The recitation ended, his body contracted to meagreness and the glow of ecstasy purpled into spleen. I sensed the advent of a storm.

His fingers curled about my neck.

'Hah! Look out there, into the street, at that... that rabble that thinks itself literate when all it reads are the sports pages of the papers and thinks it can write when it scribbles filth on lavatory walls. Who reads Shakespeare today, tell me? Or Dante, Dostoyevski or Tolstoy, ha? And who today can even write like them?'

The breath lapping my face smelled of cinnamon, the cinnamon with which Mother had spiced his fruit.

'Forty years!' he exclaimed, his hand become a claw gripping my shoulder. 'Forty years was I a teacher, and what did I have of it? Class after class, year after year of blockheads, chaff; children of their parents turning their backs on knowledge, beauty, truth in pursuit of pettiness and prattle, blind—my God, how blind—to the power that stirs in Man.'

His eyes, anchored to the depths of chiselled sockets, pierced. His vibrating voice burred more harshly.

'Sometimes, there is a star, a boy, a girl with a gift—a gift for speech, poetry, art. But where are they now? Tell me. You, *you* tell me.'

I would have shrugged my shoulders but the clasp of his hand strangled movement.

'Out there!' he cried out, though his bambooed body could scarcely contain his thunder. 'There! Burnt out, nobodies, shells of what they might have been. Doctors, yes, and architects, plumbers, nurses, mechanics, lawyers. My children! All of them at one time my children. But how humdrum have their lives become, how commonplace, hollowed out, genius a foreign word. If this... if this be the fruit of my work, then may the world be extinguished before it crumbles from insipidity.'

He turned more squarely to me. With a crooked finger, he propped up my chin.

'And you, my young friend. You. Will you be more than they?'

My gaze fell as once more the words stirred inner depths and resounded as echo. *Will you be more than they... Will you be more than they...* Yes. Yes. I *will* be more than they.

———◆·▸◂·◆———

At school, after school, my friends called to me.

'Wanna kick of the ball?' Ricky Boxall tempted.

'A game of cricket?' Stuey Rivett coaxed.

'Hey, let's play marbles,' Robbie Ferguson pressed.

'No thanks.' 'Some other time.' 'Can't now,' I answered them all.

I stood outside their paths for I had begun to circle other orbits. First Shakespeare, Dostoyevski, and Tolstoy. Then Chekhov, Maupassant, Flaubert, all thrust into my hands by Mr Cleanslate who kindled, then pumped the bellows upon the flickering flames that glowed with the ardour to be some day more than 'they'. Into the nights I read, during recesses, lunch breaks, even in class while Bertie Quayle, hissing, 'Cissy', prodded me in the back, and shortsighted Mrs Myrtleford taught the principles of quadratic equations, square roots, and sines, cosines and tangents. Mother fretted that I was growing pale, plied me with vitamins and tonics, and advised air, sunlight, exercise and friends. I heard the words, but for the actual counsel my ears were filled with wax. I clung to the indoors, with books, books, books before me, and when I foundered beneath the weight of literary genius, I turned to the piano or immersed myself in a sea of rondos, largos and andantes kept at high tide by Mr Cleanslate who showered upon me his Beethovens, Mozarts and Bachs with the fervour of missionary zeal.

I continued to bring him his portions.

As always, he led me into his dingy lounge-room where journals, books and records lay in chaotic heaps on the frayed settee, the coffee table and floor.

Paganini dispelled the gloom.

'You are a precious lad,' Mr Cleanslate said, grazing my cheek with the crumpled hide of his hand. His face was pixie-like at that moment, the chin honed to pointing, the ears high, thin and protruding, the faintest hint of hairy fluff at the temples. 'If only Anthony... Hah!'

That little explosion clung to him as with swift jerky movements he mince-stepped to the bookcase from which he removed a large white-jacketed volume, its cover illustrated with paintings, sketches and tapestries.

'Take it, this is for you,' he said. 'A gift. A store of genius. Michelangelo, Da Vinci, Rubens, Rembrandt, Goya.'

The pages crackled with virgin crispness. On the flyleaf was an inscription: 'To Anthony. To your growth. May you reach the blessed heights. From your father.'

'Hah!' he huffed again. 'A son. A nobody. A drop in the multitude. A speck of dust. A grain of sand. But you, will you dare to be different?'

He rapped at the volume. 'Look! Study!'

Before me, colour followed colour as, his hands pitching and descending in paroxysms of motion, Mr Cleanslate frisked through the pages.

'The Mona Lisa! The Sistine Chapel! The Prodigal Son! The David! The Maja!—That is art! Not the trash in our galleries. Those Willy-nilly shapes, splashes of colour, distorted faces and landscapes without depth—all flatness, emptiness, the effluent of wishy-washy minds and wretched talent.'

He moved towards the window and pointed outside.

'What do they know of art, those rag-pickers out there, those philistines who, would they but know it, would they but care, could be free, could be great?' He beckoned to me. 'To be great is to create, to dive deep for the pearls within one's soul, to cultivate them and bring to the surface the treasures present in every man and transform what is raw into the colour, harmony and grandeur of music, of literature, of art. Had I but known this at your age... or had I been able to persuade Anthony...' His hand upon my shoulder slackened. 'How easily a man fails himself; how easily a son fails his father. For myself, forty years a teacher, where's the gain? And a son a bank clerk, where's the future?'

He searched my face.

'But you... You, so young still with the pearls waiting to be salvaged from the depths. Scorn the tastes of the masses! For that is the way to ignorance and enslavement. The way to greatness is through freedom. Will you dare be free? Will you, will you dare be great?'

Will you dare be great... Will you dare be great... The words rang, and my fantasy, fired, promised to dare.

The seas of genius in which I swam swelled into oceans. Names luminous in their greatness tumbled through my brain. Gorky, Turgenev, Balzac; Dvorak, Vivaldi, Brahms; Vermeer, Titian, Hals. And in their midst was I as my piano yielded to the zealous assault of my fingers and the library at school failed to sate my appetite.

In those oceans I swam alone, drifting from companions I had swum with before. The distances from them which I attained exceeded their vision, the depths I reached were to them unknown. And there was pride in that and satisfaction and superiority and, in the full glare of that adolescent sun, I glowed to myself as I harnessed gorgeous treasures to that surface from the very deepest of those fabulous depths.

But how to quell the swelling loneliness and the taunts?

'Wanna throw a ball?' Ricky called.

'I'm reading.'

'How's about noughts and crosses?' asked Stuey.

'No.'

'Comin' to the footy, Saturdy?' said Robbie.

'Don't care for footy.'

'What about Bertie's party?' asked Mickey.

'I'm not invited.'

And the taunts.

'Snob.'

'Highbrow.'

'Mr Stuck-up.'

'Peacock.'

'Fop.'

The names stuck to me, names that barbed and pricked and pinioned me to whatever barrier I set between my classmates and myself in the resolve some day to be more than they, to rise above their mediocre commonality and exult, lustrous magnet to their awe; while, away from school, ensconced behind a book in the haven of my home, I fell to Mother's plaints and admonitions as, fretting, she dragged me to Dr Barnett complaining that I was becoming unnaturally thin, pale and moody and that I was weakening my eyes. Could she but have known the pride she would one day reap from her son!

'It's his age,' Dr Barnett said, the portrait of benevolence, delivering his diagnosis with bold authority. 'He has nothing that a little sun and fresh air cannot remedy.'

How I hated him for that! But for Mother his words became a commandment to be consummately observed. My homework completed, she drove me into the street.

'The light is God's gift to growing bones.'

'I've got nothing to do out there, no one to play with.'

'What about your friends—Robert and Michael, and Richard and Tommy and Stuart?'

'They're dull.'

'And you, hiding your face behind those books, are a brilliant star, I suppose.'

'Mother!'—I wanted to shout—'I am! I shall be! One day you shall see!'

But her sarcasm cut deep and the sting in the wound silenced any attempt at such a declaration or promise. My future, to me so luminous, stifled into secrecy.

'Now go outside,' she pressed. 'Enjoy yourself. Be like the other boys.'

'And what about Mr Cleanslate?' I asked, clutching at another reason for remaining indoors, clinging to another hope.

'I'll see that he doesn't starve,' she answered, her palm pressing against my back, advancing me through the front door. 'From now on, leave that to me.'

And, indeed, it was Mother who now carried the portions to Mr Cleanslate, remaining there just long enough to transfer the food to his plates and rinse her own and ask, in her bustling practised way, after his well-being and his needs.

Once more, then, the streets and parks claimed me as I yielded to Dr Barnett's and Mother's prescription of sun and exercise and fresh air. I did not forget the miracles and magic woven by the 'Greats', but treasure and eternity now mingled with the earthbound and the temporal as, falling in with the sport of regained friends, I chased again those oval balls of bouncing leather and puffed once more in races after school and joined as before in their chatter of football, parties, rock'n'roll and girls.

In our games, they led, I followed. Into the streets, the parks and nature-strips. On playing fields and footpaths. Outside their houses, outside mine, and in the lanes where we ran and kicked and leapt and in stealth pursued our footballs over fences and gingerly retrieved them from rooftops or recklessly salvaged them from trees. No garden, yard or flowerbed was sacred. Wherever our feet could stand, there was our domain. And neither the reprimands of the Thompsons and the curses of the Macdonalds nor the warnings of the Kenneallys bothered us one bit. If to fly were within our power, we would have claimed even the stars. The quiet of the suburb being ours to violate, we penetrated its every interstice, which led us one day, too, to the nature-strip before my house.

There, Tommy kicked the ball. Ricky and Stuey soared. I scouted at their feet and snatched the ball. Weaving, I ran, bounced the ball, kicked. Now, Mickey marked it and, with a resounding whoop, sent it back. It fell into Ricky's hands. Kicking high, he brought down rain, and Robbie, dashing in, scooped it up, twisted, turned and dummied and skewed the ball over a rolling shoulder. Back and forth, the ball oscillated while we in turn chased after it until, with a leg-breaking kick, Mickey sent the ball careering on to Mr Cleanslate's verandah where it bounced, leapt, thudded at the window and came to rest beneath its sill.

The nearest to his house, I scaled the gate and scampered up the path. Robbie laughed, Tommy squatted, Stuey executed a cartwheel, Mickey did chin-ups, Ricky leaned against a tree. The sweat warm on my face, I picked up the ball, turned and began to run back when, in my haste, unseeing, I collided with Mr Cleanslate standing before the door.

Warmth became cold. Words of explanation formed frenziedly in my brain but, released into the open, dissipated into incoherent mumbling. I tried to pass him, but thin and wizened as he was, he seemed to occupy the entire breadth of the verandah. He stood immobile before me, a book in his hand, his pointed face contracted, his brow furrowed, his eyebrows drawn together, his pixie ears more prominent than ever. He frowned, his teeth clearly set on edge, but, in the depths of his expression, there lingered something less tangible, elusive, yet close to pain.

Face groping at face, he riveted me with his gaze, glanced with hatred swift and indisputable at the football in my hands, then once more fixed his eyes upon me. The whole episode may have lasted a mere instant, the briefest flicker of an eyelid, but in that moment, there passed before me the image of the teacher transported by the magic of Mozart and Michelangelo, of the teacher turned actor reciting Hamlet in a voice that sent goose pimples through my flesh, of the recluse pointing a lean-tubered finger at a world outside replete with host upon host of humdrum lives, the dross-laden lives of men who, would they but know it, could be free, could be great and rise to be as gods.

And in that instant, he reached out, cupped the chin of my shame-bowed face, nodded slowly and sadly as if at something lost, and said in a voice muted with regret, *'Et tu, Brute, et tu?'*

PAUL DAFFEY

Home and Away

Paul Daffey is a journalist who has written about footy for fifteen years. He's written two books, *Local Rites* and *Beyond the Big Sticks: Country Football Around Australia*, and has contributed to several others. In recent years he's been co-editor of the *Footy Almanac*, an annual book on the AFL season, and in 2013 he was co-editor of *Chewy On Your Boot: Stories From Australia's Game* (Malarkey Publications). He's travelled throughout every state during his footy wanderings and his favourite footy state is Tasmania, where the stories are richer. He loves the grandstand at the Queen Elizabeth Oval in Bendigo and the ambience at Tanunda in the Barossa Valley. He felt most wanted when he covered Swifts Creek v Benambra in East Gippsland and both teams asked him to play. He lives in Melbourne with his wife, two sons and a daughter. The family is split between Richmond and Hawthorn. This essay is an edited extract from *Beyond the Big Sticks* (Lothian, 2003).

Kevin Sheedy has a predilection for looking at football grounds on his journeys around Australia. If he is talking at a function, he might stop off to check out a nearby oval. If he is driving on holiday with his family, he might nudge the car through the gates of the local home of footy for a quick look-see. Some people think that poking around footy grounds is an eccentric, somewhat baffling thing to do, but many of us know better. Maybe there is a lovely row of elms behind the goals or a kink in the forward pocket. The grandstand might reflect a glorious age or the tin shed might need a spruce-up. No two footy grounds are the same. All reveal something of the local foibles and triumphs. Each one is a delight in its own way.

The Swifts Creek Recreation Reserve was built in a gully in Victoria's East Gippsland around the time of the First World War. Local sportsman Neil

McLarty had created a legend by running around tree stumps during his training for professional foot races. Eventually, bullock teams removed the stumps and an oval was built. The slope of the ground was unfortunate, but a compromise was reached by placing the centre circle ten metres towards the uphill goals. In 1972, a Benambra contractor was called in to reduce the slope. He used earthmoving machinery rather than a bullock team, but just before the job was done he was summoned to Orbost to repair damage caused by the flooding Snowy River. Refurbishment at the western end at Swifts Creek remains unfinished.

Throughout its existence, the Swifts Creek oval has attracted as much interest from wildlife as from footballers. Up to thirty kangaroos share the ground with the team during training. Wombats and rabbits might join in the drills as well. On match days, robust flames light up the valley. The fire is the work of supporter Neil Clark, who gathers stumps and branches from local farms and stacks the wood between the social rooms and the dressing sheds. His woodpiles are two metres high. 'It's just rubbishy wood nobody wants in the paddock,' Clark said. The fire is lit during the second half. The game recedes while the flames climb, seeming to keep the hills at bay. The blaze and the surrounding beauty create an ideal setting in which to dissect the game. Supporters chat around the fire until about nine, when the flames begin dying off. The supporters then leave the valley and retire to the pub.

The bar at the Tanunda Oval in the Barossa Valley is surely among the wonders of the football world. Built beneath a grandstand of lumpy bluestone, it features honour boards the length of the room and memorabilia cabinets filled with old footy boots and yellowing programs. Most strikingly, though, it features a wine list. Many football clubs struggle to provide heavy and light beer, let alone a blackboard listing the local drops. Around the ground, pine trees offer shade under which bottles are uncorked and picnic baskets unloaded. Two hours before the senior match, there is a festive atmosphere and few remaining car parks. Tanunda on a sunny day appeals as one of the leading grounds in Australia for watching the footy.

In northern Queensland, the bar in the Port Douglas clubrooms offers a languid contrast to the jostling verve at Tanunda. High ceilings and louvres allow the breeze through, which keeps supporters cool. Outside the bar, a wide veranda offers a view across the oval to the Great Dividing Range, which continues down the east coast to the Grampians in faraway Victoria. Around the ground, a ring of tropical trees protects spectators from the beating sun. Amid such tranquil splendour, you would never guess that the ground was built on a rubbish tip.

Visitors to the Rosebery oval in western Tasmania once thought the ground was built on a sewage farm. Pipes beneath the oval drained water into the Stitt River, which runs behind the ground. This river was the main outlet for the town sewage. Sometimes the river flooded, and the water, bearing sewage, was pushed along the pipes before settling beneath the oval. The term 'foul conditions' had strong resonance at Rosebery. Opposition players would walk off after the final siren and discard their shorts in the river.

The problem was averted when sewage was sent into waste dams, but this had little effect on the condition of the oval during the 2002 season. While most of the mainland was parched by drought, more than 2,300 millimetres of rain fell on Rosebery over 221 days, prompting milkbar owner Judy Mackerell to keep a rainfall chart by the counter to satisfy the questions of saturated tourists. Rosebery residents live in the shadow of Mt Reid, the wettest place in Tasmania, and expect a life of moisture. But the precipitation of 2002 struck them as excessive. 'It was depressing,' said Mackerell.

At the height of the football season, rain fell almost every day. Players sank to their shins in mud and umpires battled to find a spot on which to restart play. The condition of the oval increased pressure on hydroelectricity operators to stop seeding clouds with chemicals that induce rain. The practice of seeding keeps dams full and cuts hydro costs, but in an area already ranked among the wettest in Australia, it's no good for football.

Locals report that Kevin Sheedy once described the Rosebery oval as the most attractive in country Australia. They say Sheedy made the claim at a sportsmen's night in Burnie after visiting the

Rosebery oval earlier that day. Sheedy can't remember making the claim, which is unsurprising considering his extensive travels as a football evangelist over four decades, but he does remember that it was a beautiful ground. The valley of rainforest gums in which the Rosebery oval is nestled would support any claims of beauty; six inches of stinking mud would not.

About fifty kilometres south, the Queenstown oval is like nothing else in football. Known as The Gravel, for the good reason that its surface consists entirely of gravel, the ground at the heart of the famous mining town has hosted matches for more than a century. Mainland tourists stop to spoon a sample of the ground into small bottles to take home. The visitors are fascinated by the sand and loam surface, which enables the oval to withstand rainfall that would float Noah's ark.

Rex Powell played on The Gravel for two decades after the Second World War, in the days when it was still laid with silica from the smelters. Now a gatekeeper at the ground on match days, he said working bees used to be held to comb the surface for larger rocks, but mostly the ground was left to its own devices. Players accepted the inconvenience of scarred skin as the price to pay for a surface that provided true bounce in all conditions. 'You'd always lose a bit of bark around your knees,' Powell said, 'but that never hurt anyone.'

Even if The Gravel is under water two hours before a match, you can be sure it will be ready for action by the first bounce. Games are held during a cycle of five minutes sunshine, five minutes drizzle and ten minutes downpour. The hills surrounding the ground are often capped in snow, even as late as December. Sulphur emissions from the gold and copper mines have denuded the hills of growth. There is little comfort to be found at The Gravel, or anywhere around it.

The custodians of the ground, the Queenstown Crows, a club that was formed from the remnants of the west coast competition in 1993, now face resistance from some opponents. Several clubs in the Burnie region believe The Gravel is a health hazard. In recent years they have pushed for the oval to be laid with grass. Some players refuse to play there. The Crows exacerbate the problem by hurling opponents into the crunchy surface, sorting out the fearless from the faint of heart in a ritual that casts doubt on their suitability as hosts.

After the match, trainers move from player to player with a wire brush and a bottle of Friars Balsam. Stones are scraped from elbows and knees before disinfectant is applied. Some Queenstown players spend the entire season with weeping sores. No sooner does a scab look like healing than it sticks to the player's trouser leg. If the scab does survive until the next match, it's usually knocked off in the first quarter. No wonder the west coast of Tasmania is known for breeding tough footballers.

Just as the Queenstown oval is known as The Gravel, the oval at Derby in north-east Tasmania should be known as The Slope. Tourists stop to take in the rickety grandstand and the glorious view over the valley towards the town. But invariably they find equal wonder in the gradient of the oval. It's going too far to say that the Derby oval should be set up as a ski run, but only because it receives too little snow.

Derby had a ground within the trotting track that was on a bend in the Ringarooma River before a mining company diverted the river through the ground after the Second World War. The company promised a new oval to match the one that now had a river running through it, but fell some way short of its promise. One of the mine's stone dumps, high on the hill on the other side of the river, was levelled off in a fashion. Dirt was spread across the stones by piping water onto the hill and washing the dirt down. Goalposts were then erected. John Beswick, a former Derby centre half-back and member of state parliament for two decades, admitted that the oval made a mockery of the company's promise. 'Mining was king in Derby in those times,' he said.

A grandstand believed to have been at the trotting track since early in the century was shifted to the new football ground, where it offered a lofty view over the valley. You could stand on a saucepan and the view over the valley would still be magnificent, but Beswick was eager to point out that the steep drop never affected a result. Both teams, after all, kicked downhill for two quarters. Besides, plenty of goals were scored against the gradient. 'You got used to it,' Beswick said.

The closure of the main mine in Derby after the Second World War prompted a gradual decline in population until the football club folded in 1972. Local farmer Ron Hayes bought the grandstand and the oval—or he thought he was buying the oval until he was informed that the law would prevent him. Stuck with a grandstand, he stored hay in it. After several years, he sold the grandstand to the cricket club for $100 because he wanted to avoid possible liability for a visitor losing a foot through the floorboards. The Derby cricket club, aiming to return the stand to its considerable glory, held many working bees for more than a decade before lack of players forced the club to fold in 2001. The future of the Derby grandstand, which some Tasmanians regard as a state treasure, remains unclear.

Back along the Ringarooma River from Derby, the Ringarooma oval offers postcard views towards surrounding mountain ranges that are capped with snow during winter. Red and orange leaves dot the valley in autumn. The oval itself once featured a stump near the centre circle and a stream that babbled across the volcanic soil when it rained. The stream reportedly ran through the goals and out the gate. The stump was removed but nothing could be done to shift the submerged rocks that create a rise away from the rooms and towards Mt Victoria. A blast of dynamite might have solved the problem, but it would also have jeopardised the grandstand.

The grandstand is a delight. Besides offering the view towards the mountains, it features a bell suspended from its roof. Early in the twentieth century, members of the Krushka family used the bell to summon workers on their North View property for meals, and occasionally for emergencies. After a while, the family donated the bell to the football club. Timekeeper Alf Krushka rang it at the end of every quarter until he was too old to climb the steps into the timekeeper's box.

The ground at Osborne in southern New South Wales is notable for being in the middle of nowhere. There is no town and no pub, just lots of paddocks split by straight roads. Clubs exist in similar isolation around Australia, but few reap the success of Osborne. In recent decades, the club has accumulated many premierships against their rivals from town clubs in the Hume Football League.

Osborne doesn't pay rates. Its oval is built on four hectares that the club bought from a local farmer in the early 1980s. A few years later, Osborne ruckman Chris Ralston stuck a picture of his cherished home ground on the players' noticeboard at Moorabbin after St Kilda had asked him to try out. 'I just wanted to show them where I learned my footy,' Ralston said. St Kilda teammates such as Danny Frawley and Geoff Cunningham, both from the lush Ballarat district, scratched their heads. The Osborne oval appeared so brown and barren that it looked to be almost unplayable. The lack of any sign of life greatly worried them. 'They were concerned that there was no town,' said Ralston, who returned home after a few games with the St Kilda reserves. 'I said it was a farming community—everyone pulls together.'

Hume league opponents also struggle to comprehend the barrenness of the Osborne oval. With no council groundsmen to water the ground, the club relies entirely on rain to sustain the turf. Opposition clubs complain if they are drawn to play at the ground before the autumn rains bring relief. But then a game at Osborne brings dread at any time.

The death of soldiers during the First World War is honoured through monuments and memorials in cities and towns around Australia. Few memorials are linked with football, but in Victoria's Western District the passing of six Port Fairy sportsmen in the war prompted the people of their hometown to build the Sailors and Seamen's Memorial Grandstand at the Gardens Oval. The idea for the memorial in Port Fairy prompted similar tributes at smaller Western District towns.

The Allansford Memorial Pavilion was once a church or hall in Orford, a small town north of Port Fairy. The building was hauled through Warrnambool and across to Allansford by horse and cart, then placed on top of a shed, where it served as a grandstand. Both teams changed beneath the stand, on either side of a shaky partition. A stone chimney blew smoke from the rooms. In recent years, Allansford footballers have used the room below the grandstand as a gymnasium. Sadly, the chimney has gone.

However, refurbishment has revived the grandstand to its rightful place in the hearts of the region. On a day of gentle winter sun during a Warrnambool and District match of limited interest, the Allansford grandstand was bubbling. Spectators of all ages basked in the sun and delighted in sitting in such a charming old relic. The Allansford grandstand has that effect: people just want to sit in it. There can be no greater recommendation for what cynics might describe as a bunch of old seats.

The seats in the memorial grandstand at Port Pirie in South Australia are also inviting. Queen quests and ugly-man competitions raised money to build the roomy grandstand before it was finally opened in 1927. Celebrations included an exhibition match between a combined local team and Adelaide club West Torrens. Newspapers reported that everyone from the mayor and police chief to the baker's wife attended the gala opening.

The grandstand remains stout and hardy, offering a view across the oval to the blue flanks of the Flinders Ranges. Beneath the stand, a large concrete pylon interrupts a sea of wooden floorboards that hosted cabaret evenings. The bar beneath the grandstand was the swinging centre of Port Pirie for decades.

Grandstands in the goldfields of Victoria celebrate the vanity of men rather than the valour of fallen soldiers. Towns such as Bendigo, Ballarat and Maryborough created ostentatious displays of wealth that contrasted with the mood of the depression in Melbourne in the 1890s. The stand at Princes Park in Maryborough was the first. Built in 1895, it was modelled on a grandstand at the Lake Oval in South Melbourne that was later destroyed by fire. Collingwood modelled a grandstand on the Maryborough version before it was demolished during renovations at Victoria Park in 1966.

The gardens around the oval in Maryborough are landscaped. Pines and willows form a fringe around Lake Victoria, which tends to attract the footy when a westerly springs up, while elms frame the rotunda that was built as a war memorial. Other landscaped recreation reserves in Victoria include Melville Oval in Hamilton, but nothing really matches the grandeur of Maryborough. Even the toilets at Princes Park are of interest, being art deco in design.

The gardens surrounding the Eastern Oval in Ballarat earned the ground its ranking among the treasures of the colony during Victoria's boom years of the 1880s. A century later, however, the soil was dead. Even experts from the botanical gardens were unable to revive it. Any grass was washed away at the first hint of rain, prompting the Ballarat council into several failed attempts to redress the problem, including laying pipes—but those blocked up almost straight away. Finally, in 2001, the moribund turf was dug up and sand-based soil was laid down. The ground was widened and lengthened, and new drainage was installed. Ballarat historian and former football administrator Wayne Hankin said it was noticeable that water was running into Yarrowee Creek immediately after rain had fallen. 'The ground really is first class now,' Hankin said.

The Eastern Oval's rival for premier status in Ballarat, the City Oval, was the source of great controversy around the time that its grandstand was built in 1898. Before the grandstand's completion, Alex Bell, the mayor of the City of Ballarat, renamed the ground Bell Park, much to the anger of his citizens. The resultant uproar ensured that the name of the City Oval was restored.

More than a century later, in 2002, an uproar was created in Bendigo by the proposed redevelopment of the Queen Elizabeth Oval. Few disagreed with plans that included refurbishing the oval, but it was the plan to alter the shape of the oval that aroused great passion. The ground is more or less rectangular because it hosted concurrent cricket matches until the early 1980s. In the clear, baking heat of the central Victorian summer, one bowler would approach one pitch at the top end, and another bowler would approach a second pitch at the bottom end. Two decades later, the Bendigo city council decided that, with one central pitch, there was no need for deep pockets. The council voted to chop nine metres off each pocket, allowing the oval to assume the shape of most grounds in Australia, and bring in the picket fence to follow the new contours. The football co-tenants, Sandhurst and South Bendigo, as well as most clubs in the Bendigo Football League, made it clear that they liked the shape of the ground, and many Bendigo football fans agreed. The drought delayed refurbishments and gave the objectors time to muster forces.

Advocates of change wrote letters to the *Bendigo Advertiser* arguing that the shape was effectively an aberration of history. Others insisted that such history should be maintained. In the end, the Bendigo Football League presented the council with a case for sticking with tradition, and the decision to cut the pockets was reversed. Refurbishment was due to start after the 2003 season.

Besides the straight wings and square pockets, the Queen Elizabeth Oval is renowned for the impressive grandstand that was built in 1901. Down the road, the Bill Woodfull Reserve in Maldon doesn't have a grandstand like its celebrated neighbour, but it does have a courthouse, the only one in Australia at a football ground. The brick building was built on the wing in 1861. Maldon historian Brian Rhule said, 'What you see now is essentially what was there then.'

The last case at the courthouse was a minor traffic offence heard in 1969. The building then fell into disrepair before refurbishments were completed in 2001. Among the leading problems was rising damp. On the field, footballers must deal with a rising surface. From the eastern end of the reserve, which includes the botanical gardens, the land rises eight metres. Earth was gouged out of the rise to create the oval.

The rise of the oval is now far less than eight metres, but it is still considerable. Spectators in the shadow of Mt Tarrengower, where gold was first found in Maldon, hover over the players from the top of a steep wall. Forwards at the botanical gardens end look uphill and anticipate a flood of attacking moves. However, they look uphill while shielding their eyes. The problem is especially acute in the last quarter, when the sun dips low on the horizon. This inconvenience balances out the advantage of the slope. At the only ground in Australia to feature a courthouse, a measure of justice is assured.

RAMONA KOVAL

Thighs and Whispers

Ramona Koval is a writer, journalist and broadcaster. Her most recent book is *By the Book: A Reader's Guide to Life*, published by Text in November 2012. She presents *The Monthly* book podcast at http://www.themonthly.com.au/ramona-koval and blogs at ramonakoval.com. She edited *Best Australian Essays 2012*, published by Black Inc, and for many years was the presenter of ABC Radio National's *The Book Show*. 'Thighs and Whispers' first appeared in *The Greatest Game* by Ross Fitzgerald and Ken Spillman (eds., 1988).

I had to hold hands with the wartiest boy in folk dancing. This was because I was the New Girl. And because my parents were New Australians. And because I didn't know about football and teams. At St Kilda Park State School, even with blonde curls and blue eyes, I was the woggy kid. My mother gave me the crusty bread sandwiches with salami or herring salad. All I wanted was Peck's Paste with the crusts cut off. I begged her to throw away my little red lunch box and wrap my lunch in newspaper like the Aussie kids.

They asked me, 'Whojabarrakfor?' I did not know the answer to this question. Neither did Mama. Eventually I understood that this referred to football teams.

'Which team do we barrack for, Mama?'

'Don't get into any fights. Say you barrack for all of them. No favourites!'

Mother was worried that football was like politics. You shouldn't show your preferences: the Nazis would come and shove you up against the wall if you gave the wrong answer.

I told the kids I barracked for all of them. This was not the right answer. You had to barrack for only one, and that one had to be the team that your family had always barracked for. Even when they were bottom of the ladder. Even if they had always been bottom of the ladder. Kids might feel sorry for you, having such a hopeless team, but you weren't allowed to change it ever, or you were a rat.

'What team did we barrack for in Poland, Mama?'

'We barracked for the winners.'

'Did we barrack for Collingwood?'

'No, we barracked for the liberation forces of the Red Army. And then we barracked for the occupation forces of the American Army. Okay? Now eat your soup.'

Team sports were not part of our Way of Life. First of course, it was every man for himself—'Teams? Ha! They always let you down.' This was based on the true fact that Mama's best friend told the Germans that she was Jewish. That's team sport for you. Games—these were the province of those who didn't know what real life was about. Gin rummy, yes. Football, no. Anyway, I was a girl.

But even Aussie girls barracked. They had scarves. And streamers. I learned the nicknames diligently. The Bombers. The Cats. The Magpies. And I even knew the teams they stood for. At playtime we had to reel them off like a litany.

I worked out that most of the kids barracked for St Kilda. I thought that was safe. I lived in St Kilda. Could you get gassed in a concentration camp for barracking for St Kilda? I resolved never to tell them I was Jewish and took a St Kilda cover. No one would ever know. We made a new Greek girl hold hands with the wartiest boy. We asked her what team she barracked for. We laughed when she didn't know. I had finally picked the winning side!

Then I wanted a scarf. In the St Kilda colours. Red, white and black. I asked my dad. He hardly ever knew about anything Australian, but he was a tailor in a factory in Flinders Lane, and I thought I could trust him with this one. Although I had to admit, in my heart of hearts, that the coats he made for me every year were terrible. Not one year would pass when my winter coat would actually fit. There was always one arm short and one side longer than the other. He said it was my fault for not standing straight. No one ever believed me, but I can to this day proudly show them proof. There in the family album is the evidence. Me, at five, in a vile shade of yellow. The picture is in black and white, of course, taken with the box brownie, but the colour of pus oozes unmistakably out of it. Of course, we have no photos of me after that. Dad broke the box brownie, and he never replaced it.

But before it broke there's another picture of me, in my St Kilda scarf, crying uncontrollably. Why? Because the scarf was red. Just red.

'But I said red, white and black!'

'It's got red!'

'But what about white and black?'

'Red is nicer for children!'

'But I barrack for a team; I need red, white and black!'

'Why do you want what the others have? If they all jumped off a moving train, does it mean you would have to?'

'But the team has red, white and black!'

'You know, in the war, children died, little children smaller than you they were, because they didn't even have a scarf, and you tell me now about red and black and blue?'

'White, not blue.'

Although I always made sure I had the last word, I never won one of these arguments. I was always outnumbered by the poor, innocent, dying children in any of a dozen concentration camps.

Okay, forget the scarf. I took a square of white paper, drew a black and a red stripe, and stuck it to the inside of my desk lid. Mama made me wear the scarf, anyway. It was cold in St Kilda, and you might die of exposure if you didn't have a scarf wrapped around your throat three or four times. I threw it into someone's garden on the way home. I told them an Italian boy stole it.

At nine, I saw the little boys play footy as I wandered past the oval. They had little matchstick legs and baggy shorts. They had grubby little faces and blackened knees, and their shoelaces were always undone and far too long to be safe. And they shouted and never had baths. And the football seemed to go off in any direction. I had a few kicks once.

I preferred a game you could control. Like 'Fish' or 'Old Maid'. I could control these games by playing with my sister. And cheating.

Jewish people very rarely played anything that meant they had to go outside. Only at the beach, after enormous meals and coffee and ice-creams, the men would play Volly Bolly. This was a game where you didn't have rules, but you belted a ball over a net. I later came to recognise that this must have been an adaptation of volleyball. The rules and the pronunciation had been corrupted in the translation.

Cards seemed to be the national sport of my parents, played in smoke-filled lounge rooms on Friday night, with the men and women at separate card tables. At ten o'clock they would stop and have a rest with lemon tea and cheesecake. And poppyseed cake. And chocolate cake. And apple cake for those on diets.

In the morning there were lots of matchboxes upturned with the matches out. My father won millions of matches like this. But never any money. The kids played Monopoly or that one with all the questions and a magnetic pointer to tell you the answer. We were allowed to play those games because they helped to make us clever, and we would win scholarships and be famous doctors. Or at least marry them. Footy was for Aussie boys, and for knocking your brains out.

Even as a teenager, none of the boys I knew was a team sport type. They were good scholars with glasses and pimples. I was happy to overlook the pimples, because those boys lent me their physics notes. They preferred to make radios on Saturday afternoons with their electronic sets. If you came up real close to them, they smelt nice and earthy. They were beginning to get hair on their faces, and their voices were breaking.

Anyway, the boys at school who played in the team were always after the Cheryls and Elizabeths and Denises, who pashed on with them at dances and wore their friendship rings. They had those thoroughbred good looks that fresh air could bring. If I had ever brought home one of them, and a friendship ring, Mama would have slashed her wrists. Once, when I asked to go to a dance, she said that Hitler couldn't kill her, but I would.

If we ever drove past a football ground on a Saturday afternoon, my mother would click her tongue at the poor women who were being forced to go to the game with their men. They hadn't even had time to remove the curlers from their hair. The nylon scarves over the gaudy plastic display on their heads didn't fool anyone. We felt so sorry for them. Mama said that men at football matches got drunk and then bashed up their wives after the game. Even worse when their teams lost.

At university I avoided the boys who lived in college. They were called Ashley and Andrew and Lloyd and played for the university football team. But I did notice that they had long outgrown their baggy shorts and long jumpers. Times had changed since St Kilda Park State. They had teeny weeny shorts and muscular thighs. With hair on their legs and shapely calves. And those little jumpers with the sleeves cut out. And long arms with biceps and hairy armpits. Fabulous teeth and the most wonderful bottoms. I imagined them in the showers after the game, as they soaped themselves and tossed towels around. They were never circumcised.

The footy boys were the embodiment of all those things that made me different from them. They were the symbol of badness. I imagined that doing it with one of them would be like eating pork and shellfish with a milkshake, all at the same time. They were lamingtons at Passover.

Sometimes, even now, I'm drawn to the footy replays.

Ah, those thighs are still there. Big ones and bigger ones.

They're probably terrible lovers, all of them, grunting and working out the next handpass strategy.

And they do look silly, don't they, in those pictures at the end of the season. When they all line up like schoolboys, pushing their biceps out with their fists behind them. Don't they know we're not looking at those arms? We're all transfixed by those thighs—the way the muscles divide into twos and threes, the exquisite hardness of them.

I've grown out of wanting the scarf, or needing to belong to a team. I have never been to a football game, and I don't expect I ever will. But it's still a little thrill for a Jewish girl to imagine being sandwiched between a pair of those thighs, eating Peck's Paste on white bread, with the crusts cut off.

Go, St Kilda! Car'n, the Saints!

MARK O'CONNOR

Under Martian Eyes

Mark O'Connor was born in Melbourne in 1945, and graduated from Melbourne University in 1965. He is a professional poet and author of some fifteen books, with his poetry showing special interest in Italy, the Great Barrier Reef and the environment. Editor of Oxford University Press's much reprinted *Two Centuries of Australian Poetry*, he was Australia's 'Olympic poet' for the Sydney 2000 Games, with a fellowship from the Australia Council to 'report in verse on the Games'. O'Connor has been the Australian National University's H.C. Coombs Fellow and a visiting scholar in its Department of Archaeology and Natural History. Like his father, he is a Collingwood supporter. 'Under Martian Eyes' first appeared in *The Herald*, 6 May 1988.

The players, swathed in their overcoats,
push the incompetent celebrants on with voice,
with bitter love and indignant sorrow:
'Go in, you bludger!', 'Don't feel *sorry* for him!'
The ball they manoeuvre is stitched to keep
the oval shape of chance,
where every bounce demands good luck.

The players stand in the weather
under six compound-eyed Martians.
Their ground is ringed, a cyclotron
with walls to intensify the sound.
A minor kill. The stands rock with fury:
'Oh you mongrel!'—seagulls flung
aloft like exclamation marks.

The victim strapped to stretcher poles
is removed at the trot by tiger-coloured men.
Above, around, the Martians stand in prayer,
heads bent like elders.

Players are arbitrary.
White priests are trained to save them
from the haggard weight of justice; the square flags signal
from a world of adult fairness.
Their celebrants are immortal numbers, seasonally reborn
—giant 12, nuggety 7, legendary 4—
jostling forever in half-predicted patterns.
Their temple-in-the-round is open; the full moon,
day-pale, floating beyond the stands,
recalls them in tragedy or glory
to planetary perspective.

At the climax, surviving celebrants
change totem; skinning off colour,
each other's trophy.
Cars tidy the teams away; from nearby lairs
dull trains clank in at walking pace
and gulp their fill.

TERRY LANE

Dropping the Ball— The Original Sin

Terry Lane trained as a clergyman but is best known as an ABC radio broadcaster and writer. He presented local radio in Melbourne, Sydney, Newcastle and Hobart. *The National Interest* was heard on Radio National and Radio Australia. He wrote a weekly opinion column for the Melbourne *Herald* from 1987 to 1989, then for *The Sunday Age* until his retirement in 2007. He now writes a weekly page on digital imaging for the Livewire technology supplement of *The Age* and *The Sydney Morning Herald*. Lane is the author of eight books, including three novels. This essay was first published in *The Greatest Game* by Ross Fitzgerald and Ken Spillman (eds., 1988). In the same year, it was judged by the Anti-Football League to have done the least for football in the best and fairest way, earning Lane the Wilkie Medal.

> *'Not enough football and the boys will become pansies.'*
> —*Councillor Basil Fitch, March 1987*

Football is the metaphor for life. Beyond question. Absolutely. It is cruel, humiliating and savage. The rules are capricious and based on the Rightness of Might. It is vulgar, macho, nasty and brutish. Regrettably it is not also short. It is anything but. Even when summer is at its searing height the *Sun News Pictorial* will be running pictures of sweaty footballers toiling up and down sand dunes. It is omnipresent and inescapable. Most of all it is boring. Tedious, dull, tiresome and monotonous. I only regret that there are not more synonyms that I can call to my aid.

Here is how I came to this dismal view of football.

When I was a young man aspiring to be a Shepherd of the Lord's flock, studying in a theological college, mastering the rudiments of hermeneutics, eschatology and homiletics, we were presided over by an ecclesiastical version of Jekyll and Hyde.

On all days except Wednesdays our principal was a wise, good Christian gentleman. He was an eloquent man who taught us to value the power of the spoken word. He made church history live. He always sympathised with the underdogs—the non-conformists, the reformers, the pilgrims. He gave Holy Roman empires short shrift. He was a pacifist, prizing peace, gentleness and love. So persuasive was he in his ethics lectures that it was a rare bird who graduated with any enthusiasm for war.

He valued independent thinkers. He supported conscientious objectors. Conscientious objectors to everything but football, that is.

On Wednesday afternoons we were conscripted. Once a League footballer himself, the principal believed that the game would make men of us. He was that curious anomaly, the Muscular Christian. Football was compulsory. Obligatory. Inescapable. Utterly miserable.

'But, sir,' I would argue, 'how does compulsory football differ from compulsory military service? How does violence on the football field differ from violence on the battlefield?'

It was useless. And not only was he our principal, he was also, every Wednesday afternoon, the Umpire. God! The arbitrary punisher of sinners. The giver and interpreter of commandments. Chastiser of wrongdoers. And so on.

On Wednesday afternoons this gentle Christian pacifist became a fascist. A tyrant. The Franco of the football field. Genghis Khan. Hitler. Ivan the Terrible. A Pharisee. A Sadducee, even—and you know how bad they were! Don't you?

So every Wednesday afternoon we would assemble on the Glen Iris oval. You could easily pick the real footballers from the reluctant conscripts. The genuine article wore athletic supports and elastic bandages around their knees. To this day I have no idea what purpose is served by either of these accoutrements.

The reluctant conscripts, on the other hand, did not even own a pair of regulation boots. Impecunious student though I was, I was forced to destroy several pairs of perfectly good shoes on boggy ovals on Wednesday afternoons. I also never took to the oval without a decent book in hand to mitigate the boredom, and even on some occasions carried a brolly if the weather looked doubtful.

I was always assigned a position near the fence where the ball was least likely to come. In fact, it's not going too far to say that the regulars went to some lengths to keep the ball away from my patch on the field.

The Chief (as he was known) would blow the whistle, and away we would go. I could usually make a pretty good fist of keeping out of the way of the action. No one in his right mind would kick the ball towards me. But every now and again the speed of the melee would take me by surprise, and I would find myself in the midst thereof.

Once, in self-defence, I dropped my book and umbrella and grabbed the ball and kicked it towards the goal. I scored a behind. For the other team, it seemed. I had lost track of the direction during one of the changeovers. In my defence I must point out that it was a very foggy day—a pea souper, the sort only Melbourne could turn on back in the days when we still burned coal in our fires.

Never mind, I treasure that behind as the only score I ever recorded in football. I do not intend to be deprived of it.

Now I come to the capriciousness of the rules of this wretched game. What I hated and feared most of all was the thunder of the herd—huge, hulking, hairy chaps, more like Barbarians than Christians. The ground shook under their boots. Although they were my Brothers in Christ, I have to tell you on Wednesdays they were truly horrible.

Anyway, on another miserable day I got in the way of the ball again and actually had it in my hands, looking round for some way to dispose of it as quickly as possible, when the Herd arrived! One of the largest managed somehow to hit me in the kidney with his right shoulder. I 'oofed' loudly and dropped the ball. The Chief blew his whistle and— you will scarcely believe this—awarded a free kick to the oaf who had assaulted me. When I eventually got my breath back, I sought the theological justification for this outrage.

'Dropping the ball!'

Dropping the ball? Of course I dropped the bloody ball. I was just about in terminal renal failure, wasn't I? I was suffering. If anyone deserved the consolation of a free kick, it was I. If anyone deserved to be penalised, it was the oaf.

I wasn't going to take this lying down—well, not for long. I waited my opportunity, and eventually it came. He came running down my side of the field, bouncing the ball with nonchalant arrogance, and I hurled myself into the middle of his back.

Beeep went the umpire's whistle. The ball would be mine. Justice would be done.

'Free kick to Mr Harvey!'

What? Free kick to him? He dropped the ball.

'No, no,' called His Eminence the Umpire. 'You pushed him in the back. Free kick to him.'

And that's been more or less the way life has gone ever since. I don't understand the rules, but one thing I do know for certain, the umpire's decision is always outrageous, arbitrary, unfair and inexplicable.

Teetotallers are killed by drunken drivers who get off scot free. Innocent children die of leukaemia and warmongers live to ripe old ages. The wicked prosper. The Good die martyrs' deaths. The rain falls on the just and the unjust. It's all just like a game of football.

And like college football, it's compulsory. You can't get out of it. There is no other game on that they will let you play instead.

But this is a digression. I really want to consider the formation of national character based on the sin of dropping the ball.

Dropping the ball always seemed to me to be either inevitable, as when the kidneys are under attack, or prudent, as when the Herd is thundering down. But it's against the rules to do the prudent thing. The rules demand that you hang onto the ball, no matter what threatens. It's a rule for drongos. And it's a rule that has guided our national destiny.

Consider this. Australians have been in just about every war since the Mahdi got Gordon in the Sudan. Australians went to that one. Then to the Boer war. The Boxer Rebellion. The Great War and the nasty excursion into Russia afterwards to put down the Bolsheviks. Then the war in the North African desert, followed by the war in the Pacific, arguably the only one in which we had a legitimate interest. After that it was Korea, Malaya and the madness of Vietnam.

I have never been able to understand this enthusiasm for other people's wars. I certainly cannot understand why thousands of apparently sane young Australians keep going over the top to almost certain death. Except as some sort of obedience to the dropping the ball rule.

I once made a radio programme about football. I interviewed a bloke who had almost played for Fitzroy and another chap who had been a champion player, much sought after and owned by three different clubs at various times.

The almost-but-not-quite player was waxing lyrical about the virtues of the game. 'Embodies all that is best in the Australian character,' he boasted.

'Yep,' said the genuine article. 'Male chauvinism. Vulgarity. Love of violence. Mindless obedience to authority. Anti-intellectualism. Drunkenness. It's all there in the Great Game, no doubt about it.'

I couldn't have put it better myself—and I don't even like the game.

I used to say to the principal: 'Why not compulsory music appreciation? Art lessons? Literature groups? Surely these also are necessary for the well-rounded man or woman? I guarantee that a spot of compulsory Beethoven will do wonders for our spiritual development.'

He thought that I was just being cheeky. Football does that to you. It makes you lose all sense of proportion. The footy replay becomes more important than music, art or literature, the Grand Final more significant than a great performance of the 'Ninth'.

A couple of years ago the VFL proposed playing the Grand Final at Waverley Park rather than at the Melbourne Cricket Ground. You would have thought that they were proposing to overthrow the democratically elected government. The Premier of Victoria, the dour and abstemious John Cain, treated it as a serious threat to the stability of his government. There was a Showdown. Never mind that industry was in its death throes; that the education system was a shambles; hospital waiting lists a mile long; public transport a vandalised disgrace. Here was a Crisis, demanding the intervention of no less a person than the Premier of the State.

All over where a football match was to be played. It was page-one news for weeks as the advantage to-ed and fro-ed between the VFL and the Premier. At last the Premier won. The Grand Final stayed at the MCG. The apocalypse had been averted. Life would still have some meaning. Civilisation was saved.

This is a game?

The other day I heard that in the little town where I grew up (pop. 700), they now pay has-been League players to play for the local team. Once upon a time my father used to play for the fun of it and to enhance the good name of the town. Now foreigners are brought in—mercenaries. To play other little towns (who also field their mercenaries) in the most minor of all leagues.

Even small children with sufficient ferocity are paid to play these days.

What good can come of this?

Well, just as I was pondering these existential questions, the answer came from an unexpected quarter. Launceston, of all places. Where Councillor Basil Fitch laid it all out before us. Once and for all, the Meaning of Football.

It is simply this: Boys who don't play enough football become pansies!

So that was what the principal meant when he said it would make a man of me. He was concerned about my sexual preferences rather than such abstract ideas as courage and chivalry and the ability to kill and die for worthless causes without complaint.

Councillor Fitch was upset by a school ruling in northern Tasmania that limited boys to one footy match a week. This, said the councillor, was simply not enough. The link between homosexuality and insufficient football was obvious, he said. His reasoning, reported by the Melbourne *Sun*, went like this:

'If the kids can't play football at weekends, then they'll hang around video parlours and sleazy hang-out joints. When kids hang about at the weekend with nothing to do, then the problems start. You get vandalism and underage drinking.' (Please note the hierarchy of degeneracy here.) 'These lead to muggings and drug abuse and naturally homosexuality follows on from this.'

Well, naturally. QED.

GEOFF SLATTERY

Gentleman Jack

Geoff Slattery has more than forty years' experience in publishing. He worked as a journalist on Melbourne's major metropolitan dailies and was sports editor of the Melbourne *Herald* (1987) and *The Sunday Age* (1989–90). In 1991, he co-founded the Text Media Group and, in 1995, he founded The Slattery Media Group (SMG), which until 2012 was the official publisher of the AFL. SMG has published dozens of books on Australian football, including the official publication celebrating 150 years of the game, *The Australian Game Of Football* (2008). Geoff also established five highly rated restaurants across Melbourne (including the Italy 1 group) and is the author of two cookbooks, *Simple Flavours* and *Good Food, No Fuss*. This essay is a revised version of Slattery's 'Jack Dyer', which appeared in *Legends of the Australian Football Hall of Fame* by Bruce Eva, Nick Bowen and Peter Ryan (The Slattery Media Group, 2012).

There is sadness and joy about this story, originally published in *The Age* in 1981 and amended for this book. I researched the yarn for some weeks in the middle part of that year, interviewing Jack Dyer and many of his great mates and colleagues; those from his playing days, and those from his media days. The joy comes from the memories—the warmth and humour of Dyer, and the wonderful repartee he had with anyone, but in particular with his regular and reliable jouster, the unyielding Lou Richards. The sadness is clear with so many of these wonderful people, so much part of the Dyer story, no longer with us. Dyer himself died in 2003.

In 1981, Dyer was in the fiftieth year of the sport he loved, having made his debut with the Tigers in Round 2, 1931 as a raw seventeen year-old. He was still fit and strong, and looked years younger than his age. There was no hint of the illness which, in the late 1950s, had him close to death.

I was lucky to have known Dyer from his days as a *Truth* 'columnist'. On my first day on the job, as a young and green cadet, I made my way upstairs to the sports department of *The Truth* office at 277 William Street, conveniently located next to the Metropolitan Hotel. There was only one person there: Dyer. He greeted me cordially and resumed his task, single-finger typing ideas for his twice-weekly column of gossip, gags and gold, which had the peerless title of 'Dyer'ere'. Those ideas were put into vivid prose by his great mate and ghost, Brian Hansen. Dyer and Hansen had a wonderful relationship, almost symbiotic. Dyer had a rare talent to gather news from his vast array of contacts in the world of footy, and Hansen, the young news breaker, would turn these delicious dollops into front-page and back-page leads.

I worked for *The Truth* for seven years before moving on. During that time, all of us who worked around Dyer grew to love him as a kind, gentle, caring individual. We drank with him at the Celtic Club (Dyer always drank ponies, 140ml glasses) and we drew on his long life in sport, not just footy. We laughed along with him, at his marvellous sense of the beauty of life.

While still a football columnist with *The Truth*, Jack Dyer was called to give evidence in a Victorian Court. In a defamation suit against the newspaper's boxing writer 'The Count', the court was having difficulty finding out the defendant's identity.

Dyer took the stand. His police days helped him race through the oath; then he was asked the identity of 'The Count'.

'I don't know, sir,' he replied. The court was flabbergasted.

'You mean you've worked there for so many years, and you don't know who a fellow writer is?'

'Yes sir,' said Dyer.

'Well,' continued the barrister for the aggrieved party, 'who are some of those you work with?'

'Aaah,' said Dyer, 'there's Mopsy, and Pogo, and Bluey, and Big Steak and...'

The judge cut him short. 'Mr Dyer,' he intervened, 'you are turning this hearing into a Roman Holiday.'

According to *Webster's Dictionary*, the jurist was describing Dyer's testimony as an 'entertainment acquired at the expense of others' suffering, or a spectacle yielding such entertainment.' It was probably accurate.

———❖———

The phone rang for ages before the familiar voice answered: 'Dyer speaking'. We exchanged a few wisecracks before we got down to what Dyer liked to call 'the business'. It was time for the Jack Dyer story to be reconsidered, I said. After all, it was sixteen years since his life story *Captain Blood* had been published and the legend was bigger than it had ever been before. Dyer was momentarily taken aback.

'After all these years,' he said, 'someone wants to talk about me.' Then he laughed. Dyer couldn't be serious for long.

We began at South Vermont, where Dyer had been living for a couple of years. Wide, quiet streets, rolling hills empty of life, big cars in big garages, brown bricks sitting in clay, and a day's march to the nearest pub. Dyer lived out here with his daughter Jill, son-in-law Warren and their three children. It couldn't have been further from Dyer's beloved Richmond.

Two pairs of low-cut footy boots stood drying on the front porch, immediate evidence of the tradition continuing. There was a long wait before the door opened. Dyer never seemed to worry about haste or time.

'Hello-how-are-you-are-you-well?' he said.

It was a typical Dyer greeting, covering the lot in one mouthful. Ten years earlier, when I met him for the first time, he had used exactly the same words. And not much else about Dyer had changed. The wide nose, big ears, grey sideburns supporting the brushed-back steel-grey hair, the kind eyes, the fast-moving mouth, the slow laugh and the delight in stories from the past. Dyer was cleaning potatoes, getting things ready for tea. It was strange to watch the vegetables treated so tenderly in those big, rough hands. But that's Dyer—the Captain Blood part of him started and finished on the football field.

The invitation to start from the beginning was all he needed. 'Right,' he said, 'right from the start—Yarra Junction State School.' He went on:

> *Mum wanted us to go on, so she sent me to Richmond. Put me into St Ignatius's, to see if I could play football and cricket. Brother Peter was the sports master. He took me straight down to Surrey Park, and arranged a scratch match. He was very happy with the performance. We went on to win the premiership. He said he had only wanted a ruckman. After six months at St Igs, he was transferred to De La Salle, so he took me with him. He said 'we might as well go on with the business.'*

That last line sounded more like Dyer's than anything the esteemed Brother Peter may have said.

Memories of school days for Dyer didn't go much further than footy and fighting. Big wins and big losses, interspersed with tales of hiding his college cap and blazer as he came home to Richmond, for fear of 'mobs waiting for you on the corner'. It was the Depression and, whether he liked it or not, Dyer had to leave school after his Intermediate year (Year 10) to provide for the family. I gained the impression it didn't worry him much.

'I wasn't a bad scholar, but I lost interest,' he said.

It's probably fortunate that Dyer went into the workforce at fourteen. Had he taken the option of a scholarship on offer to Xavier, Melbourne's prestigious Catholic private school, and perhaps further, his great broadcasting lines would never have caused so much mirth for so many. It didn't worry Dyer in the least that his quaint use of the English language—his so-called Dyerisms—created so much humour. I had taken great delight in publishing quite a few lines from his broadcasts— 'Bartlett, he's older than he's ever been before' (on the occasion of Kevin

Bartlett's 300th game in 1980); 'the ball's in no man's land and the loose man's come from everywhere'; and so many more. Did he feel he was being ridiculed, I asked him. Not at all, he said. 'We [note the royal 'we'] were starting to slip away a bit. You put us back on the map.'

———◆◆◆◆———

Dyer's amazing ability to 'slip the tongue' lasted as long as the man himself. He started on radio in 1952, three years after his retirement from the game, after much persuasion from Phil Gibbs, who later became a sports director at Channel 10. 'He wasn't keen to do it,' said Gibbs:

> *He reckoned he couldn't speak on radio. So we finally convinced him to have a practice first. We went to a game at North Melbourne. Jack was terrible. Even then he had a language of his own. I'll never forget him saying: 'Pass the ben-i-colars, Phil.' But we went back and listened to the tape, and despite it all, you could tell even then he had that quality about him.*

Part of the deal with Gibbs was that he would teach Dyer the art of radio if Dyer would teach him the finer points of football. Gibbs recalled:

> *The lesson started at a social match at Keilor... All the old stars were playing. Jack told me to play in the ruck with him. We were waiting for the first bounce and Jack said to me to take the knockout. Up I went, and I felt this whack across the ear. It nearly knocked me out. Dyer had hit me a beauty. I couldn't believe it. I said to him: 'What was that for?' He replied: 'Now you know what it feels like.' It was part of his teaching.'*

Of all his later media activities—radio, TV, newspapers—Dyer preferred radio. 'It's just like playing the game,' he would say, 'you're always with it, and you can abuse the umpire.' People listened to Dyer not for what he said about the football but how he said it; some found him infuriating, most didn't.

No story on Dyer would be complete without a few of his lines from that lengthy media career on radio and television, and of course print.

This comes from the 1978 Grand Final between Hawthorn and North Melbourne:

> *On the kickout, it's out towards the wing position, the pack fly again, over the top of the pack and a good mark has been taken here. It looks like… it is… Cowton with the ball. He immediately handballs it in the air, away they go as Henshaw comes down the ground. He's going for the short pass. It's not a good one at all. It's punched away by Martella [sic]. Another punch up in the air. In goes Demper…dipter… ier…domenico…in after it again.*

Can't you just hear him saying that? As Lou Richards told me, 'You couldn't buy what he's got, you couldn't make it up.'

⊷•◉•⊶

Dyer is universally acknowledged to have been a champion, in the real sense of the word. In the foreword to *Captain Blood*, the late Hec De Lacy of *The Sporting Globe* wrote of Dyer: 'Jack Dyer, Richmond's giant, was the greatest big man in Australian football. He stands supreme, he's the greatest of the great.' Not surprisingly, given his errant elbows, and penchant for the shirtfront, Dyer rarely polled in the Brownlow Medal, although it is not generally recognised that he finished fourth to Marcus Whelan in 1939. In his 312 games, he kicked 443 goals, many with the famous drop punt that he always reckoned he invented, although the truth is somewhat hidden in time.

In a profile written for Perth's *Western Mail* in 1949, when Dyer and Richmond were in town, it was reported:

> *Jack Dyer has specialised in an unusual kick, which he calls the drop punt. He says it's the straightest kick in the game. For this kick he holds the ball vertically instead of horizontally, and drops it point downwards. The ball is kicked with the toe and instep, just above the ground and is propelled with a spin. On one occasion at practice, Dyer got 12 goals from 12 shots with the drop punt, at distances about 40 yards (35 metres) out.*

A great ruckman, performing in tandem with Perc Bentley, and later a forward as his body started to fail him, Dyer won the Richmond best and fairest award six times, and the trophy now carries his name. He played in Richmond's 1934 premiership, and was captain-coach of the Tigers' 1943 champion team—dominant Grand Final winners before a packed house at the Junction Oval. He captained Victoria in 1940, represented his State fourteen times, and is also in the AFL's Team of the Century, formed in the same year he was inducted into the Australian Football Hall Of Fame. His legacy is apparent when each Richmond team goes on field—the skipper is now dressed in the famous No. 17 guernsey, a wonderful memorial. The *Western Mail* profile concluded:

> *Jack Dyer takes his place with the greatest players the game has produced. Just over six feet in height and about 15 stone in weight, he represents the rare vintage in football—the good big man. When we talk about 'the good big man' we usually mean the big man who has everything in the football sense, plus speed. That is—or was—Jack Dyer, except that Dyer goes further. In addition to his magnificent physique and great courage, he has a remarkably astute football brain. This endows him with a capacity for leadership possessed by few players.*

There *was* more to Dyer's life than football, but it needed considerable prodding to get it out of him. Ask Dyer about football and he'd talk forever. Ask him about his family, his friends, his other life, he'd just smile, mumble a few lines and look blankly at you, waiting for the next question. His wife of more than thirty years, Sybil, died in 1971. His friends say her death left him flat. Dyer said to me that 'everything was all nice until she died. Suddenly it was...' His family kept him going. 'I'm pretty lucky,' he said, 'I've never had to live by myself.'

By 1981, however, it seemed that Dyer could not be happier with life. He was forever smiling, joking, always relaxed. He'd talk to anyone about anything, and was forever confronted in pubs by people talking about football or, more accurately, wanting to talk with him about football. He was never more content than when holding forth at the bar with friends or, more likely, drifting acquaintances. Friends Dyer knew by name. Others—acquaintances or minor colleagues—by nicknames. Those who know him are always amused by his inability to remember names. The story of Dyer in court was no different to when Dyer was at work, at the pub, or in the street.

Every week, Dyer used to make the trip to Richmond for lunch at Craig McKellar's pub in Swan Street, about equidistant from the Punt Road Oval and a milk bar Dyer ran in the forties, in Church Street, down the hill from St Ignatius church. It was at McKellar's that he picked up all the gossip, maintained the links. If it had been up to him, he'd have lived in Richmond. 'But the kids love it out there [at South Vermont],' he said. Dyer's closest friends remained the men of his playing days, men like Essendon's Ted Rippon, South Melbourne's Laurie Nash and the Magpie marvel Lou Richards, although Dyer said: 'Don't say that (about Lou). He's my bread and butter.' Richards countered: 'You're writing about Jack. That'll take about three paragraphs'.

Dyer and Richards were the two who kept TV's longest-running program, *World of Sport*, from tedium. Ron Casey, the show's compere and later HSV-7's general manager (Casey was also inducted into the Hall Of Fame's Media section in 1996) described Dyer as 'the gentle humourist'. But there was nothing gentle about a battle of wits between Richards and Dyer after a Collingwood-Richmond contest.

One measure of the popularity of the duo was the number of advertisements they did together—and the number they knocked back. Richards described Dyer as 'the funniest bloke in the world to do advertisements with'. He continued:

He's forever changing the script in midstream. We were doing an ad for a chain saw, and I'm saying something like, 'you use it with your partner', and Jack's supposed to reply with: 'Is it any good for camping?' And lo and behold, he adds after camping 'and fishing'. I nearly fell through the floor. I had to ad lib to Jack's fishing line. I ended up saying: 'yes it's great if you catch a whale, it really makes the filleting easy'. The funny thing is, whenever he throws in these lines, the ad is always much better.

Casey was another at *World of Sport* with undisguised affection for Dyer. One year, Casey recalled, he wanted Dyer to do some promotion for Channel Seven:

He wasn't on the phone, so I sent an urgent telegram to ask him to come to the studio. We received no reply, so I sent another. Still no answer, so in the end I went over to his house in Richmond. I knocked on the door, hardly knowing what to expect, and Jack answered. Behind him, on the mantle, I could see the telegrams—unopened. I said to him: 'Jack, I sent you those urgent telegrams, why didn't you open them?' Straight away he replied: 'Oooh, I never open urgent telegrams, you never know what might be in them'.

———————⋄✦⋄———————

Most of Dyer's stories from his playing days have been heard or read before. One he told me seemed new:

We were playing out at Carlton, and I had to catch the train to the ground. You had to in those days. I only had a deener (one shilling/10 cents), and I caught the train out there. Then I looked out the window, and I couldn't see any houses. I thought 'This is not Carlton.' Eventually the train stopped at Reservoir. I didn't know what to do. Eventually a bloke put me on the right one, and I arrived just in time. I was so riled up, I had a love-r-ly time. Blokes were going down everywhere. Anyway, we won easily, and I've left the ground feeling marvellous. On the train again, and you wouldn't believe it—the carriage was full of Carlton supporters. They never stopped abusing me—kids, old ladies, the works. One bloke said to me: 'You must have eaten your babies, Dyer.' I said to him: 'Me. I'm gentle. I go to church on Sundays.' The train stopped. I was out like a shot, and into the next carriage. It was full of Richmond supporters. The rest of the trip home was love-r-ly.

It was about this time, during the 1935 season, that Dyer was saddled with the nickname Captain Blood: it came from a cartoon drawn by *The Age* cartoonist John Ludlow the Monday after Dyer had dispensed with a few Fitzroy players in a rough affair won by the Tigers at the Brunswick Street Oval. This was the era of Errol Flynn and the movie *Captain Blood*: it seemed natural that the ruthless Dyer would be compared to the swashbuckling Captain Blood/Flynn of that time. Strangely enough, Dyer was only reported four times (once for throwing the ball away) and suspended just once—for striking Jock McHale's son, John, in a match against Collingwood at Punt Road late in his career.

———◆◆◆———

In 1981, with his media career winding down, Dyer remained a busy man. During the week I interviewed him, *The Herald* tried to get him photographed with the new Liberal Premier, Lindsay Thompson, an avid Richmond fan. Dyer wouldn't be in it: 'Don't they know I'm a Labor man?' he wailed. Another day, he was up at dawn, filming a commercial for Tattslotto with Richards. 'That's the first time I've seen a million dollars,' he said. 'We tried to pinch some, but they had two armed guards'. After that it was out to St Albans to present some guernseys to a primary school on behalf of 3KZ. Then to North Melbourne to do his column for *The Truth* which, he said, revealing his competitive streak, was getting harder. 'Once upon a time there was only one writer you had to beat. Now there are thousands.'

After he'd been to Richmond for some photographs one day, we met at McKellar's pub. The old blokes around the bar cheered when Dyer arrived, forty minutes late. Dyer was prepared for anything. We went from one bar to another, then for a walk down Swan Street. Dyer was self-conscious as he posed outside Dimmy's.

Several people went past. He knew none of them. Occasionally one would greet him.

'Hello-how-are-you-are-you-well?' asked Dyer.

COLIN TALBOT

Smoking in a House of Mirrors

Colin Talbot grew up near the Flinders Ranges and, but for a serious knee injury flying for a mighty mark in the Under 10b team, would perhaps have made the All-Australian team in later years. Instead he was a rock music columnist for *The Australian* in the 1970 and wrote for many other journals. Talbot now writes novels, his latest being *Sweet Mystery* for Arcadia/Press-On. He has also directed a feature film, *Sweethearts* (1990), from his novel of the same name, and co-written songs that have appeared on albums by some of Australia's finest musicians. This piece appeared previously in *Colin Talbot's Greatest Hits* (1977).

A*t 1pm on a fine and warm Saturday a league footballer smoked marijuana. About two hours later he was on a ground ready to play 100 minutes of senior football. About 2500 people were at the game. He smoked pot for a few hours the night before and had only a few hours' sleep.*

'When I ran out with the side everything looked brighter than usual, it was almost glaring,' the footballer said yesterday. 'When I moved into position I felt detached from the whole scene. There were no pre-match nerves, and I felt relaxed.

'I felt a little tired, probably because of the late night. I wasn't aware of my opponent and I felt I wasn't taking part in the game.

'It was like a daydream. I kept fixing my eyes on certain objects around the ground...

'The reason why I took pot before the game was because it was my reaction against the whole football scene.

'I had been brought up to be nothing else but a footballer. I was pushed into football from the time I was six...'

The Sun, 9 May 1972

Looking out from Melbourne's Glenferrie Oval you can see the trains go by. The railroad track runs close to the oval and Hawthorn Oval is close too. Brent Crosswell is playing football for Carlton today.

He stands, somehow vacantly, up near the Carlton goals. Closely watching trains. Up on the hill the crowd is watching the play. Crosswell is digging the trains.

Some of the young Carlton supporters on the hill are sharing a cigarette with each other. The cigarette has hashish in it and it is being clandestinely passed back and forth along a line of about ten people. The more times these cigarettes go up and down the line, the less guarded becomes the manner in which these cigarettes—joints—are passed along. Behind and around are more easily recognisable supporters drinking from cans. If they looked, they would see a dozen longhairs smoking hash. But they are watching the game. If the television crews trained on this part of the crowd, thousands of people watching the football replay would see cannabis being smoked at Glenferrie Oval during the Hawthorn v. Carlton match. But the cameras are trained on the action on the oval. And the dope smokers are watching the football.

Meanwhile Crosswell is still digging the trains. They flash past. The trains look... really good. Now he watches the crowd. There are so many people up there. Thousands.

The dope smokers are watching Crosswell now. They notice he hardly seems to be aware that the ball is nearing him. The ball comes closer. The crowd roars. Crosswell is staring out at the trains, and the crowd, and the sky. They think... 'What's Brent doing? He doesn't seem to be concentrating on the game. He looks blocked. Would that be remotely possible?'

Brent Crosswell looks up at the crowd. Man, if he could only be up there, if only he weren't on this field. If he could be up there somewhere in that crowd. Watching the game, digging the trains...

A recruit from Launceston in 1968, Crosswell played a prominent part in the side's premiership that year, despite several clashes with coach Ron Barassi. He was dropped from the senior side for disciplinary reasons early in 1969 but found his way back.

In 1970, as a ruck rover, he was an almost unanimous choice for best man on the ground in Carlton's magnificent win over Collingwood.

The Age, 16 March 1971

⬥

Brent Crosswell came across from Tasmania when he was seventeen. A star schoolboy footballer, he had been brought up in a family which worshipped the game. Football was *it*.

His father was a butcher; the family lived in Campbelltown and Brent was sent to the best college so he could get the best education. Whatever trouble Crosswell got into, his ability to kick long, mark big, play hard, got him out. There was talk of expulsion, but Crosswell had to stay to win the big game for his school. He learned that college kids were one up on high school kids. He learned that the sons of the wealthy landowners, of doctors, of lawyers, didn't want to associate with any son of a butcher. But the same people dug knowing footy stars. With these unfortunate facts of life weighing him down, Brent was packed off to Melbourne to be a star. He hadn't yet finished his secondary schooling. He began matriculation at University High, in Parkville. He was signed to Carlton.

Crosswell had been told by his folks to train hard, learn fast, go in with determination, so he would work his way up through the Seconds and into the Carlton Firsts. A league player in the VFL. He would have made it. A big star. So much for the master plan. With little trouble he went straight into the league side.

'When I first arrived at Carlton, I looked at the guys in the league side. I was still a schoolboy, and they seemed to be very big and tough. But in less than three months I was in the side. I'd achieved what I came over to do easily. My whole world just... crumbled.'

Brent was told he was future captain material. Suddenly there was nothing much left for him. He had breezed in.

Being a footy star isn't quite like being a cricket star or a tennis star. For you can't tell when you've reached the top. It is too nebulous. Cricketers and tennis players know when they are regarded as being about the best in the world. But football has eighteen men in each team, twelve teams in Melbourne alone, and then Adelaide and Perth have more league teams. When you're there you're just there. One of the boys.

With a few runs in the firsts notched up, Brent journeyed to Adelaide with his team on a trip. It was a freak-out. He vowed never to be caught on an airplane with footballers again.

'Going across wasn't too bad. But coming back was bad news. Just not my scene. A lot of the guys were drunk. We were travelling in a small plane and I was sitting up front trying to get as far away as possible from what was happening. The hostesses were getting troubled.'

At the end of this year the Carlton footballers will be going to Russia for exhibition matches. Crosswell won't be on the trip.

Crosswell is what the football pundits call a 'temperamental player.' This means sometimes he goes out on the field and kicks hell out of the ball, and marks like John Coleman and generally plays like a tearaway. No one can touch him.

And sometimes he goes out and is almost not worth his place in the side. He seems vague, spaced. Tired from the trip. Thinking, 'what the fuck am I doing out here? What am I doing playing league football?' He is lackadaisical. He is unconcerned. Bored. He just plain doesn't want to be there.

When he started in league, Brent was enthusiastic. He listened intently to what the coach had to say. He tried hard. He flashed into the play and showed he was as brilliant as anyone. On his day.

Now he moons, while coach John Nicholls delivers his tactical address.

He thinks of other things. Not football.

He stands where the coach can't see him.

On the field he invariably can't wait until he is off. He did have big ideas. Now he doesn't care. Football doesn't really interest him. He suggested Carlton footballers should wear lighter guernseys so they wouldn't sweat so much. No one wanted to know. He thinks League sides should have only sixteen men on the field so the game is not so crowded. No one was much interested. The VFL is not exactly forward-thinking. You might even say, apathetic.

And Crosswell? Well, the game almost disgusts him.

'It's terrible when you set out in a game to hurt some guy. But this is what happens. You see a good player and run out to him. You know if you hurt him, you can ruin his effectiveness, put him out of the game. And feel no remorse because you know you're just doing your job and you know the club is pleased.

'I've done some terrible things, like kicking players. And players should feel ashamed to put someone in hospital. To break bones. But they don't feel ashamed.

'Anyway, I've had enough. I've broken my collar bone, collected bruises, stretched ligaments. I'm sick of guys trying to rub me out on the field and sick of the violence. It's supposed to be a sport. I've had enough injuries. I don't want to end up a physical and mental wreck.'

Brent Crosswell doesn't want to play football anymore. This will be his last season in VFL. The ribbons and the bows have fallen.

———◆◆◆◆◆———

To paraphrase Gertrude Stein: 'Carlton is the top team, is the top team, is the top team...'

Hawthorn in fact is rigid and unthinking, fascist in its terrible certainty that it can bulldoze effete football liberalism...

It is a strange thing how accurate the Carlton football team translates the picturesque character of the area it evolves from. Carlton supporters include the ranks of the unshaven, the unwashed, the academic elite, the student poets and quite a few of those sturdy proletarians for whom football is a religion.

The élan with which Carlton plays football is a physical translation of the heterogeneous voice which shouts from behind the pickets.

Maurice Carr, Melbourne Observer, 27 August 1972

The footballer lives in a Carlton terrace house. He lives with friends and has the front room, facing a heavily trafficked street. On the wall is a poster of Che Guevera; under this, a guitar.

Brent plays a little classical guitar, a little folk. By the bed is a stereo outfit and in an opposite corner is a Match II footy. The room is tidy.

A footy and a poster of a Cuban revolutionary.

He says his teammates generally don't understand him. They think he is a little silly. This year Crosswell turned down an offer to be contracted with Carlton Football Club, do the club's thing, play the game the club's way, jump when he was told to, and in return for that earn $5000.

Silly? Maybe, maybe not. Instead he played on a game-to-game basis. He played only nine games and didn't bring in much money. The other players, the club, can't understand him. He exists on jobs like bartending, cleaning, factory work. Yet he could be a star. Get on a contract, maybe win a car, get set-up in a cushy job by the club. Do the bourgeois trip.

But these are the things he wishes to forget were ever even speculated upon. The club, friends of the club, have offered him a lot of incentives—good jobs. He turned them down. He prefers to do things his way, or not at all.

In his wardrobe are racks of shirts he can't begin to wear out. Everyone wants to give him shirts. When a footballer steps on a TV sport program, he gets shirts or after-shave or belts or brushes—all sorts of stuff. Now Brent has so many shirts he gives them away. He gave six to me to 'clean out' his wardrobe.

So here he is, rejecting all the things which football brings—material gains, glamour, kicks. No wonder that most of the footballers can't relate. On the field, Brent's kicks are getting harder to find.

Does the attitude of the others to him cause much concern? Well he seems to sleep okay. He gets by in Carlton. Life is liveable. Crosswell has friends the footballers would find weird and foreign to them.

A while back the Melbourne *Sun* ran an article on its inside sporting pages about a mystery footballer who smoked dope. The mystery footballer was approached by the *Sun* and given money to tell the story. But he wasn't allowed to say the stuff was enjoyable.

The Carlton supporters on the hill wonder who the footballer was. They pass another joint. Crosswell flies for a mark. They grin. It's okay.

Earlier this year Brent Crosswell was summoned by Carlton Football Club officialdom and given a testy warning. He was told that following conversations with two Commonwealth police officers, certain information had been relayed concerning the linking of his name with that of hashish. The officials apparently told Brent he had been advised to leave the State immediately—within twenty-four hours—and not come back for a while.

Brent split to Tassie for five weeks. Hung about in the countryside and enjoyed himself. Away from the MCG. Away from Princes Park. But he wasn't worried about getting busted. Can you imagine how thousands of young fans would greet the news that Crosswell's name had been linked with drugs? If Crosswell had actually been busted?

A mass turn-on for Victoria's budding school-age ruck rovers. An endorsement of the stuff.

'*This must be the end*', sings Jim Morrison.

When he leaves the game, Crosswell will have maybe two bucks to show for his years of footy, and a few shirts. He could have been amassing thousands and he could still be doing it. But no.

He's just turned twenty-two, and he owns a motorbike. If that machine breaks up, he'll have to get a pushbike, or walk. His studies were interrupted by his footy career. Well, not so much interrupted as pushed aside. A schoolboy league footballer finds the sudden change in lifestyle must be examined. By the time this footballer realised the lifestyle was not for him, his earlier aims were not so easily picked up on.

So he is studying again after a four year absence. It's hard to get back on one treadmill while still trying to get off the other one. With football now not one of his scenes, he doesn't know what he might do.

Maybe, says Crosswell, he'll just float around until he dies.

———◆·✦·◆———

A conversation with a young Carlton supporter on the hill about the game of Australian Rules Football—

'What's your impression of this game?'

'Far out scene man. Get to wear the club jumper man. Star trip, man.'

'Do you feel there is commendable tension between the individual and the team—and that the individual is subjugated to the team?'

'Yeah man. It's the team, man. Gotta get the goals. Have to get the old ball up between the sticks for a lot of majors, man. Can't have the players running all over the ground chasing kicks man. They have to play the man, man. I mean it's good to see a guy taking the big marks man, but the team's got to win man. It's not just a game, man. It's life.'

———◆·✦·◆———

Crosswell is a brilliant footballer. He can amaze spectators with his play. Yet he feels he has never been allowed to play the game he could. There was always the thought of what he could do, and what he was expected to do. He knows which players in the league can compete against him, and knows there aren't many of them. But still, he can't go like hell for the mark. Because it's a team. He's just a number, and the team is what has to win. He can't fly. He's stuck on his feather.

And there are players in his team whom he feels shouldn't be there because they aren't good enough. But he can't ignore them. He has to work with them, talk with them. Gradually getting more pissed off with the double bind, Crosswell found it harder and harder to cope.

Before John Nicholls took over, Barassi was coach. The player and the coach never actually exchanged blows, but almost. Continuous bickering, fighting, tension. Crosswell said Barassi threatened him once and he decided that was it. He said if Barassi wanted it, then they could fight it out in the gym, with the boxing gloves. But it didn't happen.

This year an incident involving Crosswell caused a minor footy sensation. During a Carlton-Geelong game, with the ball at the other end of the ground, Crosswell and Vin Waite, another Carlton player, exchanged blows.

Crosswell fell down.

Waite and Crosswell had exchanged a few words earlier in the game when Crosswell had been disturbed at Waite's strategy. Later it was Waite who was disturbed by Crosswell, and he ran across. They struggled briefly, and Crosswell took the easy way out and fell down. He didn't want to fight—with a teammate—on the oval.

———◆◆◆◆◆———

Up on the hill, the dope smokers are screaming with Crosswell to take the mark because they know he can.

A bearded man with lots of black hair takes a joint from his mouth and screams, 'Order of Lenin for Crosswell.'

The group raises hands in a clenched salute. The footballer is a cult hero.

'Smash the fascists Brent!'

'Up there brother.'

They are out of it but they identify with him. They want to be into it. Down on the ground, kicking the socialist punts, marking over the bourgeoisie, out on the field, eating the oranges, wearing the guernseys, in the team. Kicking on.

But down there it's Crosswell with the guernsey.

Sick of the footy orgasm he is digging the trains. Looking up at the crowd, he wants to be part of it. Out of the game. Gone, and not fooled again.

KATHY SKELTON

The End of a Fine Romance

Kathy Skelton (1946–2002) grew up in the Victorian seaside town of Sorrento and learned early in life that it helps a woman in an Australian man's world if she can say, 'Bill Bloggs played a bottler in the back pocket.' She wrote this piece while living 'two drop kicks and a chain of handpasses' from Windy Hill. Skelton worked in the areas of school support and curriculum for the Ministry of Education, as a member of the University of Melbourne's Faculty of Education, and as writer and editor of the Curriculum Corporation's *EQ Australia* magazine. An *EQ Australia* obituary marking her early and sudden death read: 'Kathy believed in the power of language, she being wise and antic, learned and funny, rich in ideas and generous to the ideas of others.' University College at the University of Melbourne remembers Skelton with an annual Kathy Skelton Scholarship. This essay first appeared in *The Age*, 18 April 1987.

On a mantelpiece in my inner-city house is a tattered, fly-spotted photograph of the 1949 Mornington Peninsula Football League, C-grade premiers. In contrast to their contemporary counterparts, fifteen of the nineteen Sorrento players wear long sleeves. My Dad is one of the four who don't, and he stands in the back row, jaw set, arms folded, muscles bulging and hair receding. He's thirty-four years of age, and somewhere out of the photograph I am three.

I often study this photograph, searching for some clue to my passion for football. I am reluctant to look too hard. Perhaps the answer lies in whatever one calls the reverse of an Oedipal complex. How else can I explain my unashamed appropriation of the Walter Stringer trophy, a shapely, silver-plated teapot, awarded in the same year to the best and fairest C-grade player?

And I've made no secret of my desire to inherit the President's Cup, something of an art deco number, presented by Sid Baker in 1946, the year of my birth. Not only do I share its age, but it was instrumental in the survival of our beloved budgie, who was felled in one of his nightly periods of liberation by *The Concise Oxford Dictionary* falling from my sister's lap. He rose from the Axminster on faltering wings, made two stunned circuits of the room at picture-rail level, then dropped like a stone into the President's Cup.

Puffing, with one eye open, he remained there for two days on top of the cigarette papers, tap washers, carpenter's pencils and cotton reels, then appeared on the rim of the trophy, whistling, miraculously recovered. In our family, we make few distinctions between Sid Baker and St Francis.

My earliest memories of football are of the Sorrento grandstand in winter and, underneath, the ladies' auxiliary selling afternoon tea and the almost sexual mystery of the two doors marked 'Sorrento' and 'Visitors'. Around two on Saturday afternoons, these doors would suddenly fly open and a long line of bums in shorts, above glistening thighs, above red and white hoops stretched over taut calves, would ripple by to a cacophony of car horns. (I didn't pay too much attention to the other team.)

I can't recall a single incident or passage of play from a match of my childhood. Except, of course, the day our dog, a border collie-kelpie cross, which, in the absence of sheep, chased anything that moved, rushed on the ground, grabbed the ball by the lace and, after some nifty dodging and weaving around a couple of lumbering ruckmen on the half-forward flank, tore off into the pine trees and sat down with the ball between his paws. I am grateful to this day that he didn't bring the ball to me. By the time the cry went up, 'That's Skelton's dog!' I was ensconced in the Ladies'.

Somewhere around the start of high school, I realised I needed other heroes. I found the credibility gap between the giant who soared above the pack to mark, goal and put Sorrento in front and the boiler-suited plumber digging next-door's septic tank more than I could cope with. I needed more distant gods whose romantic aura I could manage and manipulate without the intrusion of too much reality. So, goodbye Sorrento, hello Melbourne. Why Melbourne? Alack and alas, it was my father's team.

Every Thursday night it was 'League Teams' on the radio, and every Saturday afternoon it was Norman Banks or Doug Heywood or Phil Gibbs or Jack Dyer bringing me agony or ecstasy. My school exercise books were filled with cuttings and photos of the Melbourne team. The features of a warm temperate east-coast climate, intricate diagrams of strip-farming in pre-industrial England (meticulously coloured with borrowed Derwents), the causes of World War I, stories about birds with names like the Yellow-spotted Dotterel, concocted for Gould League certificates, and how to make blancmange, were all obliterated by Bob Johnson manoeuvring his posterior in the goal square, or Geoff Tunbridge caught in mid-flight on the boundary line, or Norm Smith staring stern-faced into the camera.

Our budgie added 'Car'n the Demons' and 'Hassa Mann' to his existing repertoire of 'You stupid boy!' (my mother to my brother) and 'What do you want in your lunch?'(my mother to all of us).

All this adolescent passion for the game (and the players) climaxed in the 1964 Grand Final, when Neil Crompton made his legendary run from the back pocket and goaled to give Melbourne victory. With a standing-room ticket, I stood pressed against the wire fence somewhere in the Southern Stand. Had the Almighty exacted a price for victory in those last agonising minutes, I would have willingly been crushed to death having savoured the exultation of the winning goal and the final siren.

I have to confess, with considerable shame, that football took a back seat during my university days. I became a closet fanatic, because One didn't admit to caring about football, let alone going to a match, unless One had entrance to the MCC at finals time, and then in the company of some callow youth in checked jacket, moleskins and elastic-sided boots.

So it was clandestine checking of the teams in Friday's paper and nonchalant attention to the scores on Saturday night's news. Watching *Pelaco Inquest* was a rare pleasure, but even then it was necessary to sit very close to the old AWA in case a sudden intrusion called for a bit of dexterous dial-twiddling.

In the early seventies, with university thankfully behind me, I met a man who, among other things, went to the football. He went every Saturday. Terrific, I thought. I've always liked Essendon; they'll do. And they did. The man has gone, but Essendon lingers.

I learned the pleasure of standing with the same group of people every week—some friends, some unknown to me except for Saturday afternoons in the outer; of conversations with strangers that you'd never start on the tram, or in the cinema, or even at a protest rally; of post-game drinks under the old Cricket Club stand, where a brandy and dry is a beer glass of brandy topped with a centimetre of dry; and of match post-mortems which, after a loss, always begin, 'Put a pencil through...' All but half a dozen of the Essendon team have had a pencil through them at some time.

I also learned how watching football concentrates the mind. I have known myself to compose the weekly shopping list or mentally re-arrange the lounge-room furniture while engaged in other acts of passion, but never while watching the football—though the day I realised my marriage was over (round 9, 1981, Essendon v. Melbourne), I was having trouble concentrating and felt compelled to go home at half-time. Usually, however, from the bounce of the ball to the final siren, life beyond the boundary line does not exist. All that matters is the art and conflict of the game and the prospect of victory. And loss makes victory sweet.

That is why Essendon's seventeenth-round win over Carlton in 1986 was particularly beautiful. It was good to beat Hawthorn, too, but in the taxonomy of teams worth defeating, Carlton is close to the top. It wasn't a 'hugging strangers standing on the seats belting out the theme song rocking home on the Broadmeadows train' victory. That's premiership stuff. But it was the kind that washes small quantities of vindictive pleasure through the veins. Unfortunately the season ended badly, and Essendon's crisis extended beyond the loss of an elimination final to Fitzroy.

Football's crisis, on the other hand, appears to be mid-life, brought on by men who could be having their own. The good doctors (Aylett and Edelsten), the executives of Powerplay, and those at the top of the VFL, are all around the dangerous age of forty-five, when success and fame are desperate and attractive compensations for the passing of youth. That a game with years of tradition and attachment to people and place can be expropriated by captains of industry and advertising wheeler-dealers to become an 'entertainment package, the flagship of our marketing programme' (as Bob Pritchard once said of the Sydney Swans) represents everything I loathe about the path football is taking.

I keep meeting people who feel the same way. The other night in a Melbourne restaurant, two of my dinner companions were men who, migrating to Australia in the fifties (one from Greece, the other from England), have followed Footscray almost from the time of their arrival. In separate conversations, they both expressed the view that football had changed so much and seemed so open to manipulation that they couldn't take it seriously; they could no longer care about it. Both felt their interest in future would be confined to checking the scores on Saturday night's news and going to the occasional game.

Whatever Essendon's fortunes, I'm wondering how much longer I can sustain my passion for them and for VFL football. In 1987, I was offered only eight games at Windy Hill, six trips out to that monstrous mausoleum off the Mulgrave freeway and the chance to get excited about beating 'instant' teams with names that sound as Australian as the Hollywood Superbowl.

So, I'm starting to insure myself against the day when I can tolerate it no longer, when the mergers and interstate moves have obliterated half the traditional Melbourne teams; when, if you still have a team to watch, you'll see them more often on television than locally; when 'standing-room' is swallowed up by discreet glass booths with waiter service for those most traditional of football followers, business executives; and when the antics of the Bluebirds and the Swanettes are the order of the day and not just small-time aberrations.

Then I'll give it away, if I haven't done so already. I've decided to follow Coburg. And a woman has persuaded me. Deserted by South Melbourne, she's switched to the VFA and says Coburg's the go—in the finals in 1986 and a captain-coach with a socialist perspective on the game.

Some people will think that none of this matters. And in the context of poverty and injustice and AIDS and war-torn Lebanon, the demise of league football is a mere bagatelle. But no less a thinker than Albert Camus once said, 'All that I know most surely of morality and the obligations of man I owe to football.' And, equally surely, I know he didn't come to this realisation watching Versailles versus Montmartre on television or in a super box surrounded by Lacoste or Pierre Cardin whiz-kids. He learned it in the outer, or behind the goals, standing, probably, with his mates Simone de Beauvoir and Jean-Paul Sartre.

STEVE HAWKE

The Consummate Competitor

Steve Hawke grew up in Melbourne barracking for Geelong, though unfortunately he is just too young to remember the 1963 premiership. He found his way to the Kimberley as a young man, and worked for many years with Indigenous communities and organisations. Writing *Polly Farmer: A Biography* was a welcome reintroduction to the world of footy after the Kimberley years, when scratchy shortwave broadcasts and week-old papers were the only access to the game. He has also written two histories, *Noonkanbah: Whose Land, Whose Law* and *A Town Is Born*; a children's novel, *Barefoot Kids*; and a play, *Jandamarra*, which was a highlight of the 2008 Festival of Perth. This essay is extracted from *Polly Farmer: A Biography* (1994).

He [Polly Farmer] was the player that caused more concern to all players and coaches than any player I have known. And that includes the Colemans and the Wades and the Hudsons and the Locketts and the Dunstalls. Farmer created more concern for coaches and opposition players than anybody I have ever known. They couldn't set themselves a way of retarding his brilliance.

These are the words of Ted Whitten, who had good reason to know, as the captain-coach of Footscray during the time Farmer was at Geelong. Farmer had done at Geelong the same as he had at East Perth earlier. Using the creed that defined his own role as 'to get the ball and give it', he played a brand of football that was all his own, but simultaneously could make a whole team hum.

He was impossible to stop because he had such a wide range of attributes as a player; they could not all be countered. He was so feared not only because of his unstoppability, but because his style of play was so productive. In the one sentence his disciple John 'Sam' Newman describes Farmer as both 'the consummate team player' and a 'selfish player'. Selfish because 'he worried about one thing only and that was how he played and how he handled the person who played against him'. But 'all the rest followed... because of the way he played football he brought people naturally into the game'.

Father Brosnan, a knockabout priest who boasted of being dropped from the Cudgee State School football team that only had twelve kids in it, perhaps comes closer than any to defining the way Farmer worked. Though he was actually talking at the time of Farmer off the field, it applies equally well to his football. Reaching back to his seminary training in the philosophy of causality he cites the proposition that, 'The formal cause has its effect by its mere presence.'

This is obviously not to suggest that Farmer was a passive force on a football field, but rather that he was a natural force in his own right whose presence and play inevitably created its own effect. The great forwards named by Whitten were feared less than Farmer because they relied on others up the field to create for them. Farmer created in his own right. He was almost always the originator of the play.

This comes back in part to his position as a ruckman, at the bounce or throw-in that starts the play. But it has more to do with his particular creed of 'get it and give it'. Farmer was not a receiver. He believed that once the ball came anywhere near him it was his. He could scrabble in the packs with the best of the rovers and shoot the ball out.

Much modern coaching is built around a theory expounded by the great Allan Jeans of St Kilda and Hawthorn. Some credit the theory to him, though others trace it back to Len Smith. Jeans says, 'In football, from the time you bounce the ball until the end of the game the ball can only be in one of three phases. It's either in dispute, we have it, or they have it. It can't be in any other area.' From this analysis the coach then lays down 'fundamentals', as to how players should move and respond in any given phase and its many variations.

The most critical phase is the one where the ball is in dispute. Herein lay half of Farmer's genius. He was amongst the best there have been at winning this ball. Throughout a game he consistently shifted the game from the 'in dispute' phase, to the 'we have it' phase. The possession that does this—wins the neutral ball, or creates the turnover—is the critical one whose worth never shows up in mere statistics. When this is combined with the other half of his genius—his acknowledged status as the best user and disposer of the ball in the game—his value to a team can begin to be appreciated.

Farmer's ball-getting ability was even more critical in the hard-slogging, relatively low-scoring Victorian Football League than it had been in Western Australia, where a more free-flowing, open style of football prevailed; the ball was in dispute more often, and tended to be disputed more fiercely.

Newman scoffs at those who deny there were deliberate attempts to nobble Farmer in Victoria:

> *Absolute bullshit... It is sheer folly to suggest—whether they would be fair or not in using tactic—[that] they didn't spend hours trying to work out how to combat Farmer. Some stepped out of the bounds of what was asked of them, and others wouldn't. Those who didn't step over the bounds would have no flat chance. Those who did step over the bounds, you would find that they spent a lot of time in the medical room after the game, nursing injuries that no one ever saw them get. He was a professional.*

Rod Olsson succeeded Farmer as the coach of Geelong in later years, but also played against him as a Hawthorn ruck-rover. One of the best-known incidents of Olsson's playing career came when he was knocked cold by Ted Whitten, receiving severe concussion. When asked in his Geelong days whether Whitten was the toughest footballer he had played against, he apparently replied that there were two tougher, Darrel Baldock and Graham Farmer, whilst noting that between the pair they were only ever reported once. Whitten himself tells a story:

> *One day I fixed up Denis Marshall down at Geelong, and Polly leapt over and said, "You shouldn't have done that EJ." "It was an accident." I said. "No it wasn't," he said, "you shouldn't have done*

that." Before the game [finished] I was in a pack. Geez, he gave me a beauty—quite legitimately though. He was pretty strong. And nobody saw it. But you accept those things, just things we all do during the course of a game. You don't bitch about it because, I mean, they're only receipts.

Farmer passed the acid test of the VFL tough men with flying colours. And the opposition could find few other ways to frustrate his effect on a game. Whitten again: 'We were very jealous because he had created something within himself that he could control and we couldn't.' Newman commented that:

Farmer worked on the basis that if you have had your opponent change his game to try and combat you, the thing that they had to concentrate on—the football—was out of their mind. A lot of ruckmen used to look at the ball and look at Farmer. They used to be preoccupied with what he was doing, where he was. That is what he worked on, the fact that you play your opponents on their weaknesses, not on their strengths.

Even Farmer's arch rival, Carlton legend John Nicholls, was forced to play on Farmer's terms during their meetings:

I probably didn't jump as early as [Farmer], but when I played him I did... With Polly, I never gave him any advantage because I'd do the same things as he did... We would both jump early for position— particularly at centre bounces—and quite often the ball would come down and neither of us would get it.

Nicholls feels that the two of them tended to nullify each other, and for all the hype their confrontations created, in many Carlton-Geelong games, neither would have a great influence:

Probably I used to regard him as a better player than I was, and probably more skilled than I was, so I really had to dish it up to him all the time in ruckwork. At the centre bounces and boundary throw-ins I had to be aggressive to him every time. If I didn't attack him on an aggressive basis every time, he would beat me. We used to play it very hard, and because we both used to jump early and use our arms and things, we quite often had blood noses and things. But we've always been good mates... I've always said that Teddy Whitten was the best all-round player I've ever seen, but certainly Farmer was the best ruckman without a doubt. A lot of others have been very good and come close, but there was only one Polly Farmer and he was the best.

Farmer came to Geelong virtually as a finished product as a footballer, merely adding the touches he felt he needed of additional strength and a greater mental and physical toughness. He played the same game that he had at East Perth of feeding the ball out to the running players. Through his first couple of years one reads in some of the match reports that his handball was astray, and being sharked by the opposition. Farmer takes umbrage at this. As far as he was concerned his handballs always went exactly where they were intended. What he was trying to do was educate his teammates to his style of play, to be moving towards goal as they received the ball from him. Even now watching an old video he gets annoyed at a commentator saying that a handpass missed its target. 'The ball was in the right place, Alistair Lord just didn't move to meet it.'

Newman comments that it took about a season and a half for this to sink in with the whole team. 'Farmer never sat down and said that he was going to do this. He would just do it, and many times Farmer would hit guys who didn't realise what he was doing.' Some, like Goggin, adapted very quickly, but after a time they all 'learned that when he got the ball they had to be on the move'.

Bill Goggin's understanding of Farmer's way of playing football was instinctive, as if the pair were made for each other. Goggin's mate, long-time Geelong trainer George Clark, conjures up a Schwarzenegger and De Vito-like image:

They were almost like twins—this sense between them. And it came out of nowhere. And they were magnificent to watch. Billy would say, 'I knew what he was doing before he did it, and he knew where I was going to be'... Billy would just run, and he'd just hit him on the chest.

'I knew it was coming. I'd look over my shoulder, and here it comes.'

'Farmer revolutionised the game of football.' This is a statement one hears and reads over and over. It is a claim made about no other player. It is by no means universally accepted as a statement of fact, but the fact that it is heard so often says something about his impact on the game. It is usually taken to mean that he was the pioneer of the art of attacking handball that has become such a central feature of the game, or that he was the progenitor of play-on football.

Some argue that this had begun with the Len Smith mosquito fleet at Fitzroy, where flick passing and quick movement of the ball at close quarters had taken a team of ordinary players to the finals in 1960. Footscray under Ted Whitten played this same style in reaching the 1961 grand final against Hawthorn. Others say that Farmer was unique unto himself, and though some tried to emulate his style, handball did not come of age as an integral part of football until the historic 1970 grand final when Carlton came back from the dead to steal the premiership from Collingwood, thanks to a half-time instruction from a desperate Ron Barassi to handball at all costs.

What all the insiders agree on is that Farmer opened their eyes to the possibilities of handball, and what it could do when used so well. No one had utilised it in the same way, and to the same effect before Farmer arrived. In this sense, even if he was not a revolutionary, he was a central figure in the evolution of the modern game.

The effect that his handball had on the patterns of play and the way the ball was moved down the field was just as important as the use of handball as a technique. Essentially football had been a straight-ahead game. The flick passing game could get the ball out of packs or manoeuvre it to advantage, but essentially it shared the ball between players running down the same line.

The long handball that Farmer introduced had the capacity to completely change the direction of play, to cut right across the field. This would provide increased options for the receiver, by throwing defenders out of kilter and opening up new lines of attack. At its most perfect it created football that was beautiful to watch. It became one of the classic football passages—Farmer to Goggin out wide, streaming downfield, delivering perfectly to Wade, mark, goal.

Farmer's insistence on putting the ball in front of the receiver, forcing him to move forwards as he took the ball created a new pattern that gradually became more and more important: lateral movement to create the space for a forward thrust. Barassi's triumph in 1970, initiated to overcome Collingwood's superior aerial strength by going around their big men, gave coaches and players the courage to use the same pattern of play out of defence. As the game has evolved further, so the understanding and usage of the tactics have developed. Barassi makes the point that:

> *There has to be someone to give it to. The guy running past was the key; not so much the handballer, but the handballee, so to speak. When Barry Davis went from North Melbourne back to Essendon [in 1979] to be a coach, he began to take stats on who were the receivers of a handball, indicating that he wanted to know who the hell was running past.*

But it was Farmer fifteen years earlier, when Barry Davis was just beginning his football career, who had opened the eyes of the football world to the real value of the handballee, the man running past.

It has come to the point where good sides will chip the ball backwards and forwards across the field by hand and foot until the right opening is created for the movement forward. But now, as then, it still works best when giver and receiver have the speed, the vision and the understanding to create the movement quickly and unexpectedly, catching the opposition off guard. Farmer made the moves more quickly, more unexpectedly, and more tellingly than anyone. *He hated to waste a possession* is another of the recurring statements made about him. Yet he needed no time to make the assessment of the best option. With uncanny peripheral vision and knowledge of where his team-mates were, and lightning hands, the ball would be on its way almost before he had it in his hands. Ted Whitten describes the process in almost mystical terms:

He had some magic about him whereby he had full control of the football... You could sort of tell that he would bring it down with him. He had the amazing sense of being able, when he was in the air, to know where his men were situated around him, because the moment he hit the ground it was either a kick or a handball directly to his team men. He got up in the air and he would think about it coming down, 'What will I do with this one?' And he had that unique sense, he would mesmerise players. You would really think they were stopping to see, just to watch him, just for a split second—and bang—and then they would start again.

On top of all these attributes was his phenomenal consistency. 'He did the job every Saturday,' says Bob Davis. 'He never dropped below 75 per cent,' says Newman. 'He never had a bad day when people could have said that he was thrashed or didn't contribute. When he was having a bad day he would always be competitive, his effectiveness would never drop below seventy-five per cent. He was the consummate competitor.'

MANFRED JURGENSEN

Highpoint Carlton

Manfred Jurgensen was born in Flensburg, Germany, in 1940. He is a bilingual poet and novelist whose latest publications are the autobiography *Five Weeks at "Humanitas"*, the novel *The Last Australia Day* and the collected poetry volume *The Otherness of Words*. Jurgensen is Emeritus Professor at the University of Queensland and lives in Brisbane with his wife and the ragdoll cat, Shelley. He is currently working on a novel about Ludwig Leichhardt. 'Highpoint Carlton' first appeared in *The Greatest Game* by Ross Fitzgerald and Ken Spillman (eds., 1988).

It's one week to the Grand Final. A block of units in Brisbane announces the names of its transient residents. Looking for mine, I notice the many foreign words waiting to be buzzed. I had to lose my key to be confronted by them. In an absurd hope I press my name wondering whether I am at home.

'With a name like that you'd be able to kick a ball!'

He examined me with a mixture of amusement and respect, or perhaps it was the kind of mockery in which college students specialised. I could not tell. Why didn't he just go on bouncing and kicking his leather bomb? Instead he threw it at ·me just as I was about to get back into the house. Luckily I caught it, or my landlady's front window would have been broken. That would have been the last straw seeing it had taken me seven weeks to get a room at the top end of Swanston Street in a run-down terrace house.

'Good mark!' he shouted. I was angry and kicked the ball across the road into the grounds of Newman College. Who did he think he was, awarding marks like a teacher? Pompous twit! I went back inside.

'Is Jurgie home?'

David lived two blocks away in Faraday Street, and this time he had come with a friend. Mrs McLeod was unsure whether she should call me down. The boy had come all the way from Germany to study, not to play football with the neighbourhood louts. She felt responsible to his mother on the other side of the world.

As I came down the hall, David ignored my landlady and yelled, 'That's him, Bert.' I felt like a criminal. And as before he threw a ball at me, narrowly missing Mrs McLeod. To escape her swearing I ran out of the house and joined the intruders. They took me to the university field. On our way David played the teacher again. He wanted me to remember mostly foreign names that didn't make much sense to me: Kekovich, Silvagni, Barassi. They were their heroes of 'Australian Rules', not a game but, it would seem, a migrant's path to identity and recognition.

I learnt to contest marks that afternoon, practised the punt kick and bounced an oval ball as if my future depended on it. My gym shoes were in shreds, my boiling feet swollen and stiff. But I felt curiously relieved. It was as if I'd kicked my name into the spring air of a city that did not seem to want to know me.

Princes Park smelt of human bodies, pies and beer. Bert showed me how to stand on cans to catch a view. I chewed my first Four'n'Twenty as Big John Nicholls led out the Blues. From the other side of the ground I could hear the roar, 'Carlton! Carlton! Carlton!' David and Bert were busy emptying cans in honour of the home team.

In appreciation of the training I had received and to show that I had understood the meaning of loyalty, I yelled at the top of my voice, 'Up the mighty Blues!' It was like kicking—I kicked a verbal punt sixty metres in the direction of Big Nick. All he had to do was mark it. It wasn't my name any more that curved into a torpedo punt above the heads of spectators. I barracked for a team and passed the ball to Bert and David, my mates who introduced me to Australian Rules. I yelled for them while they remained silent. We too were a team. 'Up the mighty—!' At the bounce of the ball someone kicked the cans on which my view depended. As I fell into the crowd in front of me, I was surrounded by mustard brown shawls and beanies. What was left of my pie landed in the neck and hair of Hawks supporters. My mates pulled me up again, ripped open a Carlton Bitter, raised a mumbled toast to the cloudless August sky and said, 'Let that be a bloody lesson to you!'

The following year I went to train with Carlton. I remember one cold afternoon when we were joined by a soccer player from Canberra. The way he marked he must have been a goalie. His press-ups seemed a kind of ballet. He shook hands like an arresting officer, and he ran faster than all of us. What was he trying to prove? I tried to think of him as just another newcomer to the code, a convert like myself. No one understood his name when he introduced himself. It sounded un-Australian.

Alex Jesaulenko soon became naturalised; he became 'Jezza'. Aussie Rules was a translation of European scepticism and ambition into a new mythology. It not only played with words, it had its own language. The natives spoke it as they learnt the syntax of eighteen interdependent positions; the migrant spectators copied their pidgin re-enactment. Communication between them may have lacked elegance, but the desire to make yourself understood was overwhelming. Everyone had a rough idea what was going on.

There were Saturdays when the game turned into poetry for both the team and the crowd. The ball was recited in a metre of inevitable beauty. For once there was precision, even among supporters. And I went home alone kicking words, booed by the barracking of dusk.

'Not a game,' I began, 'but old dreams re-enacted. In its drama of endeavour, life became the ballgame it reflected. High marks in the Never-Never. Suddenly meaning depends on a kick twenty metres out dead in front. How to be full-forward at last and quick to convert while taking the brunt in defence, roving cleverly to death. With time-on the bounce of the ball is past tense. Undefeated, out of breath, the players heed their coach's call.'

The lines disappeared in the fading light. Jezza was taking a shower with the rest of the boys.

There were nagging games like stubborn arguments and quarters of sophisticated rhetoric. Sometimes the afternoon was rescued in a single mark. Or a fifty metre pass restored faith in the impossible. We always played for someone else and, when we watched, it was us who were playing. Australian Rules. Perhaps that was one of the reasons for its attraction. For three years I was taught the sport of re-enactment.

On television no amount of instant replays or fancy lingo of Lou the Lip could capture the conspiracy between players and spectators, the excitement of sensing that the bounce of the ball was really about something else. Maybe the canned applause and laughter of American TV shows had made an authentic telecast of VFL football impossible. As it was, the crowd sounded sterile, part of a visual package to fit into the frequent commercials. Even live coverage looked edited. The camera angles excluded most of what was going on.

Back on the ground, careers, marriages and domestic tragedies were entrusted to the chosen few. Parliament met at the MCG, Windy Hill, Kardinia Park, Glenferrie Oval, Arden Street, Moorabbin, Princes Park. The Blue Boys were considered bluebloods, Menzies was club ticket holder Number One. Carlton playing Collingwood or South took on ideological dimensions for some.

In the early sixties club loyalty was strong, even if it was interpreted differently. It was a sensation when Ron Barassi left Melbourne for Carlton. I remember reading the monstrous headline in the *Sun* and knew the game would never be the same. When the Number 31 guernsey ran out on the Carlton football ground, all hell broke loose. Public adultery had been committed. Barassi's goals did not count. Norm Smith's adopted son had turned Judas. In the Carlton dressing-rooms I listened to Ron explaining ball-handling and tagging. His confidence and boyish grin made me forget that he had betrayed the code.

A quarter of a century has passed. The nature of Australian Rules has changed. Local and interstate players sell their loyalty to the highest bidder. The game has become more and more like an American television show. Private entrepreneurs are buying and selling teams. VFL is played outside Victoria. The very name and identity of a club are changed.

But other names have remained that have accompanied hundreds of thousands of fans throughout the years, Schimmelbusch,

Dipierdomenico, Ditterich, Catoggio, Kourkemelis, a new Silvagni. First, second or third generation Australians chasing a ball to score someone else's elusive goal. Jezza became player-coach of Sandgate, Brisbane, for a while, Big Carl played at the Sunshine Coast and Gary Dempsey just won a premiership for his new side, the Southport Sharks. Old VFL footballers don't die; they make Queensland their interchange bench in their final games.

Heroes are quickly forgotten if they don't become television or radio commentators. I find it a relief that most players do not allow themselves to be considered 'experts', made to serve on know-all panels discussing the ifs and buts of success or failure. It proves, I think, that to them the secret is still alive. For they remember that once a string of names could stage the ecstasy of dreams. Rovers and followers, back-pocket players, full-forwards and ruckmen wrote plays of loyalty, bravery and deceit. Teams could act as one body. Life was an eternal search for this body. We joined a club, a team to find ourselves again, we depended on others. Their names were adopted as part of our own identity.

Hawthorn has kicked the decisive goal against Melbourne after the final siren and will play Carlton in the 1987 Grand Final. A fifteen-metre penalty was awarded on a technicality and only because the umpires did not hear the siren. The heartbreak of miracles continues: Australian Rules. (Perhaps it was all a television plot.)

———◆◆❁◆◆———

It's one week to the Grand Final. When I discovered Carlton in 1962, the siren sounded for first quarter. Although I was young, I did not make a name for myself. When I press the buzzer, no one answers. I may last the third quarter. It's harder in front of the TV. There's nobody there to shout, 'Ave a go, you mug!' And David has also stayed in Melbourne. Wonder what's happened to him. He hasn't called to ask, 'Is Jurgie home?' Could've kicked a ball around, for old times' sake. Drop-punted a few names and marked one or two.

JOHN HARMS

Epiphany at the MCG

John Harms is a writer, broadcaster, historian and publisher. Having spent most of his life in Queensland he now lives in Melbourne with his wife and three young kids. His books include *Loose Men Everywhere, Memoirs of a Mug Punter* and *Confessions of a Thirteenth Man.* He is the editor-at-large of www.footyalmanac.com.au and of *The Footy Almanac,* which has been published since 2007. This essay first appeared in *The Footy Almanac 2007.*

It is Grand Final morning. I am walking through the Fitzroy Gardens. Past the river god fountain up to my left. Past the cenotaph. I look up at the majestic trees. I'm trying to understand my state. My thoughts. My emotions. My smallness.

It is overwhelming—the deepest of feelings: that life matters, and that people matter. And I wonder why I am in such a heightened state of awareness on the morning of a footy match. Just a footy match. Why do I find such meaning in this?

I keep walking. I cannot remember life without footy. I cannot remember life without hoping Geelong would win on Saturday, and eventually be the premiers. I cannot remember life without yearning. I cannot remember life without an underlying sense of melancholy. I know *La Condition Geelong.* But I also know that the human spirit is found in the fight to live a passionate life in the face of the human reality—that eventually we are no more. And, as the ancient writer Paul reminded the people of Rome, 'Suffering produces endurance, and endurance produces character, and character produces hope, and hope does not disappoint us.'

I have never lost that hope.

So many of my childhood memories are connected with footy. Great family days when we all wanted so much for Geelong to win. Sitting around together watching the replay on an old black and white TV. Even days by myself, listening to Geelong on the radio, reading the paper, keeping a scrap book.

The first Geelong game I can really remember attending was at VFL Park against Footscray in 1971. By sheer fluke ('These seats look alright') we sat right among the Geelong cheer squad.

Gee-Long CLAP CLAP CLAP, Gee-Long CLAP CLAP CLAP.

We were part of it, stirred by it. The Cats lost by two points after Billy Goggin's goal was disallowed in the dying minutes. Ripped off. It was a shocking decision, and we drove home wondering why that always happened to Geelong.

As I get closer to Wellington Parade the crowd swells. Generations of Geelong supporters walk together. I feel I know them. I know they are struggling with this. Trying to be confident. Years of failure haunting them. 'Is it me?' we ask ourselves. Feeling inadequate. Feeling no sense of entitlement. Why? Why do I feel I don't deserve this? Why have the gods chosen the people of Carlton and Hawthorn and Essendon? Why does the world belong to them?

But I admire these Geelong people; that they are not embittered. I admire their loyalty. I admire the gentleness of their souls, and their understanding that profound relationships are born of shared suffering. I admire their capacity to forgive. But, God forbid, what if we lose today? Is this to be just another test?

Only grace will save us, and the sausages and beers in Yarra Park. J. Dunne has gathered with C. Allan, B. Kane, and Brian Miller. G.C.J.D. Haigh and Tim Adam turn up. Amber arrives ('I'm so nervous'). Then The Handicapper, eight months pregnant with our first child, waddles up the path from Jolimont Station like a Grand Final veteran. We all chat. We discuss the team. Young Mark Blake has been dropped. The selectors have opted for the experience and stronger body of Steven King. The Cats must match Port Adelaide's Brendon Lade and Dean Brogan. We must get the footy before their classy mid-fielders get it.

We tell ourselves it will be fine. We've been terrific all year. We shake hands and embrace and wish each other well. Then the group disperses, heading to the particular seats, flung far and wide, that each has managed to secure (somehow). We walk down the tree-lined path towards the mighty MCG.

Inside people rush about. Some have found their seats and have sent a scout out for pies and beers. The Handicapper and I are three rows back from the fence, behind the point post at the city end. We are next to the Geelong cheer squad.

We wait. Past players, each holding a premiership cup, form a long line in the centre of the MCG. Some are very old. Bobby Davis is introduced holding the 1963 cup. He looks humble and proud. My tears well. Not because he is the only surviving premiership coach. Just because he is a wonderful man; a true elder of the tribe. He has the grin of a man who knows he has been blessed with a rich life, and is thankful for it. The Handicapper holds my forearm.

At last the players appear. Port run to the Punt Road end. Tom Harley leads the Cats through the banner. It's almost too much. I feel uplifted and ready, and also deeply at peace, like that moment after a funeral where you've shed your final tear, and you are at one with the people about you. Look at Otto. Steve Johnson. Joel Corey. Nervous. Come on boys.

Gary and Nathan Ablett make me think of their father. His brilliance. His restlessness. I think of my own parents. My father's lifelong love of the club. Him sitting with my mother in a little house in the Adelaide Hills. My brothers and their families. I think of the thousands gathered around Australia and the world. Please.

The players warm up and then line up for the anthem. Geelong people are in a state of baffled wonder, but we love our team, and we just hope they play well.

Ottens and Brogan face each other. 'Come on Otto,' I say. The noise builds. Siren. Thud. The game starts like a Grand Final. Physical scrimmages. Max Rooke smashes into David Rodan, who doesn't flinch. Nervous handballs go nowhere. Tackles. No one has any time.

The Cats start to make their own. They win clean possession and spread the footy. Quickly. Precise handballs. Accurate kicking. They make space. Chappy bombs, Mooney marks. Goal. Mooney marks again and dishes to Johnno. Another one. The Cats look okay. Johnno is alert. He intercepts a handball and bananas towards goal. Just off line. Gary Ablett spoils the kick in, paddles, steadies, and goals. We're out of our seats. The players are washing away our fear.

But Port fight back. Lade's tap finds Shaun Burgoyne on the fly and he streaks into goal to reduce the margin to seven points. Around the ground, though, the Cats look comfortable.

'They're on,' a bloke behind us says.

Hunt sprints along the southern wing holding the footy inside the boundary line. He squares to Ottens, now up forward. The crumb spills to Chappy. As he's about to launch one home from fifty he sees Johnno on his own in the pocket. He passes with the outside of his foot. Johnno marks and pops it through. Then Selwood gets it, and has two to beat. With the poise of Robert Harvey he shows the ball to one tackler who takes the bait. He lets the other tackler come to him and pops a delayed handball into the path of Bartel who snaps and goals. The Handicapper's eyes speak the unspeakable, 'I think we've got this.'

When Port gather the footy they are under immediate pressure. Late in the quarter Michael Pettigrew runs from the back pocket. Ottens sets off after him. He has ground to make up. He gives everything, and runs the Port speedster down. Holding the ball. Ottens, at that moment, is spirit personified.

We're feeling pretty good about things, and what follows the quarter-time break is ten minutes we will never forget. It is a time of transcendence. Geelong plays the most beautiful, free-flowing footy imaginable. They win the ball deep in defence, and have such belief in each other when they attack. They play with the purest skill. Hunt to Corey, back to Hunt, footpass to Rooke. Who handballs to Enright in an instant. To Stokes. Out to Johnno. Goal.

Minutes later Enright wins a skirmish in the last line of defence. He squirts a handball to Bartel. Even though he is in the last line of defence he has the confidence to loop a handball to the running Wojcinski who doesn't break stride. He hits Rooke with a sharp left-foot pass. Rooke puts the footy out in front of Mooney who doesn't stop. He wheels around on a Brownless arc and pumps a Polly Farmer handball to Selwood running wide on the flank. Selwood bombs long to Nathan Ablett. The footy has moved the length of the field so quickly that the defence is in chaos. Free kick. Goal.

Out of the centre again. Gary Ablett to Selwood who is streaming forward. He puts the footy to Nathan Ablett's advantage in the square. One-hander. Just like his dad. Five goals in no time and the Cats are 53 points clear at the eleven minute mark of the second quarter.

The crowd is alive: *Gee-Long CLAP CLAP CLAP, Gee-Long CLAP CLAP CLAP.* I am nine again. I sigh. The tears come. The Handicapper looks at me. I feel like we are chosen. At last. I feel like the boys are playing so brilliantly that something drastically awful would have to happen for us to lose. They are showing us what is possible. They have had an epiphany. They have invited in the football spirit. They've come to believe that people are at their finest when they denounce the tyranny of self, in the interests of the team. These are the fruits of that spirit.

And I'm part of it. Just in case I'm not convinced, when Chad Cornes kicks for goal the footy lands a couple of rows behind us. It bounces high, and I reach up and grab it. I hold it tightly. I have the Grand Final footy in my hands. The actual footy. I handball it back to the boundary umpire.

Port are shattered. The Cornes brothers try to lift them. The Burgoynes get the footy, but often deep in defence and they have few options. They too are giving everything. Salopek runs down Gary Ablett. But the Cats are just playing so well.

If any Geelong fans are still concerned, straight after half-time Cam Mooney takes a mark and goals. Port's hopes are snuffed out. The Cats continue to dominate, and we begin to celebrate. The Geelong heart opens. There are tears around us. People look at each other wondering whether they deserve this; this gift. The overwhelming mood is gratitude. The thanksgiving begins. It is a celebration which honours the players and what they have done. Blue and white people are clapping and laughing. Families hug. Friends embrace. A balding man from the front row introduces himself to me, and then returns to his family. As Geelong sweeps the ball forward the crowd directs, pointing out the players who are free.

To add to the moment Chapman flies over Tredrea to take a classic high mark; one of the great Grand Final marks. 'Chappyyyy,' says The Handicapper. Even in the last quarter the Cats keep running and continue to kick goals. This is how the game can be: great team footy played with a free spirit. By the time the final siren sounds, I understand hope fulfilled. I feel my own joy. And the joy of others. I look around the stadium at these people whose happiness has substance. The players. Mark Thompson. Us fans. You must understand suffering to know the fullness of that joy.

Tom Harley knows suffering. He and Cameron Ling were the only two players to speak publicly when things were tough. But they have led these boys, and have helped them find their best. This is a players' premiership, assisted by a coach who has learnt much about life over the past two seasons. He has also learned what footy can mean to those who love the Geelong Football Club.

The players are gracious in victory. A six-year-old presents each player with his premiership medal. In return the player puts a premiership cap on the kid's head. Jimmy Bartel beams. So do the kids. Johnno is awarded the Norm Smith Medal. It could have gone to Matthew Scarlett or Chappy. But Johnno is the creator; the man who sees the game differently. Einstein said imagination was more important than knowledge. Johnno has a footy imagination like few others. We are fortunate he was given a chance to express it. Tom Harley, a man of substance, makes a simple speech. The light in him shines. 'We are Geelong,' he concludes. The boys do a slow lap. Geelong fans stay. When the players return to the race they link arms and form a circle. They sing the club song.

We are Geelong.

The Handicapper and I walk back towards the city.

We are blessed.

JEFF GUESS

Mark of the Day

Jeff Guess was born in Adelaide in 1948, and is one of Australia's most acclaimed poets. His first book *Leaving Maps* appeared in 1984 and was hailed by Judith Rodriguez in *The Sydney Morning Herald* as 'a major collection'. Since then eleven other collections have been published, the most recent being *Autumn in Cantabile* (2012). The recipient of many writing awards, Guess has edited numerous anthologies and written several textbooks on the teaching of poetry. 'Mark of the Day' first appeared in *The Greatest Game* by Ross Fitzgerald and Ken Spillman (eds., 1988).

watching him go up the sky as if he
    held some secret toe-holds in the crowd-rung
air   long fingers   stretching into all the
    grey and difficult distance   glistening

robed with rings of rain and silver
    light   he knows his own degrees   less than a
go-between for gods   nevertheless   were
    this the very port of Mars   this warrior

rises   risking all our soft Saturday
    fears of losing more than the match   he flies
for all of us   clutching at the stars   way
    out of reach   but catching any piece of sky

is not enough   what counts is still the worth
    of what he does with it   back here on earth

ORIEL GRAY

Loss of a Homespun Legend

Oriel Gray (1920-2003) was one of Australia's pioneering woman playwrights, a progressive whose work engaged with major social and political issues including gender equity, the environment and Indigenous issues. Early plays included *Lawson* (1943), *My Life is My Affair* (1947) and *Had We But World Enough* (1950). *The Torrents* shared the 1954 Playwright's Advisory Board prize with Ray Lawler's *Summer of the Seventeenth Doll*, while *Burst of Summer* won the J.C. Williamson Theatre Guild Competition in 1958. In the 1960s Gray became a television writer, and for nine years was a writer for the popular serial, *Bellbird*. Her autobiography, *Exit Left: Memoirs of a Scarlet Woman*, was published in 1985, and her work continued to attract interest many years after her death. This essay first appeared in *The Greatest Game* by Ross Fitzgerald and Ken Spillman (eds., 1988).

---

*W*ebster's Dictionary defines a legend as 'a traditional story popularly regarded as historical or myth; lives of saints or similar stories; inscription or motto, especially on coin or medal'. Frazer's *Golden Bough* is nearer for me—a fantastic but believable story, a word-of-mouth history, an accepted ceremony that is part of our lives.

Legends can stay within a family or illuminate a world, as the wanderings and conversations of Jesus or Don Quixote have done. They might begin with a tribal scuffle or suburban game and grow into a tradition on which heroes can hang their shields or their football boots. The more commonplace they seem, the more identified with people's collective life, the more important they may be when they are needed.

Before my three sons were born, my branch of the family knew nothing about Australian Rules football. But we knew a good deal about legends. The family album was treasured, though the names of most of the Edwardian bucks and belles had been lost or forgotten. Ghost stories were told and re-told, of Grandfather Sheehan who had seen and spoken to Andrew Fisher's ghost; of Little Claire (dead before my time) who was given to appearing in front of Catholic aunts before impending deaths in the family. She often appeared before weddings, too, so she could not have been a morbid child.

When my sister and I joined the Communist Party in 1940, we hid the shameful fact that we were traditionalists at heart. Although we talked about everything else, we could not admit to each other that family legends would have to wither away along with the state. Vague as we were about dialectical materialism, we were glumly certain that it would not stretch to cover Fisher's ghost or little Claire.

Actually, the Communist Party had a sneaking liking for legends, too, so long as they were spoken (like our family ghost stories) and not written down in theoretical works. When the cottage lecture was over and the speaker from Marx House had gone home, when a few drinks got mixed with the respectable coffee, then someone would tell of Lenin listening to Beethoven's 'Seventh' and declaring, 'Life is joyous, comrades!' instead of the grim policy speech expected. And someone else would talk of Rosa Luxemburg stopping to pick a red carnation on May Day, as though he or she had been there. These stories seemed so wonderful, yet so close to us, so available, that I found myself wondering why, if Marx and Lenin, Rosa Luxemburg and La Passionara could come across with such inspiring one-liners, they wrote such prosy pamphlets? I was very young then.

Later, when I lost faith in the humanity of theoreticians and policy-makers, I decided that these things might have been said and done and shared with people in the street, but the theoreticians would leave them out lest their quirkish humanity detract from the weightiness of the work.

But the people remembered, as they remembered Hector on the walls of Troy taking off his helmet because the waving plume frightened his baby son. They remembered as they remembered a common soldier tying two sticks together and giving the cross to a girl who was being taken to be burnt as a witch in Rouen. The people have always been the keepers of legends, whether they passed them round the campfire or the pub bar. I hope they realise that in Victoria they are in danger of losing one right now.

Although my three sons were born in New South Wales, they came to Victoria early enough to grow up convinced that Australian Rules is the only civilised way to play football. They regard other codes with tolerant condescension, considering them necessary steps in the Ascent of Man.

My eldest son, Stephen, follows Fitzroy with the same dedication that Galahad showed for the Holy Grail. In this case, the Premiers' crown. Steve has been a dedicated republican since the age of sixteen. But when the Queen was present at a match when the Roys, near the bottom of the ladder, beat Richmond, the reigning Premiers, he came bounding home singing 'We Are the Boys of Old Fitzroy', assuring me that in all fairness you had to admit that the Queen was not a bad looking sort at all, and anyone could see that she was very interested in the game. He did stop short of saying she was wearing maroon and blue, but one more tinnie and he would have! Given a few more generations, the family will tell it as a truth that Elizabeth R snatched a Fitzroy pennant from Great-uncle Stephen and waved it frantically, acknowledging the Lions' right to bear their place in her own coat-of-arms. That's how legends are made.

I must not lean too heavily towards the Lions as legend-makers. For many years my other two sons barracked for South Melbourne. They inherited South from my first husband, actor John Gray, when he left to live in New Zealand. 'Stand by the Bloods!' he said in the resonant voice that earned him many a quid on stage and radio. 'I can't ask Steve to desert Fitzroy, though he is my only son. But I can trust you two boys to stand by the Bloods.' They were deeply impressed.

I do not know how South Melbourne—'The Mighty Bloods'— became the Theatricals' team. It may have been because the individual rorty battling aura of old South Melbourne was a defiant challenge to the belief that all actors were poofters, as all actresses were tarts. (Though it is considered sexist, I use the term 'actress' deliberately. It is a fine historical term defining great women who lifted the standards of and ennobled their profession.) It may have been because the Bloods were the eternal losers to Fate, as Theatricals were the eternal losers to Management in the days before Actors' Equity and the Australian Writers' Guild.

I remember vaudevillian Frank Rich threatening to break a long-time friendship with actor Keith Eden because Keith had said that next year would be the Bloods' year to howl. 'Whaddya mean?' bellowed Frank. 'Next year? This year!' Keith conceded that, of course, they would win this year, though the season was half-way through and the Bloods second from the bottom of the ladder.

When Jeff Underhill wrote his delightful vest-pocket opera, *The Ballad of Angels' Alley*, he called his unheroic heroes, the lovable, inefficient, losing rogues of Tom Tiddler's gang, 'The Bloods of Angel's Alley'. A wry tribute to the Theatricals' favourite team. Jeff knew about as much about the game as I do, and probably applauded a goal at the wrong end if he went to a match at all. Still, he would tell you sincerely that he barracked for the Bloods. Why? It was tradition, it was legend, it made you one with that band of outsiders, the Theatricals, yet one with the rest of the cheering or despairing tribe.

They barracked for South Melbourne, *old* South Melbourne. Then the Bloods passed into the hands of Dr Geoffrey Edelsten and became the lordly Swans, possessed of cash reserves and a chorus of primping 'Swanettes', who would have brought down on their heads the wrath— and the handbags—of the lady barrackers for old South.

Perhaps the Sydney Theatricals support them now—Jeff Underhill's Bloods were never down *their* alley anyway. They were denizens, in their time, of Little Bourke and Little Lon, loungers on the corner of Gore and Gertrude streets. In Melbourne, a good deal of that allegiance seems to have passed to Fitzroy, so often the battling underdogs, yet carrying the image of the legendary Haydn Bunton before them like a fragment of the True Cross. In my brief tour on *The Sullivans*, a kind of miasma would hang over the Crawford Productions canteen on a Monday morning. It rose from the gloom of the Roys' defeat—or from hangovers occasioned by their victory.

As I write, I realise that the Game has been more part of my life than I thought; that some motherly interest I pretended, that some of the loud arguments and even louder laments that were poured into my ears must have taken effect. And there are so many links with the theatre that I have loved with the same despairing devotion that my neighbours give to their teams.

There is Ray Lawler trying to explain 'Up there Cazaly!' to the respectful but uncomprehending cast as *The Summer of the Seventeenth Doll* was being prepared for productions in London and New York. Dennis Miller, playing Pierre in *War and Peace* at the Russell Street Theatre yelling, 'They've won! They've won! St Kilda's won the Premiership!' when he was supposed to be announcing the result of the Battle of Borodino. Russell Street Theatre giving Melbourne its first play about Australian Rules with its season of *And the Big Men Fly*, Alan Hopgood's saga of the boy from the bush who plays in bare feet. David Williamson writing *The Club*, which could be about any football team and any power struggle. Barry Dickins's *Royboys*, which could be about only one club, but everyone's lost hopes and dreams.

Oh yes, the Theatre has its connections with the Game—and the Game is theatre in itself. It has high drama and low comedy, with many of the best lines delivered from the audience. Cold and bored as I was at the time, I have treasured the memory of an obligatory game I attended when Fitzroy's Owen Abrahams made some fatal mistake that meant yet another defeat. It left the whole crowd silent, except for a solitary voice in the hush, perfectly pitched, perfectly timed, a line delivered in sorrow not in anger, eloquent as the Eli, Eli: 'Abey! Abey! Abey, my boy... !' And if an umpire should 'Exit, pursued by a bear' as Shakespeare once called for, there are many times when it would find favour with the groundlings.

It has high romance, in our family anyway. When Stephen, that boy from old Fitzroy, was courting journalist and film critic Annie Gillison, he converted her to the Game. Old friends from intellectual days were startled to see Annie sporting a badge bearing the face of Bernie Quinlan (known to his admirers as 'The Boot'). They were married on a Saturday, and Fitzroy was playing a desperate game. None of the wedding guests knew that under her elegant wedding gown Annie was wearing 'The Boot' badgepinned to her borrowed blue garter.

There is a favourite theatrical story about the manager of the London theatre where *My Fair Lady* had been playing for eighteen months to full houses, with a six-month waiting list at the box office. He was so intrigued to see an empty seat that he remarked on it to the elderly lady beside it. He was most embarrassed when she explained that her husband had booked many months before, but had died in the meantime.

'Forgive me,' said the manager. 'But—surely you have one friend who would have come with you today.'

'Oh, no,' the widow replied. 'They're all at the funeral.'

Like most theatrical stories, it is best acted out. When I had finished my performance, Stephen said, 'They tell the same story about seats at the Grand Final.' He made his point, and I took it and became a little more tolerant of the passion that sweeps over Victoria every winter, with the flu.

But it took the hysteria that accompanied the America's Cup win to really open me to the homespun merits of our native game. I made myself something of a social outcast, hissing contempt at the ocean-yacht enthusiasts (which meant almost everybody). 'The Yanks buy up Australian brains, Australian enterprises, swamp us with experts and dictate our foreign policy! Now, when a few rich men buy the skills to win an elitist race, you act as though it were a national victory. And where are *you* mooring your yacht these days, in the Darebin Creek?' And when the cup was lost I said, 'Good riddance! If only they would take their bases with it!'

The people in the Housing Commission area in which I live did not get excited about the America's Cup. It roused nothing like the communal enthusiasm that runs through the shopping centre as Grand Final day approaches. It is taken for granted that you have a team to barrack for, and it would be churlish to say you haven't. You are trapped in discussion about players and form and injuries and umpires. Even a discussion on the weekend weather takes on a thrilling intensity, and everybody joins in. Many of these people have little enough to get excited about—the pensioners, the unemployed, the single mums searching the Blue Cross Op Shop for bargains. There is the single hope of a bet on the TAB, but there is nothing communal about that. It's every man for himself, and you don't want to cruel the chance of a good dividend. Footy is different. You share it, even in dissent.

On a Saturday morning, the kids are out in their team jumpers, often with the number of their favourite player on their backs. The housewives swap personal details about identities, and fortunate is she who can say, 'My auntie knows Peter Daicos well. She lives just behind his cousin. Oh, that knee is giving him a lot of trouble.' Or terrible threats are uttered to Mr Wong, our Chinese chemist: 'I tell you, Mr Wong, if they lose today, on their home ground, well I've *finished* with them!' Would Mr Wong, who plays tennis, say that about Pat Cash, or think it would matter if he did? Never! But his customer feels as though she has uttered significant words, and her team must somehow take notice. Does the childhood belief still flicker, that words can be magic, that this time the spell might work, the wish might come true as it does in all legends?

Aussie Rules matters deeply to these people. They understand how lack of finance is crippling some clubs; they know about being short of money. They are suspicious about the entry of business tycoons, but resigned to it. 'The bastards are always in for the gravy, aren't they?' They want to see Australian Rules made popular, but they do not want to see it taken away from them, promoted, nationalised, internationalised, bounced off a satellite, out of sight of the game they know and love. 'It is our game really,' they will say, and the MCG is the heart of the world that one day of the year.

Many Aborigines have played Australian Rules, a wry paradox, you might say, when so many Australian rules were set against them winning or even surviving. But the game was open to the best, and they played it and added heroic names. Doug Nicholls (later Pastor, then governor of South Australia) for Fitzroy; Polly Farmer for Geelong; Syd Jackson for

Carlton; Jimmy and Phil Krakouer for North Melbourne; and Maurice Rioli for Richmond.

The Aborigines know that a people losing its legends loses its soul. With everything against them, they have managed to hang on to their oneness with their ancient heroes, their Dreamtime. I wonder if the fans and barrackers of today's Aussie Rules have as much stamina. Or will they resign themselves to sitting at home with their unrationed tinnies and an academic interest—letting the old team spirit, the fierce protective clan loyalty, die away with the stories?

Legend is one thing the press or the business moguls cannot create. People are needed for legends—not only to make but also to tell and argue again round the campfire or the public bar or to pass on to a grandchild who has come with a question.

'Don't you believe what you read in the papers. That mark was *so* high—that punt was *so* far—they *did* come from forty-eight points behind at three-quarter time, to win! And you can tell *your* kids that your grandad vouched for that. I *saw* it! I was *there!*'

GERALD MURNANE

Land of Dreams Come True

Gerald Murnane has spent all his life in Melbourne and country Victoria. He matriculated from De La Salle College, Malvern, in 1956 and trained briefly for the priesthood before becoming a teacher. After two novels in the 1970s, he began teaching creative writing at tertiary level in 1980. Novels such as *The Plains* (1982), *Landscape With Landscape* (1985), *Inland* (1988), *Velvet Waters* (1990), and *Emerald Blue* (1995) established Murnane as one of Australia's most thought-provoking writers of literary fiction. Murnane's latest novel is *A History of Books* (2012). He is also the author of a collection of essays, *Invisible Yet Enduring Lilacs* (2005). Murnane's many awards include a Patrick White Award (1999), the Australia Council's emeritus award (2008), the Melbourne Prize for Literature (2009) and an Adelaide Festival Award for Innovation in Writing (2010). This essay first appeared in *The Greatest Game* by Ross Fitzgerald and Ken Spillman (eds., 1988).

In the winter of 1946, when I was seven years old and living in Bendigo, I acquired by chance a wad of coloured cards, each bearing on one side a richly tinted photograph of a man hugging to his chest, or dropping towards his boot, or leaping upwards to grab, or looking as though he had just mislaid, a shining leather football.

Until the day when I acquired the cards, I had been in a state of innocence such as few male children in Victoria or the Riverina nowadays experience—I knew nothing whatever about the football competitions of Melbourne.

I learned a great deal from my wad of cards. I learned that the city of Melbourne was divided into twenty-two principalities or city-states, each with its own coloured uniform. The twenty-two should have been twenty-four, but I had found two irregularities that annoyed me from the start. I knew that Geelong was not part of the entity known as Melbourne, and I could not think where the territory of the team named Melbourne lay. (Later I came to think of Melbourne, the team, as being immanent or spiritually present in every suburb—rather like Almighty God being present in the world.)

Did I not think of the twenty-four as being divided by a deep gulf? Did I not know the difference between VFL and VFA? No, I did not. And how could I have known? My parents knew nothing about football; I had not begun to read newspapers; the kids at school talked mostly about the rivalry between South Bendigo and Sandhurst.

I doubt whether I had actually kicked a football myself at the time when I played with my coloured cards. I considered football less a sport than a branch of geography. Football enabled me to see the great city of Melbourne as divided into brightly coloured zones. Shuffling my cards and re-arranging them on the mat in the lounge room was more interesting than staring at the map of Europe in an atlas.

Of the twenty-four names, only Melbourne, Geelong, and Preston were previously known to me. (Preston was the stony paddocks north of the Tyler Street tram terminus where my family had lived before moving to Bendigo.) The other twenty-one names brought to my innocent mind no image of any actual place. They were names as vague and mysterious as the *Suomi* and *Sverige* and *Helvetia* on the postage stamps in the window of Mrs Linane's toy shop. From the sound of the names and from the all-important colours attached to the names, I put together a Melbourne of dreams—a marvellous kaleidoscope-city that I gloated over for several years. My many-coloured city disappeared almost wholly when I first saw a map of Melbourne and when a well-meaning friend of my father's heard me babbling about Williamstown or Camberwell and took me aside and told me the facts of life that my irresponsible father had neglected to tell me: that as a boy grew towards manhood he ought to think of settling down with a steady VFL club.

Before I learned the facts of life, though, I was free to spread out my cards and to see, far away on the other side of the lounge-room wall, my city of bright, shifting colours. Sandringham, I surmised, was near the sea—not just because of its name but also because of the golden stripes and the blue in its uniform. Brighton, despite its cheerful name, was a shabby place. The Brighton jumper was mostly the same maroon as the knitted cardigan that I had been made to wear for so long as a child that I hated its unravelled cuffs and the hideous, liverish colour of the wool.

I admired half a dozen sets of colours and, of these, two especially. They were the purple with the gold monogram of Oakleigh and the green with the gold vee of Northcote. I could never finally decide which should be my first choice. Even the two dream-places, Oakleigh and Northcote, seemed to attract me equally. Oakleigh's colours were the colours of the wrapper on a Violet Crumble bar, which was a precious luxury in the back streets of Bendigo in 1946. I thought it was no coincidence that the name of the makers of the chocolate bar with the golden filling should be Hoadley. The word 'Hoadley' could have been just a variant spelling of the place where men wore the Violet Crumble colours. And if that was not enough, I always heard in the first syllable of Oakleigh part of the first syllable of cocoa. Oakleigh the dream-place was a place of opulence and wealth. If I had heard the expression in those days, I would have said that the Oakleigh footballers looked good enough to eat.

Northcote appealed to me in a different way. When I saw its colours, I thought of green paddocks, of wattle in bloom, of the yellow-green of willows beside a stream. The word 'north' denoted my favourite wind; I had no doubt that the warm north wind blew freely across the green and gold meadows of Northcote. When I was tired of dreaming of the sensuous indoor pleasures of Oakleigh, I took a dream-stroll through the bracing air of Northcote.

Seven years and many addresses later, I was living in the south-eastern suburbs of Melbourne. By then I had learned the facts of life; I was a follower of the VFL. I went by train every second Saturday to the MCG to watch Melbourne. This was still a few years before the successive

Melbourne premierships, but the Melbourne that I followed was steadily improving, and the future seemed bright.

One Saturday night, when I boarded my train for home after Melbourne had beaten some lowly side, I found the compartment already occupied by a strange, wild-eyed tribe. They were football followers obviously and, just as obviously, their team had won a great victory that day. But their team was no big-name VFL team. The ribbons in the lapels of these people and the scarves around their necks were coloured like Violet Crumble wrappers. The hardy minority, the exclusive sect, were followers of Oakleigh, and they were going home from having seen their team defeat Port Melbourne. Here I explain something that might just now have puzzled the younger reader. In those days there were more than enough football followers to go around. VFL and VFA both played on Saturday and drew good-sized crowds.

One of the Oakleigh followers on the train was a boy I knew from my school. He was Vincent Rice, and he told me he had been an Oakleigh follower all his life; he had never seen a VFL game, and he never intended to. Something stirred in me on that cold evening in the second-class compartment of the Dandenong train. I dimly remembered my lost paradise of childhood dreams. I saw the cards spread out on the mat: the blues and the golds and the strange combinations that I never saw at VFL games. But did I then throw in my lot with the purple and golds? Did I then fling my arms around my long-lost tribe? Impossible. You see, I was residentially one of the purple and gold tribe already. I lived at that time within the boundaries of the city of Oakleigh. In our wanderings, my family had come a long way from Bendigo. In seven years I had travelled from the lounge-room mat in Bendigo to the place where everything was supposed to be chocolate-coated. And that place was a dreary place indeed. I had had my nose rubbed in my own daydreams—an unpleasant experience! I could never think of loving the purple and gold again.

What about the green and gold? Yes, I saw for a moment the green meadows and the yellow of the wattles and willows. But Northcote was on the far side of Melbourne... The dream drifted away.

For most of the next twenty years I was only a half-hearted football follower. As soon as I had begun to earn money, I had become a racegoer, and on many Saturdays at the races I did not even bother to listen when the VFL scores were announced at intervals during the day. I had lost interest in Melbourne when they had won their second successive premiership. Occasionally I went with some friends to watch South Melbourne struggling.

In 1976 I was the father of three small sons. Two of them had begun to call themselves barrackers for one or another VFL club. They got no encouragement from me. I had lost all interest in football. Yet I did not want my sons to feel deprived. One day in 1976 I read that the match of the day was at the MCG. That was what I had been reduced to—one of those sanctimonious puritans of football who watch the match of the day and pretend not to support either side. I could sink no lower.

We sat upstairs in the old outer stand—in Bay 15 where I had barracked for Melbourne more than twenty years before. The game had been underway for three minutes when one of my sons asked me where the ball was. I took a little time to understand. We were sitting so far from the action that my small sons had not been able to follow the flight of the ball. They would have been better off watching the TV replay at home.

We moved down nearer the fence, but then the crowd got in the way. We walked around the stands, watching the game from here and there. The boys had a bit of fun tigging one another on the stairs. We went home at half-time. The world seems a grey and lonely place when you are walking away from a crowded football ground at half-time.

The next day, Sunday, was fine but cold, with a bracing wind from the north-west. I took out the street directory and looked down the page headed RECREATION RESERVES, PARKS, OVALS. The Northcote Football Ground was less than ten kilometres from our house. A paragraph, lost among the VFL pages of the Sunday newspaper, told me that Northcote was at home that day to Camberwell (red, white, and blue tricolour, I remembered at once from my cards of thirty years before).

We went through the gate, and my two sons leaped in the air like sheep and bolted. They scrambled over the fence onto the oval and played kick-to-kick among the hundred or so children and adults. The air was thick with footballs. They hung in the air like sea-birds over a rubbish tip, and the noise was like corn being popped in a huge cauldron. While the kick-to-kickers kick-to-kicked, I looked around me. The crowd was no more than a thousand people, but what people they were: wind-bitten, grey-faced oldies for whom the 1950s had never ended; roly-poly ethnic teenagers talking a dialect made up entirely of monosyllables and four-letter words; fearsome-looking beer drinkers sprawled on a green embankment among stacks of eskies. Nowhere did I see a trendy or a yuppy. I had come home at last.

Surely I am not going to add that I saw green meadows or willows or wattles? Yes, reader, I saw everything that I had dreamed of when I shuffled the cards thirty years before. In the deserted outer ground I found a stunted Cootamundra wattle. When I looked through the fence at the western end of the ground, I saw the Merri Creek winding through its gorge, and the tops of willows showing above the level of the parkland beside the gorge.

Only one detail was not quite what I had expected. When the kick-to-kickers had finally been cleared from the ground and the two teams had lined up, the Coters (I had already learned their demotic name) wore not the green with the gold vee but green and gold stripes. I heard later that the club had discarded the vee a few years before as being old-fashioned. I wished I had been consulted.

Camberwell beat Northcote narrowly that day, but I took my sons a few days later into Alexanders Clothing Stores in High Street and had them fitted with green and gold stripes by the official patron of the club, Mr Sol Alexander. For the next seven years my sons and I followed Northcote faithfully.

Each Sunday at quarter-time and half-time we jumped the fence and joined the other men and boys huddled around the coach and the players and the trainers on the field. We saw from close-up the sweat dripping from foreheads, the blood trickling from noses; we heard the grunts and snarls and obscenities; we shrank from the sting of the coach's tongue.

About that coach... This is a story of dreams come true—of strange coincidences. My sons had only just settled in as followers of Northcote when a new boy arrived at their school and made friends with them. The new boy's name was Brett Hobbs, and his father was Colin Hobbs, former Fitzroy and Coburg and Northcote player and, at that time, coach of Northcote.

During each game I stood not far from the coach's box, but I never presumed on my nodding acquaintance with Colin Hobbs. I heard every groan and curse that came from his box. I heard many of the instructions that he sent by runner out to the field. I heard the pleas for justice that he shouted to the umpires. But I tried to keep out of sight of the coach. I was afraid that if he had to greet me he might lose the thread of some match-winning thought that was just then forming in his mind.

While I stood near the coach's box, my sons roamed the outer ground, covering as much territory as ruck-rovers. Often they ran behind the goalposts and offered themselves as markers for Northcote players shooting deliberately for goal. If an opposition player was shooting, my sons tried to distract him with screams and antics.

Whenever the ball bounced over the fence in the deserted outer, my sons ran to retrieve it. If the opposition was in attack and had broken away from Northcote, my sons would always pretend to stumble and would miskick the ball to the impatient boundary umpire, thereby giving Northcote the chance to pick up their men. But if Northcote was attacking, the boys moved swiftly and surely.

In the quiet of the outer, the lone human voice carried far. The more voluble of my sons spoke warmly to individual players of the opposition, telling them their shortcomings as players and as human beings. My son's voice would carry across the ground, and although I never saw any player respond, some trainers would tell the smart-arse to shut his mouth.

As football followers do, we developed varying degrees of hatred towards the opposing teams. By common consent, my sons and I hated more than any other club the men in purple and gold from Oakleigh. With my sons the hatred was a healthy natural impulse—they hated

Oakleigh because Oakleigh was more successful than Northcote. Although Oakleigh rarely won a premiership, they were nearly always in the final while Northcote mostly struggled just outside the four.

In my case, the hatred for Oakleigh was something nasty and perverse from the locked cupboards of my psyche. In hating the purple and gold, I was taking revenge on a world that had disappointed me. Or was I a little boy crying for his lost lollies? But these matters are too deep for a book about healthy outdoor exercise... The simple fact is, I hated Oakleigh even more fiercely than my sons and most other Northcote supporters hated the purple and gold.

We followed Northcote through thick and thin for seven years. The club had its ups and downs, but the trend was upwards, so much so that in 1982 Northcote was generally agreed to be a contender for the flag. Even my sons and I, in our cautious discussions, agreed on this. For most of the season, Northcote was in second place on the ladder. On top was the only side that was able to beat us twice in the home-and-away games. Yes, that side was Oakleigh. Twice they beat us—the first time was a thrashing; the second time was the occasion of the only accurate prophecy I ever made as a VFA supporter. Northcote had fought back strongly in the last quarter. When the siren sounded and the unspeakable Oakleigh mob had raised their victory howl, I whispered to my sons, 'When we meet these Violet Crumble bastards in the finals, we'll eat them.'

During the weeks of the finals I was either trembling with dread or dazed with bliss. Even now, I remember only brief passages of play or odd moments while my sons and I watched and waited.

We had been sure that the green and gold would have to clash twice with the purple and gold. In the event we met only once—in the second semi-final. We met on a warm spring afternoon at Toorak Park, which was neutral territory. Most of the Oakleigh supporters skulked by the pepper trees at the northern goal; most of the Northcote supporters stood on the green bank of the outer. Until half-way through the last quarter the game was in the balance. In the warm sunshine I lapsed into a trance-like state. I had dreamed all year of this meeting... no,

I had dreamed of it since 1946. Perhaps I was still on the lounge-room mat in Bendigo, shuffling my cards—purple and gold, green and gold. But then, like an alarm clock on the far side of a dream, the final siren sounded, and Northcote had won.

The taste of that win was sweet, but we still worried about the Grand Final two weeks later. We expected to meet Oakleigh a second time, but Caulfield, the forgotten third team of the last three contenders, did to Oakleigh in the preliminary final what we had done to Oakleigh in the second semi.

The Grand Final was desperately close, but even at the worst moments I felt a dreamlike confidence that all would be well at last. Northcote defeated Caulfield narrowly, and if I were an ordinary football follower I would end this piece by describing my feelings as my son and I ran onto the ground with hundreds of other Northcote followers to press around Colin Hobbs and his team. But, as I explained at the beginning of this piece, I am not an ordinary football follower.

Of all that happened during 1982 I remember most fondly the end of the second semi-final, when Northcote defeated Oakleigh. I remember my two sons running ahead of me through the crowd just after the final siren. My sons wanted to reach the players' gates before the two teams left the ground.

The two boys were wearing their green and gold jumpers. When they ran through the Oakleigh crowd, they looked like two green and yellow parrots flitting through a forest of Hoadleys' wrappers. But I had begun to fear for the boys' safety—the mood of the Oakleigh supporters was terrible to behold.

I had thought my boys were going to cheer the green and gold from the field, but no... when the siren had sounded, the boys stood ready to taunt the defeated side. Even at that moment, my sons' love of Northcote was not as strong as their hatred of Oakleigh.

I saw the danger. My sons were out of their young minds. They would be king-hit by the nearest Oakleigh supporters and then torn to pieces by the purple and gold rabble.

At that moment Colin Hobbs strode through the players' gate. He saw at once that my boys were about to commit ritual suicide. He swept them in front of him into the Northcote rooms: into the sanctuary of the green and the gold. I stayed outside in the crowd, but I was safe. I wore no green or gold.

I stood there trying to keep my face neutral. I stood, as it happened, in the narrow space between two streams of players leaving the ground. I stood while the green and gold and the purple and gold flowed around me and then to their appointed ends. I stood in the land of dreams come true.

DAVID WILLIAMSON

The Club

David Williamson AO is one of Australia's most successful stage and screen writers. Born in Melbourne in 1942, he studied engineering but rose to prominence as a playwright in the early 1970s with such plays as *Don's Party* and *The Removalists*. Other major works include *The Club, The Department, Travelling North, The Perfectionist, Emerald City, Money and Friends, Brilliant Lies, Dead White Males*, and *Up for Grabs* (which starred Madonna in its London premiere). Williamson's film work has yielded four AFI Awards for Best Screenplay—*Don's Party* (1977), *Gallipoli* (1981), *Travelling North* (1987) and *Balibo* (2009). Other screen credits include *The Year of Living Dangerously* and *Phar Lap*. He divides his football allegiance between Collingwood and Sydney. 'The Club' is an excerpt from David Williamson's play of the same name.

First performed in 1977, *The Club* was described by its director as 'a dissertation on politics' and by Lou Richards as 'a cutting play about the real business of the modern Aussie Rules back-room boys—dirty business'. The action takes place in the committee room of a top professional football club. There are six characters, all of whom are featured or referred to in the following selection. They are: Gerry, a new-breed career administrator; Ted, the club's president; Jock, a conniving ex-president; Laurie, the coach; Danny, the long-serving team captain; and Geoff, an imported star.

[There is a knock at the left door]

JOCK: That's probably Geoff. How do you want to handle this, Laurie? I'll have a chat to him first if you like.

LAURIE: I'll talk to him, if you don't mind.

JOCK: Suit yourself. I just thought that a fresh viewpoint might help break the deadlock. I was a coach for fifteen years myself, and I have had the odd bit of experience with troublesome recruits.

LAURIE: [tersely] Clear out and let me talk to him.

JOCK: Suit yourself.

[JOCK goes to the left door and brings in GEOFF HAYWARD, who is medium to tall and looks and moves like an athlete in top condition]

JOCK: Come in, Geoff. Sorry to interrupt your meal. Gerry and I are just going next door to have a drink so that you can have a little chat with Laurie. Feel free to call me if you need me, Laurie. Sometimes a fresh viewpoint can break a deadlock.

LAURIE: Thank you, Jock.

[JOCK and GERRY leave through the right door]

LAURIE: You've read the morning papers, I suppose?

GEOFF: Yep.

LAURIE: The committee are meeting in just over an hour to decide whether they're going to accept my resignation. I think they're going to ask me to reconsider it, but it's hardly worth my while if you're going to keep defying me.

GEOFF: So what are we supposed to do? Kiss and make up?

LAURIE: I don't want you to defy me in front of the players again.

GEOFF: I don't want to be told to do push-ups again.

LAURIE: If you break discipline you do push-ups. Everyone does.

GEOFF: I don't.

LAURIE: Nobody else objects to push-ups.

GEOFF: That's because most of them have got ear to ear bone.

LAURIE: I see. You've done a few subjects at university so you're out of our class.

GEOFF: If you like doing push-ups, I must be.

LAURIE: All right. Point taken. You don't like push-ups, but it goes deeper than that, doesn't it? Why are you playing so badly?

GEOFF: I'm doing my best.

LAURIE: No you're not. You played two good games at the start of the year, you went to pieces in your third game, and you've got progressively worse ever since.

GEOFF: I've lost form.

LAURIE: It's more than that. You're not even trying. Is it just that you object to me personally or is there some other reason?

GEOFF: I've lost form. That's all.

LAURIE: Look, I know there's some degree of antagonism from the other players—you came to the club with a big reputation and a lot of money, so there's bound to be, but it's not going to help matters if you lay down and stop trying.

GEOFF: You're reading too much into it. I've lost form.

LAURIE: It's more than that. Last week you stood down on the forward line staring into the crowd for over a minute. The ball came, and you let it go right past you. Look, level with me, Geoff. That's more than being out of form. What's going on?

GEOFF: All right. If you really want to know, what's going on is that I'm sick to death of football, and I couldn't care less if I never played another game in my life. It's all a lot of macho-competitive bullshit. You chase a lump of pigskin around a muddy ground as if your bloody life depended on it and, when you get it, you kick it to buggery and go chasing it again. Football shits me.

LAURIE: I wish you'd let us know your attitude to the game before we paid 90,000 dollars for you.

GEOFF: If you think you can buy me like a lump of meat, then you'd better think again.

LAURIE: You took our money with your eyes open, Geoff. Don't you think you owe us something?

GEOFF: If you're stupid enough to offer me that sort of money, I'll take it, but all you've bought is my presence out on an oval for two hours every Saturday afternoon.

LAURIE: We thought we were buying a lot more than that.

GEOFF: Took your money? It was practically thrown at me. You weren't there at that final sign-up session?

[GEOFF shakes his head ruefully]

GEOFF: It was a joke. There were three of my guys on one side of
          the table and Gerry, Jock and Ted on the other. Jock was
          looking at me, and I'm not joking, as if I was a giant pork
          chop. He was almost salivating. I felt sure that any moment
          he'd bring out a little hammer and test whether my reflexes
          are as good as they're cracked up to be. I couldn't believe
          that those three goons were for real. By the time we'd got
          ourselves through the pleasantries, I was getting pretty
          crapped off, and I decided to make myself a bit difficult,
          so when they shoved the form in front of me to sign, I read
          it through four times, put down the pen, shook my head
          and said I wanted more money. I didn't really expect to get
          any more—I just wanted to establish myself as something
          more than a tailor's dummy—but it was marvellous. All hell
          broke loose. Your guys called my guys cheats, Jock thumped
          our president on the snout, and Gerry sat there stirring his
          coffee with a retractable biro. I was just about to burst out
          laughing when I looked across and there was Ted Parker
          sitting in the middle of all this pandemonium, his face as
          white as a sheet, scribbling frantically in his cheque book.
          'Ten thousand', he yelled. 'I'll go an extra ten thousand,
          but that's my limit.' Everyone had a ball.

LAURIE: Are you still living with that girl?

GEOFF: Susy? Yes. Why? Do you think she's a corrupting influence?

LAURIE: She didn't seem very interested in your football career when
          I met her.

GEOFF: She's not.

LAURIE: She thinks it's macho-competitive bullshit too?

GEOFF: You can't exactly blame her, when it gets to the point where
          we start coming to blows behind the lockers.

LAURIE: How's your jaw?

GEOFF: Still sore. How's your gut?

LAURIE: Likewise.

GEOFF: Push-ups are one thing but slugging me into submission just
            isn't on.

LAURIE: I know. I'm sorry. I love football, and I love this club, and
            it's a bit hard for me to understand someone who holds both
            of them in contempt.

GEOFF: Love the club? Jock, Ted and Gerry?

LAURIE: The club's not Jock, Ted and Gerry. It's nearly a hundred
            years of history.

GEOFF: Yeah. Well I missed the history and copped Jock, Ted and
            Gerry. Honestly, what's an old fool like Jock doing in a
            position of power?

LAURIE: He was a great player, and whether he deserved to or not
            he won four premierships when he was our coach.

GEOFF: Didn't he deserve to win them?

LAURIE: We're not here to talk about Jock.

GEOFF: Was he a bad coach?

LAURIE: Yes.

GEOFF: How come he got those premierships then?

LAURIE: [irritated] He got them in his first six years, in the days
            when the best talent in the country was fighting to get a
            purple and gold guernsey. By the time I took over, all of that
            had long finished.

GEOFF: Someone told me that you were responsible for getting him
            the sack.

LAURIE: I thought he was coaching disgracefully, and I did some
            lobbying. I'll admit that to anyone. He dosed himself
            up with whisky before the '67 Grand Final and half-way
            through the last quarter he took Benny McPhee out
            of the centre where he was really firing and put him at
            full forward, where he was never sighted. It cost us the
            premiership. Why are you so interested in Jock?

GEOFF: I'm not. It just amuses me to see you guys sticking around
            in this club for years, having your little power battles,
            cutting each other's throats and filling up your lives with

petty nonsense. So Jock was a bad coach, and you lost a premiership. What does it matter? It's not important.

LAURIE: I might be old fashioned, but it seems important to me to step in and do something when a great club's going downhill because of incompetent coaching.

GEOFF: I don't want to play the devil's advocate, but you've done some pretty bad coaching yourself lately.

LAURIE: Such as?

GEOFF: Such as not shifting Danny off Wilson last week. He was getting thrashed.

LAURIE: I know.

GEOFF: Wilson was leaving him for dead.

LAURIE: *[irritably]* I know.

GEOFF: Then why didn't you shift him?

LAURIE: Because he was desperate to keep trying. He's never been that badly beaten before. I know it was the wrong thing to do, but Danny's been the backbone of my team for eight years, and I felt I owed him something. Besides, I doubt whether there's anyone in the team who could've done any better.

GEOFF: I could beat Wilson.

LAURIE: You? You were down the other end of the ground staring into the crowd!

GEOFF: I could beat him .

LAURIE: *[angrily]* I'm getting pretty bloody fed up with your arrogance, Geoff. You've been paid a fortune, and you won't even try; and when I try and talk to you about it, you give me a lecture about how petty my life is, and to cap it all off you nonchalantly tell me you could beat Wilson when in the last five weeks you've hardly got a kick. I was watching you carefully last week, and you couldn't even outrun Butcher Malone.

GEOFF: I was stoned.

LAURIE: Drunk?

GEOFF: Stoned.

LAURIE:	Marijuana?
GEOFF:	Hash.
LAURIE:	Why?
GEOFF:	Because it feels fantastic. Five minutes after you smoke it, your head lifts right off your shoulders. I wasn't looking out into the crowd, incidentally, I was watching a seagull. Not just an ordinary seagull. It was the prince of seagulls, dazzling me with blasts of pure white every time its wings caught the sun. The roar of the crowd paid homage to its grace and beauty. You ought to try some, Laurie. It alters your whole perspective on things.
LAURIE:	Are you stoned now?
GEOFF:	*[nods]* I had a smoke before I came.
LAURIE:	Are you addicted?
GEOFF:	You don't get addicted to hash, Laurie. Hey, did you see me fly for the ball in the second quarter? I was so far up over the pack I felt likes Achilles chasing the golden orb.
LAURIE:	Jesus, Geoff. How am I supposed to deal with this?
GEOFF:	Just don't ask me to do push-ups.

[JOCK pokes his head through the right door. He is smiling affably]

JOCK:	Sorted things out yet?
GEOFF:	Not quite.
JOCK:	Would you like me to have a talk to the lad, Laurie? Sometimes a fresh viewpoint can help in these sort of situations.
LAURIE:	*[irritated]* No.
JOCK:	Just give me a few minutes, Laurie. I've got something I want to say to him.

[LAURIE gets up, looking at JOCK in an irritated way, and leaves through the left door]

JOCK:	He's got it in for you, I'm afraid, Geoff. Not to worry. We'll sort it out. You did some nice things last week. Not one

of your best games but you did some nice things. Glorious mark you took in the second quarter. You just seemed to go up and up.

GEOFF: I felt like Achilles.

JOCK: Who's he?

GEOFF: A Greek guy who could really jump.

JOCK: *[nods]* Some of our new Australians could be champions if they'd stop playing soccer and assimilate. Why did Butcher Malone take a swing at you when you hit the deck? Did you give him an elbow in the gut?

GEOFF: No, I blew him a kiss.

JOCK: That's good. That's subtle. I was a bit more direct in my day, although I did have a little trick that used to throw 'em out of their stride, come to think of it. You know those times when you're half a yard behind your man, and he's going for the ball, and there doesn't seem any way you can stop him?

[GEOFF nods]

JOCK: Well, the thing in your favour is that everyone, including the umpire, is looking at the ball, right?

GEOFF: Right.

JOCK: Right. Well as soon as your man leaves the ground, get your thumb and ram it up his arse. Works every time.

GEOFF: Sounds effective.

JOCK: It's a beauty. Wait here while I have a piss.

[As JOCK moves to the door he notices that GEOFF has taken out a pouch of tobacco. He stops]

JOCK: Roll your own?

GEOFF: Mmm.

JOCK: I used to roll my own.

GEOFF: Would you like me to roll you one?

JOCK: Yeah. Thanks. I'll be back in a minute, and we'll have a nice quiet smoke and a little chat.

[GEOFF nods his head as JOCK goes out the door. He fishes in his back pocket and takes out a tin. He looks at the door through which JOCK has gone, looks at the tins, nods his head and smiles. Black out and house lights up]

ROSS FITZGERALD

Never Forget Where You've Come From

Ross Fitzgerald was born in Melbourne on Christmas Day, 1944. Emeritus Professor in History and Politics at Griffith University, he is well known as a historian, biographer and social and political commentator. He is the author of five satirical novels and has worked as script editor, historical adviser and co-producer of documentary television and film, including ABC TV's *Red Ted and the Great Depression* (1995) and *The Legend of Fred Paterson* (1996). Recent books include his memoir *My Name is Ross: An Alcoholic's Journey* and two co-authored biographies, *Alan ('The Red Fox') Reid*, which was short-listed for the 2011 National Biography Award, and *Austen Tayshus: Merchant of Menace*. Fitzgerald writes for *The Weekend Australian, The Canberra Times* and *The Sydney Morning Herald* and regularly appears on radio and television. Ross Fitzgerald and his wife, artist Lyndal Moor, live in Redfern, Sydney. This is a revised and updated version of the essay that first appeared in *The Greatest Game* by Ross Fitzgerald and Ken Spillman (eds., 1988).

My father, Bill, was not a liar, so it must have been me. I always thought Dad played football for Collingwood Firsts, but actually he only played for the Reserves. He was a better cricketer. I must have blown him up in my mind to be a hero. As Peter Carey and Manning Clark said, all Australian history is based on lie and legend. That applies to personal as much as national history. Each of us creates his own mythologies.

Cricket and football brought Dad and I together. In my child's mind, he was famous. I can still see a caricature of him from the newspapers when he captained Sandringham in the Victorian Football Association, all knee bandages and broken-boned, which we kept pinned up on the toilet door for years. Placing it there—whose choice was it, I wonder?—strikes me now as most unfair.

In my mind and memory he had played cricket with Ponsford and Ryder and Billy Woodfull, my old headmaster at Melbourne High. He captained Jack Iverson when he played for Brighton. As a wicket-keeper Dad stood right up to the stumps. He played until he was quite old; as a young boy I used to come to watch him, proud as punch. Once, when I was only eleven, the Sandringham VJCA side he was playing for was one short, and Dad got me a game. He said it was the only time he ever cheated. The outgoing batsman was caught, and Dad said that they had 'crossed' (which they hadn't) so that he faced the bowling and shielded me from the fasties until I got my eye in. Dad and I put on a fifty partnership, and I got twelve not out. He was ever so proud of me, and I of him. It was a marvellous day.

When Mum first knew him—about three years before they married—Dad was laid up with a bad cartilage that made kicking difficult; but he was lucky to be able to kick with his left foot—although not as successfully as before. (When I was about eight years old, he showed me how he placed two pennies inside his elastic knee bands, to provide extra support.) After playing footy with Collingwood, he played for St Kilda Reserves, then Sandringham. Before World War II, in 1939, he had started coaching Old Brighton Grammarians and after the war he coached a Caulfield team. That was the last time he was actively involved with footy until he again coached Old Brighton Grammarians—when I was ten. After the war, Bruce Andrew, who was talent scout for Collingwood, wanted 'Long Tom' (he was tall for a player in those years) or 'Old Fitzy' to join him. As that meant he would be traveling all over Australia and away a lot, he turned the offer down, even though Mum said it was all right by her.

When I was about two-and-a-half years old, Dad started taking me to see Collingwood play (Mum played tennis). I was decked out in a

Collingwood beanie and scarf. Mum hated the endless discussions of the games. She was sad when I gave up tennis in favour of cricket and football. Poppa, my Mum's Dad—a wonderful white-haired man who told me I was like Uncle Jim, a born liar whom I'd never met—was a one-eyed footy follower of Northcote in the Association, who occasionally went to see Collingwood. But he always said Dad should have put more into cricket, as he considered him the best wicket-keeper he had ever seen.

Although he only learned one song at Clifton Hill Christian Brothers College, Dad—a lapsed Catholic—often sang me to sleep by intoning 'My Old Shackoe' over and over again. Best of all, on the radio we could listen to Collingwood play and to the Test cricket. (We didn't get television, until I was much older.) It was from hearing the footy and cricket commentators with my father that I first began to be aware of the wonder and magic of words, and the intricacies and tricks of language. 'Eat 'em alive!' Jack Dyer or 'Captain Blood' would scream. 'They say you're a star, son. You won't be shining today.' Alan McGilvray and Johnny Moyes could make a dull and boring cricket match sound like a breathless Resurrection. There was always so much going on—googlies and bumpers and new balls and no balls and little boys with dogs darting onto the field. And so much to remember. 'Do you remember Johnny... was it the Second Test at Lords in 1930 (I always thought Lords and Lourdes was the same place and at least equally miraculous) when Bradman scored 254... and a black cocker spaniel...?' Johnny always remembered.

My biggest treat was to sit up all night, with Dad and Les Shorthouse from down the road, and listen to the cricket from England. I would go to bed early in the afternoon, and get up at eight when the broadcast started. Dad always bought me my own ABC scorebook with details and pictures of the players. We would sit up all night glued to the radio set, he roasting chestnuts while I kept the score. And when it came to Lunch and Tea, we would have corned beef and pickle sandwiches that Mum had cut, and drink milk coffee out of a thermos. Then Dad and Mr Shorthouse would tell stories about other Tests in other years. I loved that.

Every Christmas Day, my birthday, Dad would recount how, in the 1938 Grand Final, Carlton's Bob Chitty, our garbo who lived nearby in East Brighton, bit the balls of Collingwood's star full forward Ron Todd as he flew to take a mark. It was, Dad said, called 'squirrel munching'. Apocryphal or not, the story was the highlight of my day.

The great Harry Collier (brother of Leeta), Alby Pannam, Keith Stackpole senior and Bruce Andrew all remember that my Dad played first ruckman for the Collingwood Football Club Districts (in other words, the Reserves) in the 1930s. He captained the Reserves for two years from 1934 to 1935. Pannam, Stackpole and Andrew all played with him, and that was in the early to mid-1930s.

Bill was also wicket-keeper for Collingwood's Second XI—John Wren's team. Appropriately, Wren, who, despite his multitudinous flaws, loved the Mighty Woodsmen, died on 26 October 1953 aged eighty-two, a month after suffering a heart attack while watching Collingwood win its first VFL premiership in seventeen years. As it happens, our greatest coach, Jock McHale, who was also at the game, died on 4 October 1953, aged seventy-one.

Although Bill played all his games at Collingwood with the seconds, according to Harry Collier he was 'bloody unlucky not to get a game'. He was always knocking at the door for selection but, as an up and coming player, had the misfortune to be at Collingwood when they were at their peak. Collingwood appeared in six consecutive Grand Finals from 1925 to 1930, winning the famous four in a row (1927 to 1930). Collingwood only missed the finals three times from 1919 to 1939. In those great decades, we won seven flags and came second seven times. That's how good the Mighty Magpies were in those heady days.

Dad's 'crook knees', which were almost constantly bandaged, militated against him. All in all, he appears to have played for the seconds for seven years between 1929 and 1935 before he went to Sandringham. In the 1935 Grand Final, when Dad was skipper, we were beaten by two points: Stacky missed a sitter the last kick of the day. Dad, who played when Leeta and Harry Collier were lifted to the seniors, was paid about four or five pounds sterling a game. Good money in those days, and lots of perks as well. In the words of the late Harry Collier, "Good Old Fitzy' or 'Long Tom' was very popular and well respected around the club and as a former teammate everyone remembered Bill and those knee bands'."

Apart from Norman Vincent Peale's *The Power of Positive Thinking*, which lay on his mantelpiece, as far as I know Dad never read a book—but he did devour comics and *The Sporting Globe*. Fit, slim and uncomplaining, he was rather inarticulate and didn't speak much. His own father having been an alcoholic, Dad neither drank nor smoked. When I went to Monash University I tried to be his opposite, repudiated all he offered me.

As a footballer I wasn't much good. At Gardenvale Central School and at Melbourne High I didn't make the first eighteen, always played for the seconds. Even teamed up against our portly, heavy-drinking, history master and famous footy coach, Ben Munday, whose motto—'Bullshit Baffles Brains'—still seems as true now as it did then.

At Monash, although I did well at cricket, at football I again played for the seconds. I did manage once to kick three goals in a quarter: one from an impossible angle, one from the centre of the ground when a gust of wind seemed to blow the ball interminably, and the other I dribbled through. I never kicked any more for the match. Thus three is the most I have ever been able to score. As a footballer, however, fuelled by rum and amphetamines, I was a 'most courageous player'. Ninety kilos and fearless I rucked for four quarters and would have run through an army tank.

In 1977, I moved to Brisbane. Under the remarkable coaching of tea-drinking Tom Hafey, Collingwood had come from wooden spooners in 1976 to playing in the Grand Final. How I would have loved to have been there (standing room was only two dollars). For only the second time in VFL history, the premiership battle resulted in a draw. I can still see 'Twiggy' Dunne at the thirty-two minute mark of the final quarter standing like an oak in a pack of seven and taking a mark Walter Mitty would have envied. From thirty-five metres out, Dunne converted by booting a torpedo punt and levelling the score 10.16 (76) against North Melbourne's 9.22 (76). North's Arnold Briedis had kicked an incredible 0.7. As this was the first Grand Final telecast, Channel Seven had a huge bonus with the replay.

Immediately after the second Grand Final, on 1 October 1977, when Collingwood lost by twenty-seven points, I sat speechless in front of the TV, half-believing there would be an announcement saying, 'There's been a dreadful mistake.' It was soon after that terrible defeat, or perhaps in 1980 when his old club Richmond pulverised Collingwood by the biggest Grand Final margin in history, that a television interviewer asked Hafey, 'What do you find funny about football, Tommy?' Tommy answered, 'I don't find anything funny about football.' I understand exactly what he meant. Such defeats gut me, utterly.

In 1987, my beloved team hit an all-time low. On Saturday 20 June, playing against North Melbourne, our firsts, reserves and under-19s managed just four goals between them in virtually six hours of football. Our seniors scored 2.6—both goals coming in the second quarter courtesy of our steel-eyed full forward, Brian Taylor, who had just returned from suspension.

After such an abysmal performance, I felt hopeless beyond belief. I even blamed myself, as if the sins of my youth meant inescapable retribution. But then I thought of Dad. 'Never forget where you've come from,' he would say, and 'You can kick goals when you see them.'

That year, I wrote a poem in his honour:

> *It is not shame this night, my father.*
> *We have passed beyond all that.*
> *I hold you, brave Magpie*
> *comforting the wild horses of my asthma nights.*
> *Proud, clumsy, gentle man—*
> *The dark won't hurt me now.*
> *No need to turn on the lights*
> *or bring Snowy near.*
> *Yet where do the fish sleep, daddy?*
>
> *I'm in the team, my follower.*
> *O to see you soar in the ruck for Collingwood,*
> *both knees bandaged, no teeth at all.*

'Where I come from, professor,
we like to see things in black and white.'
I've seen you cry, old warrior—
Of my brother Roddy's death.
The brightest star in all the skies,
Yet what does his gravestone say?

The dignity of your despair, my father.
How your silence thundered.
No tears are needed now.
Still I ask, was it all meant?
So much shame and hate and dark denying.

I'm beginning to define my needs from my wants.
The hours before midnight are the best.
I am my own man now, old friend—
I haven't forgotten where I came from.
Do the fish sleep still, my father,
In such seas that ask neither condition nor recompense?

Love's best sleep is sweet.
Be blessed then
and range well, big Woodsman.
There are many fields in which to reap.

As Dad taught me by example, Aussie Rules is a metaphor for life. In football things soon change. Hence, a mere three years after our all-time low, in 1990, we won our 14th VFL/AFL premiership—slaughtering Essendon by 48 points. Watching the game on TV was among the best 120 minutes of my life. Then in 2010 the first Collingwood-St Kilda Grand Final, played before a crowd of 100,016 spectators, was another draw. The wayward Magpies kicked 9.14 (68) to the Saints' 10.6 (68). Before the replayed Grand Final, held at the MCG on 2 October 2010, Collingwood President Eddie McGuire quipped that he had seen more drawn Collingwood Grand Finals (1977 and 2010) than he had seen premierships! Fortunately, the next Saturday we Magpie supporters shed tears of joy, when, in the replay, Collingwood trounced St Kilda by 56 points, thereby winning our 15th premiership, our first since 1990.

How true, I wonder, is our interpretation of our parents, and of our personal, tribal past? But without such questions and creations, where would be be? Six foot under—and as my dad (a positive thinker) used to say, 'Every day above ground's a good one.'

LEON SLADE

~~~~~~~~~

The Magpie

Leon Slade was born in 1931 and educated at Northcote High School, Victoria. He emerged as a significant Australian poet in the 1970s after the publication of *Wilderness* (Jacaranda Press, 1970) and *Anatomy of the Horse* (University of Queensland Press, 1972). The *Oxford Companion to Australian Literature* (1994) says of his poetry: 'Often humorous or satirical, Slade uses colloquial diction and imagery to express his urban, contemporary themes.' Slade's poem 'The Magpie' was first published in his collection *Bloodstock Breeding* (1979).

'loyally crying Car'n...Car'n...
(if feebly) unto the very end'
—Bruce Dawe

Gentleness is the commonplace
of poets: less so with me. Whole newspapers,
ripped-off sheets, cuttings clipped out are finally shredded
and burnt. Black & white is the colour of literature.
The dilemma is whether to dress up inside out
or dress down outside in, still, in either case,
undertaking to understand by understatement.
What hat am I wearing today? Akubra
no longer makes the headlines;
yet I switch my cover every day.
Saturday I wear my black & white bonnet.
Burning matches, winter afternoons,
dangle us by quarters as matinee serials
did in dodo days; hand in glove

in hand in glove, hostile to everything or one
that isn't black & white like a magpie
nesting or westerners characterised
at once by the colours of their hats.
What friends have in common
is more significant than their differences.

Black & white is the colour of friendship.
Lunch on a brace of editors,
lectures delivered to young mothers with butterflies,
dinner, Easter eve, with the directorate
and their corporate wives. Big B Liberals
was quite a good one but not stretched
through pâté, roast beef and dessert. Is this
a course record? A feast suffices. I bore
my company to tears, to silence and to death.
Black & white is the colour of premiership.
Candidnotly Collingwouldn't. Beyond age, love,
little's left (get the drift): an ending that's unfit,
boobs at least as great as mine,
a worm's eye view of the bleachers. He knows
the blondes that are brunette. Private parts
are more embarrassing than pubic. Black and white
are the colours of beautiful people. The hip's
a centrefold. What sort of a blunder did
the makers of Black and White cigarettes make?
The secret is acceptance.

EMMA QUAYLE

Draft Destinies

Emma Quayle grew up in Riddells Creek and spent most weekends at Windy Hill, reading books in the stands until the game won her over. She has covered football for *The Age* newspaper in Melbourne since 2001, enjoying more than anything the opportunity to help people tell their stories. Emma is a two-time winner of the AFL Players Association's annual award for journalism, and the AFL Media Association's feature writing award in 2010. 'Draft Destinies' is an edited extract from *The Draft*, her first book, first published in 2008 and reprinted by Penguin Books in 2013. She also wrote *Nine Lives* (2010) the story of former Essendon wingman Adam Ramanauskas' battle with cancer.

Wodonga, 30 July 2001

Trent Cotchin was tiny. He had big, baggy shorts and a buzz cut, and socks scrunched down to his ankles. He clapped his hands together twice, then placed them on his knees, looking up over his shoulder as the umpire bounced the ball.

Victoria was playing the Northern Territory, and Trent had a big job to do. It was the Under-12 schoolboy championships and he had been asked to play on the captain of the Territory team. His name was Cyril Rioli but people called him Junior Boy. Junior, for short. In a television report, he'd been called the best 12-year-old footballer in the country.

Junior was taller than Trent, and quicker. He thumped the ball forward five times in the first few minutes, dancing around the Wodonga oval on his nimble, bouncy feet. He played like he had not one care in the world, swinging his long, floppy arms and paying no attention to anything but the ball. Trent chased, blocked, tackled and stuck as close as he could, but stumbled, and at the quarter-time huddle was berated by his coach

194

for falling down and letting his opponent slip away.

Then things got better. In the first few seconds of the second quarter, Trent gathered the ball on the wing, glanced briefly to his right, took a bounce and kicked the ball deep into the forward line. Later, he was slung while hovering over a loose ball, and scored a goal from the free kick.

Victoria won by fifty-five points and Trent was named best player. But on their way back to the local caravan park, his mother remembered the reprimand, and wondered if he was thinking about it too.

'Are you okay?' Kath Cotchin asked Trent. He looked back at her and nodded. Of course he was.

'It was a team rule to keep your feet,' he told her, 'and I didn't. I deserved to be told off.'

The answer surprised his mum, and made her feel much better. Oh well, she shrugged, looking this time across at her husband. If Trent could handle it, it shouldn't bother them.

<hr>

Darwin, 24 November 2007

Cyril Sebastian Rioli the Third is in the middle of the St Mary's club rooms, surrounded by his family. The plan was to hook someone's laptop computer up to the new big screen and follow the draft on the internet, but no-one can get it to work.

The Saints are Junior's football team, not that he ever had much say in it. Most of his uncles and cousins have played there, and a few of them still do. His father, Cyril Junior, played 263 games and would have played more had he not broken his leg four years ago, and been told it was time to retire. He was in his late thirties, after all. One of Junior's uncles, Maurice Rioli, started at St Mary's in the 1970s, coming to Richmond in 1982 after a star-turn at South Fremantle which included consecutive Simpson Medals for best-on-ground performances in Western Australian grand finals. Another uncle, Michael Long, whipped down the wings for St Mary's before heading to Essendon to do that and much more. Remarkably, both these famous uncles won Norm Smith Medals.

Now it is Junior's time, a time many people have been waiting for. With Rioli and Long, he's the little prince of Territory football. He could kick goals from the pocket when he was five and hadn't yet turned two when legendary St Mary's coach, John Taylor, saw him waddling around in his tiny green and gold guernsey, and asked his mother if she realised just how good he'd be.

Today—finally—he is old enough to be drafted. In a few more minutes he'll have a new club.

Junior woke up feeling nervous this morning, which surprised him; he'd been so calm all week. He got up, went into the bathroom and started to cry—and he *never* cries. His grandfather came in from Melville Island last night, and maybe that's what made things bubble over. It all felt like too much; there were so many goodbyes to say.

The computer problems might have unsettled him even more, but instead they've eased his mind. Junior would love Essendon to pick him but the Bombers haven't made any promises, or said anything different to the twelve other teams who interviewed him. He's been wondering whether Adelaide will draft him, and would rather play for a Melbourne team. But if the Crows call his name, that's fine. He'll go, and be grateful for the chance. This is what he has been waiting for; this is what he was born for.

Right now, he just wants everyone else to calm down. 'We'll find out,' Junior says, as people fiddle with cords, wires and buttons. 'Someone will tell us what happens.'

◆＊✕＊◆

Melbourne, 24 November 2007

Trent Cotchin is full of nervous energy. His legs are shaking, he keeps tapping his toes on the floor and he can't stop smiling, or focus on anything for more than a few moments. This is what Trent was like when he was nine, and hadn't played footy all summer; it's what he was like last month, when his foot was stuck in plaster and he wasn't allowed to run around.

Trent is at the draft itself, in the front row of a Telstra Dome function room with his parents on one side, his girlfriend on the other and his sisters just behind. Every time someone important is introduced to her brother his little sister Tess slowly raises the small 'Cotchin Family' sign that showed them all where to sit. It's a cute, quiet reminder that Trent isn't the only one who's been waiting a long time for this day. The Cotchins are one of seven families invited along today by the AFL, a good sign they'll know his fate nice and early.

Even if Trent *could* focus, it would be hard to know where to look. There are player agents roaming the room with their mobile phones close, hoping to deliver more good news than bad to the boys they represent. A television crew is doing laps of the room and in almost every corner are AFL coaches, chatting casually to each other. The sixteen club tables are arranged in a large rectangle and the recruiting managers are at the top of them, pouring glasses of water and glancing over their notes. This is their big day too.

Trent had woken up early, just after six a.m. He couldn't manage much breakfast, and whenever someone spoke to him he seemed to snap straight back. He's not entirely sure why, because he hasn't been feeling nervous, and has a fair idea what will happen today. Everyone expects Carlton to choose Matthew Kreuzer, one of Trent's close friends, with the No. 1 pick. Richmond, which has next pick, hasn't said anything definite but last week Terry Wallace called his home, to find out how Trent's injury was and have a quick chat to his dad. As he called his father inside and handed over the phone, Trent wondered why the Richmond coach would call if he *wasn't* planning to pick him.

Still, nothing is official yet. None of it matters until they read his name out, and maybe that's why his legs won't stop shaking. 'I just want to know,' he keeps thinking. 'I just want to know.'

———◆◆◆◆◆———

Darwin, 24 November 2007

Junior didn't hear his name get called. The big screen didn't light up in time, but his phone started beeping and ringing, all at once, and he guessed something must have happened.

'Hawthorn!' announced his cousins, Randall and Shannon, calling from cousin Dean Rioli's place in Melbourne. 'They're joking...' Junior thought.

'Hawthorn!' said his manager, Dan Richardson, calling from Telstra Dome. 'Hmmm...' thought Junior. Maybe it really *was* Hawthorn.

After an hour, Junior saw his name on the screen which was finally fixed, and believed it for the first time. Pick 12. Hawthorn. Cyril Rioli. Standing up to thank his family once the draft was over, he got a bit tearful again. 'I started shaking,' he said. 'I can't really explain how I felt. I think I just felt like I know, finally. It was over.'

Junior's new colours meant an instant, new allegiance for those around him, which, in the first few minutes after the draft, struck his mother Kathy as strange, and a little sad. It was hard to comprehend until the moment it actually happened—out of nowhere he became a Hawthorn player. 'We've been with St Mary's forever and we love Essendon. We've never really had another club,' she said. 'We were all sort of like... well, it's not the Bombers, but that's okay. I think it will be good for Junior. He'll get to be himself.'

The next day, Junior would leave home again, no end-of-term holidays to look forward to this time. Kathy hoped he was ready for it. A few people from Hawthorn phoned during the day, checking up on his medical history and making sure he had a valid passport. The following Friday, the club was taking a group of young players to Papua New Guinea to trek the 96-kilometre Kokoda Trail. As in, *next* Friday. As in, eight days hiking along steamy jungle tracks, carrying sandbags and getting to know the group of strangers that had just become his teammates.

Kathy looked over at Junior, laughing with his cousins, so glad his long wait was over. She had been taken aback when he broke down during his speech because he'd seemed so settled all week. Later, he really did look relieved and it was only then that she realised he hadn't quite been himself in the few days before the draft. He looked happy, satisfied, and she wondered if he had any clue what he was in for. 'I don't think Junior's even *heard* of the Kokoda Trail.'

———◆◆◆———

Melbourne, 24 November 2007

Trent heard his name get called where he wanted it to be called, but the moment passed so quickly that he wasn't really conscious of how he felt when it happened. He forgot to remember, if that makes sense. Then he was swept away, thrown into a yellow-and-black shirt, and plonked in front of a camera. 'There wasn't any time to think,' he said. 'People were talking to you, taking you places and calling you over to them. Everything happened so quickly.'

Later that night at his party, a friend told him how relieved he had looked on TV and he realised that was exactly how he felt. It was like more thoughts had escaped his mind in that instant than entered it. All the 'what-ifs' vanished and he was left with the simple realisation that now he was a Richmond player. The party went until after midnight, but Trent had already slipped off to bed well before then. He wanted to think about what had happened, what was about to happen. How he was due at training first thing Monday morning; how he wanted to train really hard and get his foot right; how he might, maybe, get the vacant No. 9 jumper and how the club wanted him to live with Kane Johnson, the captain, until he was old enough to drive. How it was all going to get so much harder from here.

'I'm so happy,' he thought. He wanted to soak it up and sleep; the party could go on without him. 'It's all come to an end, and now it starts again.'

STUART MACINTYRE

It Won't Always Be Like This

Stuart Macintyre AO was educated in Melbourne, undertook doctoral studies at Cambridge and is a prolific historian with acclaimed publications on Australian and world history. Since 1990 he has been the Ernest Scott Professor of History at the University of Melbourne, where he is also a Laureate Professor. His football career was a little less distinguished. It began with Auburn South State School, plateaued when he represented Cambridge during the 1970s and finished in the 1980s when he played for *The Age*'s football team. 'It Won't Always Be Like This' was written especially for this collection.

Only one of my daughters took an interest in football. She began coming to Hawthorn's home games at Princes Park during the 1980s, initially as much for the soft drinks and treats my friends shouted her as for the game. But in the late summer of 1986 we went out to Glenferrie Oval for an early club practice match, the brown against the golds, and on our railway side of the ground Robert DiPierdomenico was trying out a prize recruit, John Platten. Until then she had been greatly taken with Dipper—she told him proudly at the family function before the game that we named our dog after him—but the springy-haired little jack-in-the box was irresistible to a ten-year-old girl.

Dipper's Brownlow and then the ten-goal victory over Carlton in the Grand Final that year sealed her enthusiasm, and I remember telling her, 'It won't always be like this'. She took no notice, and there was no need for her to do so for the next few years. By the time that era of playing late into September came to an end, she was in her late teens and had other interests, but she recalled my cautionary words when I went out to the Camberwell Civic Centre in 1996 to vote against the merger with Melbourne.

I drove there from my home in Brunswick, and decided to turn off at Power Street so I could pass along Linda Crescent and look once more at Glenferrie Oval. It is now a sylvan glade of eucalypts and grassy embankments, the red-brick grandstand a forlorn reminder of the crowds that used to cram into its tight confines. The black winter quagmire that brought the scorn of opposition supporters has gone. The asphalt embankment at the Glenferrie Road end—where I used to watch John Peck bullock his way to the ball and Phil Hay, his back to the play as he faced the opposing full forward—has been levelled. The wooden terraces along the railway wing, where I saw Des Dickson clean up Alan Aylett, has been dismantled. It is now forty years since the trains would slow to a crawl on a Saturday afternoon so the driver could follow the game.

I first started to go there as a young boy in the mid-1950s, often by myself as it was only a ten minute walk from home. My father was a Melbourne supporter and had been since he was admitted to the MCC—before then it was Carlton, but that was principally because his father followed South—and I was able to use his Lady's Ticket to see Melbourne's string of premierships from the Grey Smith stand. But there was never any doubt about loyalty to Hawthorn. My mother had grown up in the suburb, her brothers and sisters were all supporters, and my younger brothers and various cousins followed them.

My state school, Auburn South, had brown and gold stripes for the football team, thwarting Glenferrie State, which was stuck with the mustard pot jumpers. There were only two boys in my year who did not support the Hawks, one an hereditary Magpie and the other with a hand-knitted Carlton jumper. The question we asked was not 'who do you follow?' but whose number you wore. I had Speedy Peck's 23, my brother Sandy chose Alan Woodley's 24. We not only went to games on Saturdays, we went to training on Tuesdays or Thursdays. You could go into the changing-room before training, smell the liniment as the players were rubbed down, get autographs, even exchange a handball.

I was there at the right time. For a decade until 1952, Hawthorn won four wooden spoons and never finished higher than tenth. There was a sectarian schism in 1950, when the captain and coach Alec Albiston was dumped. But under Jack Hale, Hawthorn began to improve. John Kennedy and Roy Simmonds were joined by Graham Arthur, John Peck and Brendan Edwards. Jack O'Hagan provided the Hawks with a team song, and soon there was a bugler.

I went to the 1957 finals with my grandfather, who would die in the following year. Hawthorn had finished third and was playing in its first semi-final against Carlton. We were six goals up at half-time when a hailstorm covered the ground and Grandpa assured me we'd win. I marvelled at his acumen, though in retrospect I have a feeling he was keen to see Carlton go down; my father had his revenge in the preliminary final when Melbourne thrashed us.

After that we marked time but recruited well: John Winneke, Colin Youren, Morton Browne, Ian Mort, David Parkin, Ian Law. John Kennedy took over as coach in 1960, and soon the Hawks were tough. I was at Victoria Park that year when Pecky marked and put through a goal after the siren for our first win there.

Doctors' children have runny noses and historians have poor memories—I think we choose our vocation because we need to be trained to recall the past. I can still see Noel Voigt being carried off crying in pain after he broke a collar-bone in the final minutes of a game, and I know precisely where it was that I stood on the ground as the trainers supported him to the changing-room. Tears are memorable: a distressed young supporter of a team we beat in the last quarter, crying helplessly as he made his way towards the Glenferrie Road exit with his mother, left a lasting impression.

My recollection of the 1957 first semi-final is of Roy Simmonds turning back Carlton in the last quarter. In the glory year of 1961, when we finished top of the ladder, I saw John Winneke lay out Laurie Mithen in the second semi-final, or have I confused eyesight with subsequent accounts? I certainly saw Brendan Edwards gathering kicks at will in the Grand Final, and Ted Whitten trying to impose his will on a lost cause. I was up at the top of the Olympic stand, and the players were midgets.

By then I had entered my teens and become a squeamish adolescent. Did I really see the inebriated premiership team that night stumbling in crocodile file up in the members' stand at Glenferrie? I was there, with my brother Sandy, but then most of Hawthorn was. When I recorded this incident some years ago for a book of football memories, John Kennedy told the editors it hadn't happened—and I have no doubt who is the more reliable witness.

It won't always be like this. We all assumed that our first premiership would be followed by more of them, but Hawthorn won only five games in 1962. In 1963 we again finished top of the ladder but were outclassed in the Grand Final by Polly Farmer and Billy Goggin. After that we struggled, until Kanga returned from teaching in Stawell and a new generation of recruits joined—Peter Crimmins, Don Scott, Leigh Matthews, Peter Knights, Peter Hudson. By then I was an undergraduate, living in a residential college at Melbourne University, and my trips to Glenferrie were less frequent. But I went to the Grand Final with my youngest brother, stood on the seat to watch Huddo miss his hundred-and-fifty-first goal, saw Don Scott walking on his knees after the siren.

The following season began with the incomparable Huddo kicking eight against Melbourne in the first two quarters and then doing his knee when he marked for a ninth. Once again we suffered our premiership hangover and finished outside the four, but by then I'd gone to England to continue my studies. I spent a year in Western Australia in 1976, and listened to Hawthorn's premiership on the car radio while driving to Subiaco Oval for the WANFL Grand Final. After that it was back to Cambridge. There was no media coverage of Australian football in England, and the cost of a phone call was prohibitive. We relied on aerograms, flimsy blue sheets that you folded into a rectangle, and I had to ask my mother to smuggle a clipping of the VFL results into hers. I didn't hear of our success in the 1978 Grand Final for a week.

I returned to Melbourne in 1981, just as Allan Jeans took over and it seemed we might defy gravity. There were some wonderful footballers over that decade, and they kept coming. By then I was living in Brunswick and could walk to Princes Park for home games, gathering on the outer with a brother, a cousin, sometimes an uncle, and various university friends. I would meet Dinny O'Hearn at Percy Jones' Astor Hotel in Carlton to drive out to our away games, and he was always up for trouble. We met back in the pub after the 1989 Grand Final win over Geelong, our first back-to-back, on a Saturday that coincided with the annual punk pub-crawl. Percy insisted they would not be served, Dinny put money on the bar for all-comers, and the divvy van sent to sort out the argument collided with a tram outside the pub.

Football, for Dinny, was a form of standing sociability, a running conversation with those who stood alongside you accompanied by beer, pies and tobacco. He loathed the advance of reserved seating, and one Saturday when I was missing he had the group stand on seats in front of the new John Elliot stand to block the view of those in the corporate boxes behind them. But as the 1980s advanced, there were signs of decline. Dinny could no longer watch a Hawthorn player with a set shot on goal, and had to turn around until we told him the result. He came down with leukemia and died in 1993.

By then the glory days were over, the relatives, friends and colleagues dispersed. Our Dipper, the canine stray we so named because he needed all the encouragement he could get, passed away on election day 1996. I wanted to record that he was killed by capitalism, but my family overruled me. In his place we found a young Border Collie at the North Melbourne lost dogs' home, so fleet of foot that she became Tucky. But Tucky climbed the side fence onto the street, where she was hit by a car, and lost a leg.

Meanwhile I was branch stacking: two grandsons over in Vancouver, two more in Brunswick, all of them decked out in brown and gold. When the Canadian boys come over, I take them to Hawthorn games and, like me at their age, they are more excited by climbing to the top of the stand than by anything that occurs out on the ground. I rang them after our 2008 premiership and they were pleased. Tucky is now in her late teens, blind, deaf, hopelessly arthritic, incontinent: she can just manage to limp down to the end of the road and back again each morning. I hope she'll see another premiership.

D.J. O'HEARN

Interchange

D.J. 'Dinny' O'Hearn was born in 1937 and trained to be a Christian Brother before pursuing a career as a writer, academic, television presenter and administrator. He was a tireless champion of Australian writing and literary life. O'Hearn held the position of sub-dean of the Faculty of Arts at the University of Melbourne for many years and, in 1983, co-founded the Melbourne Writers Theatre with Jack Hibberd. He was founding executive officer of the Australian Centre at the University of Melbourne, which opened in January 1989, and which established a D.J. O'Hearn Memorial Fellowship after his premature death in 1993. A prolific writer and essayist, he was the original presenter of *The Book Show* on SBS TV, later co-presenting with Andrea Stretton. Friend and fellow writer Don Watson described O'Hearn as man who 'liked the human race in all its forms and was in love with this country'. 'Interchange' first appeared in *The Greatest Game* by Ross Fitzgerald and Ken Spillman (eds., 1988).

I have this friend who is a poet and a very good poet he is. Twice each year we trundle off to the Hawthorn-Collingwood game, and twice each year my friend Evan has to explain his team's failure. He has a unique way of doing it.

As soon as the game ends, he congratulates me on Hawthorn's thirty- or forty- or sixty-point win. Then he chooses one Collingwood player and announces that he played a good game and, after reflection, declaims that, on the whole, that player beat his opponent. This breakthrough allows him to consider a second Collingwood player and again, upon reflection, he muses that on the day this player too beat his opponent. By the time we have shuffled along several blocks with the post-game crowd on our way to the pub, friend poet has run through the whole

Collingwood team and, after due consideration, has come to the conclusion that each one singly has beaten his opponent.

My willing suspension of disbelief finally cracks. I meekly inquire how, if all that he has said is the case, his team went under by twenty or forty or sixty points. Such a pointed question gives him cause to pause but not to resile. 'Ah,' he says ponderously, 'I think on the day we lacked a little teamwork.' Humbled, I desist from further comment.

Outsiders have labelled this kind of behaviour as religious, but the proper study of footy lovers belongs not to theologians but to anthropologists. My friend the poet displays the attributes of a tribal member rather than a person imbued with religious belief. If he were merely religious in barracking for Collingwood, he would by now have lost his faith. As a member of a tribe, he can suffer armed incursions, scorched turf policies and even the abduction of some of his warriors, but he knows that the coming generation is full blood, that the tribe will re-group and regain its territory, that one day, in the spring, the black and white balloons will float over the MCG and that, on that day, by 5.30, his euphoria will be complete, and his cup will runneth over by the grace of Collingwood publicans.

Tribes, of course, develop their own rituals, and members of tribes are allowed a certain individuality. At Hawthorn matches, I stand with a shelf of historians surrounded by hostile natives from the visiting tribe. We listen to their garbled messages, note their fallacious views, marvel at their blindness and lack of perspicacity. My friend Dr M lights his pipe, not as a sign of peace but as a symbol of disdain: his attempts to educate the visitors are met by ignorant, even belligerent, shouts of abuse. Normally a quiet man, he is driven to loud shouting, provocative comments on the sexual preferences of the opposing team and the occasional vulgarity. His erudite knowledge of the genealogy, social and historical background of the opposition players is lost on the visiting tribe, but he is constant in his attempts to send them away better informed, even if only by a sharp jab with the stem of his pipe, and the cryptic remark, 'Look at the scoreboard, ya mugs.'

Tribes are, however, not easily subject to education by foreigners, even when such is delivered with dramatic force. Dr M or Dr R may point out to me that it was Curran not Brereton who kicked that goal at the far end and I accept their bespectacled judgement. When they attempt to enlighten the visiting tribe by pointing out that their (the visitors') perception of an umpire's decision is blatantly inaccurate, using such sensible instructions for people with poor eyesight as 'Open the other one', 'Coles & Garrards', or the more general, 'Look at the game, why doncher?', their gentle and socially well-meaning remarks provoke such animadversions as, 'What would you know, poof?', 'Get some wipers, four-eyes,' or as happened recently at the Carlton game, 'Hawthorn's full of Presbyterian Protestants.' No amount of reasoned argument about tautology, the distinctions between Presbyterians, Methodists and Baptists or the provenance of names such as Curran, Kennedy, Brereton, Dipierdomenico or McCarthy proved of any use: the variously pie or beer dribbling gargoyle behind us refused to recant. We had encountered tribal fixity, that most ineducable of diseases.

The disease is not limited to football, though it displays its finest expression on such occasions. Tribal fixity obviously inhabits the vulpine imagination of a de-tribalised writer such as David Williamson who, when desperately seeking an answer to his ordinariness, feels it necessary to invent a fictional hostile tribe called the Celtic mafia. Naturally enough, David's only play to rise above the trivial is his study of a football tribe in 'The Club'.

The anthropologists, however, had best be nifty, for the tribal elders have sold out to the marauding moguls. They started by encouraging and blessing exogamous marriage—always fatal to a tribe. Barassi to Carlton, Wallace to Richmond, Richardson to Essendon. The tribal elders cared not, as long as the dowry were high enough. At the Saturday ritual, instead of immersing themselves in the tribe, they distanced themselves, sitting aloof and apart, watching the contest from behind glass, darkly. Is it any wonder then that they believed the game was best seen, or could only be seen properly, through the glass of television? As for the tribes, well, they are poised for dispersion. There will be no more honing of the wit, no more learning of the argot, no more banter or chiack.

We will all become victims of the glass wall, seeing only what the camera tells us, missing the stoush behind play, unable to check the whole tribe at one glance. My friend the poet will become, like Brennan's 'Wanderer', an isolate in his own living room; the shelf of historians will be returned to academia, their views no longer tested by the potent fierceness of a hostile tribe's harangue. Good-humoured rivalry will become blandness, cathartic primitivism will be suppressed and lost to domesticity, and, worst of all, display will replace genuine ritual. The spirit of the Emerald Isle will have been trapped within the glass of Emerald city. *Ave atque vale*, oh Great Goddess TV.

KEN SPILLMAN

The Archaeology of Loss

Ken Spillman is the author of around 35 books and editor or co-editor of many others. His work spans the areas of fiction, history, poetry and criticism. In the 20th century he was a prolific author of local and sporting histories, but the Y2K bug caused a regression and he now works primarily in the area of books for young people. Spillman's illustrated *Jake* series for young readers appears in more than a dozen countries, with translations into such diverse languages as French, Farsi, Serbian and Vietnamese. The popularity of *Jake* in India has led Spillman to write a number of acclaimed books with Indian characters and settings. He chairs the judging panel for Singapore's inaugural award for children's books and is featured in the major US reference publication, *Contemporary Authors*. Ken still enjoys kick-to-kick with his sons and his former English teacher. This piece is an edited amalgamation of articles published in *The Weekend Australian*, 28 September 1991, and *The West Australian*, 7 September 1991.

The GPO is bedecked in blue and gold. The Lord Mayor has dubbed Perth 'Eagle City'. Billboards, banners and stickers all presume to speak for me—for all of us. The media never lets up. It's September 1991, and a new regime is firmly ensconced.

This is my home, but I'm not welcome here. I'm Western Australian, yet no longer one of 'us'. Officially, my existence is denied. White, male and heterosexual, I'm not accustomed to being part of an oppressed minority, but living in Perth and despising the Eagles you soon learn how demoralising it can be. Whichever way you turn, there is exclusion. I can take no part in Monday conversation or Friday speculation. Heretics like me get cut off on talkback radio. People even practice thought correction on my children.

Yet despite the contempt of the majority I am not a traitor, an enemy of the State. I'm a true believer. Like other true believers, I live as an outcast in Eagle City, camped on a midden that is the residue of past lives. Here, discarded artefacts evoke memories but not discussion. Dig deep and you'll find a question that made sense as recently as five years ago, but cannot be asked in respectable company today: 'Who d'ya barrack for?' Dig a little deeper, and you may find answers: the Maroons, the Cardies, Old Easts, perhaps even the Royals. Appellations from a lost time, a better world. College boys took on garlic munchers or wharfies, and it was possible to speak freely. You were entitled to your own beliefs. Nobody assumed anything. There was joy and sadness, side by side, separated only by picket fences. There was an invigorating diversity of opinion. On Saturdays, you could wear ancestral colours.

Many torpedo punts across the Nullarbor there was another, larger metropolis. In spite of the weather footy was played there, too. Victorians played it well, in their own way; if nothing else, they were exemplary in their obsessiveness. But what the West Indies were to cricket, and the entire continent of South America is to soccer, we Sandgropers were to footy. We took risks. We disdained the 'percentage' approach and gloried in sheer, ever-surprising brilliance. Slugging it out was for slugs.

We loved our boys who went east and showed wise men the folly of their ways. We were never surprised by their triumphs, and the roll call was far too long to memorise. In the 1930s alone, Subiaco's Johnny Leonard and Brighton Diggins captain-coached South Melbourne and Carlton respectively. Their ex-Subiaco teammate Billy Faul was runner-up in the Brownlow Medal in just his first season, while Claremont's George Moloney booted more than three hundred goals in eight-eight games at Geelong. Just after World War II, Perth champion Ern Henfry was appointed captain of Carlton after only two VFL games, while Wally Buttsworth won three best-and-fairests at Essendon and was later named at centre half-back in the Bombers' Team of the Century. Later, the deeds of Farmer, Jackson, Cable, Moss, the Krakouer brothers and a legion of others—yes, a legion—were confirmation of our supremacy. No matter that, in interstate footy, the Vics were our nemesis. We listened to our hearts. Quite simply, we knew we were better. It was like the automatons of German soccer holding sway against Brazil: the score was only part of the story.

Then came State of Origin. Significantly, more than half of the players in those glamorous Western Australian State of Origin sides of the late 1970s and 1980s were drawn from local clubs. We tantalised recruiting officers with our own breathtaking game. Who can forget big Stephen Michael, a proud Nyungar who captained his State but saw no need to 'prove himself' in the VFL , standing atop a podium in the middle of Subiaco Oval and saying how good it was to 'stick it up the Vics'. Not a handpass away, the pride of Victorian football peeled off socks and hung their heads, shattered by the enormity of a painful truth.

We loved it. Oh yes, we did. But tragically, the cheering throng failed to ponder what had made it all possible. We had a vibrant club scene with a hundred years of tradition. We had a competition we could respect and, more importantly, we had self-respect. We had preserved our rituals and valued our tribal culture.

The marketing people were able to seize upon the popularity of State of Origin games and deluded Western Australians into thinking the manufacture of the West Coast Eagles offered more of the same. They decorated a bandwagon and coaxed people aboard with shameless anti-Victorian propaganda. Entrepreneurs in the great tradition of Australia's western third, they didn't weigh social costs. Unlike military strategists, they didn't even bother with euphemisms like 'collateral damage'.

This was the eighties, a time of four-on-the-floor progress. Government and enterprise still breathed the can-do air that had filled the sails of a yacht named *Australia II* and brought one of the world's most coveted sporting trophies to Fremantle. The football world was there to be conquered: we would create a winged bird of prey just as we had created a winged keel. We would fatten it on the carcasses of long-established clubs. Melbourne, Victoria was simply another Newport, Rhode Island. Care of the goose which had laid so many golden eggs, the WAFL, could be left to others.

On 29 March 1987, I walked to Subiaco Oval to watch a match between traditional rivals, West Perth and East Perth. I was swimming against the tide—and it was humiliatingly clear that I would be swimming against the tide for the rest of my days. Thousands of people were exiting the ground, swaggering and jubilant, as I entered. They had just watched a curtain raiser, in which the West Coast Eagles had defeated Richmond.

Watch a WAFL game? Who, us? Not likely, mate!

Western Australian football was always going to be decimated by the creation of a synthetic team, not because it increased the number of teams drawing players out of the local competition (six members of Subiaco's 1986 premiership team had thrown in their lot with the blue-and-gold), but because it diverted the public gaze and explicitly denigrated the existing belief system. Henceforth, we were to consider ourselves second rate.

I had predicted catastrophe in a submission to the board of directors of the Western Australian Football League, pleading that a vibrant local football culture manifest in a viable local competition was a *sine qua non* of tolerable existence. It is very possible that only one director—Tom Stannage, a former Swan Districts wingman who graduated from Cambridge and went on to become Professor of History at the University of Western Australia—understood my Latin.

Another who predicted catastrophe was former Subiaco champion Mike Fitzpatrick, who had retired from football in 1983 after captaining Carlton to the 1981 and 1982 premierships. In February 1987, Fitzpatrick visited his family in Perth and asked various football officials for their views on prospects for the WAFL in the approaching season. 'They seemed optimistic,' he wrote. 'I said crowds would be down by fifty per cent, a figure they saw as unduly pessimistic.' When Fitzpatrick returned to Perth four months later, he was part of a minuscule crowd watching a Subiaco-East Perth match, causing him to reflect on his days at Subiaco and his years as a boy dreaming of league football: 'There was something attainable to aspire to, a place in a healthy competition with reasonable rewards, a little money, a little local fame and, above all, a good high standard of football in front of a decent crowd.'

The decline in crowds attending WAFL football was so dramatic that, even when combined with crowd figures from VFL/AFL matches in Perth, total attendances have remained below pre-1987 levels season after season. Do Eagles followers care? Do they even think about it? No. These are people who have lost their past, and whose concept of the future is the next live television coverage.

Yet living uncomfortably in their midst, I have learned that the chief characteristic of an Eagles supporter is not amnesia or heedlessness but ignorance about rival players and rival clubs, and even the nature of the competition. They don't understand that the AFL is an *interclub*, not an *interstate* competition. To them, the Victorian clubs are simply watered down versions of the Big V, and this year it's Hawthorn that is the First Eighteen. They forget that the number of Western Australians lining up for those clubs is greater than the number playing for the Eagles.

Victorians themselves have done little to stop the rot—to the contrary, they advanced it by not taking the threat seriously enough. In welcoming instant teams from interstate into the fold, they granted draft concessions that have already made life more difficult for success-starved Melbourne clubs. What they didn't understand is that they were dealing with people who, flushed with victory on the western front, would ravage their cultural environment and feel good about doing so. In 1986, Victorian clubs went for the quick fix of Western Australian money—there was plenty of it about—and that hideous indiscretion could become a factor in fixing some of them for good. If you happen to be a Fitzroy supporter, you should be very, very scared.

Now more than ever, Australia needs its footy clubs. They give us hope and meaning. They remind us were we have come from. They bring us together and teach us tolerance of faiths to which we cannot subscribe. Once in Perth we had the vibrancy of diverse football cultures. Now we have a terminal local competition, a voracious bird of prey, and a language laden with ideologically correct Comettisms.

It's September 1991. I'm pinning my faith on Hawthorn to pop the yellow and blue balloons that pollute 'Eagle City', and hoping that the wounds of so-called patriotic West Aussies are salted by a brilliant performance from the Hawks' star centreman, Claremont lad Ben Allan. An Eagles premiership would seem to vindicate the regime and the sacrifice of our football heritage.

But flag or no flag, we have the hegemony of the blue and gold. A state religion which oppresses the old faiths and attempts, through the media strongmen, to exercise thought control. Deep down, I know things will get worse. Better for television—very likely. But worse for local footy here in the west, worse for the most famished Victorian clubs, worse for me, and worse for my children. I'll be left on this midden, condemned, forever boning up on the archaeology of loss.

PHILIP HODGINS

The Drop Kick

Philip Hodgins was born at Shepparton in 1959, and died of leukaemia in 1995. He played on a half-back flank for Katandra West in the Tungamah Football League and, almost from the time *Blood and Bone* was published in 1986, was considered one of Australia's finest poets. Subsequent books were *Down the Lake with Half a Chook* (1988), *Animal Warmth* (1990), *The End of the Season* (1993), *Up On All Fours* (1993), *Dispossessed* (1994), and *Things Happen* (1995). A volume of selected poems appeared after Hodgins' death. His awards include the Wesley Michael Wright Prize for Poetry, the Bicentennial Poetry Book Award, the New South Wales Premier's Award, the Grace Leven Prize and the National Book Council Poetry Prize. 'The Drop Kick' first appeared in Ross Fitzgerald and Ken Spillman (eds.), *The Greatest Game* (1988). 'Country Football' first appeared in Hodgins' collection *Blood and Bone* (1986).

Extinct in the big league
because the extra time it takes
can get you unloaded
the drop kick is still alive
on a country ground
if the weather's right.
To shoot for goal with one
the way Jack Savage used to do
is a sign of confidence.
He could do it easily
from centre half-forward
and the story goes he did it once
from out on the wing.

His greatest moment
was winning the '59 Grand Final with one—
a running roost in time-on.
It was poetry all the way—
seventy yards and spinning like a boomerang.
Not bad for a thirty-four-year-old
who played the second half
with a broken rib.
Today, from the noise and warmth
of the J.W. Savage Stand
the drop kick looks a piece of cake
to these half-pissed farmers' sons.
They're going to take the field
at half-time in a ritual display.
Will anyone tell them the risk?
It's usually embarrassment—
a grubber off the side of the boot.
But sometimes it's worse.

Country Football

The ellipse, Hindu symbol of fertility,
is flanked by crowded cars
nosing up to the rails.
It suckles like a sow.

Inside the cars voices report
from significant, never been there places—
Kardinia, Moorabbin, Windy Hill.

Reflecting each other from the cusps
rise two-dimensional white cathedrals.

Today they will be temples to apostasy twice.
Their entrances are guarded by clones
whose torches blaze pure white.

From corrugated iron purgatory
many men feed out in lines like parachutists,
limbs varnished with an intoxicating wake
of eucalyptus oil.

Landing near afflatus
they disperse into pairs
of cryptic numerical combinations.

But one without a number,
as resolutely white as the cue ball,
omnipotent in a classical pose,
holds aloft a red ellipse
and whistles up
a terrible trumpeting of motor horns
for this afternoon's do or die.

FAY ZWICKY

Le Football Australien

Fay Zwicky was born in Melbourne in 1933. An accomplished pianist by the age of six, she began writing poetry at the University of Melbourne. After touring as a concert pianist for a decade, she settled in Perth and taught literature at the University of Western Australia until her retirement in 1987. Zwicky's first collection of poems, *Isaac Babel's Fiddle*, was published in 1975 and she has since published another seven collections, a book of short stories and a collection of essays. Her awards include the New South Wales Premier's Poetry Award, the Western Australian Premier's Book Award, the Patrick White Award and the FAW Christopher Brennan Award. In 2004 she was declared one of Western Australia's 'Living Treasures'. 'Le Football Australien' was written for *The Greatest Game* by Ross Fitzgerald and Ken Spillman (eds., 1988).

The text below is extracted from the preface to Une Petite Histoire des Jeux du Vingtième Siècle *de Dr Théophile Fourrage, first published in France in 2281, translated for English publication by the author in 2285.*

Many of the documents and letters used in this study were discovered in the ruins of the city of Perth, Western Australia, in the months February–December 2052, after our unfortunate misguided projectile incident in the Indian Ocean during the previous year.

The letters cited comprise a small part of an obviously longer exchange between an anonymous male painter, native of the island of Tasmania, and a female *poète de second ordre* from the city of Perth, circa 1987. The prose extracts have been collected from journals of the period, fragments of which have been recovered spasmodically in the course of successive excavations. In addition, commentaries by educational research and development experts of the time play a substantial role in contributing the necessary theoretical gender structures for the dissemination of our findings.

The veracity of these documents has been much contested. In this age beyond reconstruction, this age of *le grand pastiche*, such personal material has frequently been judged exaggerated and distorted, a wilful mutilation of the facts. For example, the violence of vocabulary in journals suggests deployment of military force rather than energy expended for entertainment and pleasure. Teams apparently engaged in ritual sacrifice before each game: 'Geelong[1] axes Turner,'[2] reads one local report. 'Killer instinct is a frame of mind that separates top teams from the also rans,'[3] reads another source. 'Get 'im, ya mucky mongrel!' is the reported cry of an angry female supporter of an earth-bound team, the Cats.[4] Those engaged in the media recording of such events were subject to no less pitiless treatment: 'ABC sport chief axed... ABC staff in Victoria learned of Berry's demise in a staff memo.'[5]

Analogies have been made to religion, to sex, and to the family. Sociologists and psychologists of the period under review are emphatically united in their belief that violent sport is a sublimation of

---

1   Geelong, a small industrialised village on the periphery of the Melbourne metropolis in the state of Victoria.

2   Turner, a former captain of the Geelong side.

3   Wimps, losers, failures. Etymologically derived from horseback racing (see Ch. 9, 'Gambolling in Australia').

4   Due to the great heights scaled by players in quest of the ball, teams were often designated by bird names e.g. Swans, Hawks, Eagles, etc. One passage should suffice to illustrate the often-mysterious use of metaphor resorted to by journalists describing such aerial feats known as 'marks':
     The real smoky of the Carlton 1987 recruits, bearing the heavy weight of Mike Fitzpatrick's Number 3 jumper, Richard Dennis, wrote himself into memories of the old Carltonians late in the third quarter. He came into an elevator over a pair of other players, got the ride to the first floor with them, then went express through the clouds under his own steam, plucked the ball, and landed on two feet. He must have gone higher than Sergei Bubka—without a pole.
     We are not to assume that a portable steam-powered elevator became available to players wishing to rise above the opposition during the course of play. The reference to S. Bubka is somewhat obscure.

5   This relates to the dismissal of a certain Kevin Berry, director of sports news for a national television organisation, now defunct, known in 1987 as the Australian Broadcasting Corporation. Due to internecine friction and continuing complaints by staff about ruthless treatment by corporation sponsors and administrators, a conservative government terminated funding in 1995.

sexual impulses. When players objected to the suggestion that sexual intercourse be rationed to once weekly, team coaches were obliged to seek the services of psychologists. The following item bears witness to difficulties encountered by coaches in relation to this issue:

> *Geelong coach John Devine said afterwards it was all psychological, and it would not be long before team psychologists were as common at League clubs as head trainers. 'I can't work it out,' he said. 'You look at them, and they look the same as before the Brisbane game; they tell you they are ready, but you can't tell what is going on upstairs.*[6]

The players themselves appear uncertain about the aesthetics and mystique of their profession, but their remarks on the subject are often more eloquent than the observations of anthropologists and psychologists seeking to reckon with this phenomenon. 'At weekends it's a bloodbath,' says one Saint who defied a club ban on speaking to the media, thereby incurring dismissal. 'It's something honest happening out there. It's the lions and the Christians[7] all over again.'

Seldom do we find recorded any in-depth analysis of the sport's innate brutality by its more sensitive practitioners. A man on the Geelong forward line in 1973, declared invalid in the same year, is reported to have said:

> *I don't realise how brutal the game is until the off-season when I go to club functions and watch the replays. Then I see my mates turned upside down, inside out, backwards, and hit from all angles, and I'm bloody amazed how violent the game is and wonder why I'm playing it myself.*

Yet another player, author of a small memoir entitled *Out of Their Minds*, writes:

> *The best footballers are psychopaths. They are very unhealthy people, but society views them as some of our healthiest specimens. When you have men perpetuating violence in sports, on television, or anything*

---

6   Upstairs, the customary venue for sexual encounters.

7   'Lions and Christians', refers to an earlier blood sport linked with the emergence of a now-defunct religious sect, followers of the excommunicated Jewish prophet, Jesus Christ.

of that nature, you can't call that sane. You can't call the people doing it sane. You can't call me sane. Show the kids some of the letters I get from people who're hoping somebody cripples me because of my moustache.

Needless to say, this player's participation in the destructive operation thus analysed was brief, his ostracism total. He was thereafter referred to in public as 'that poofter'.[8]

It is, therefore, difficult to reconcile such sentiments with those expressed by a poet in a fragment of an epic discovered in the latter half of the twentieth century during the 2052 excavations:

watching him go up the sky   as if he
*   held some secret toe-holds in the crowd-rung*
air   long fingers   stretching into all the
*   grey and difficult distance   glistening*
robed with rings of rain and silver
*   light   he knows his own degrees...*

The extract belies the notion that the romantic heroic strain perished with the Irish poet W.B. Yeats in the first quarter of the century. Clearly, it has survived in this portrait of a footballer created in the eighties by a poet bearing the ambiguous name Guess.

More light is shed on anomalous male and female attitudes towards the sport by an educator of the period. He argues that the school's relation to gender is one that reflects patterns of separation and association between male and female, but is also deeply implicated in the production of sanctioned notions of masculinity and femininity. Our authority writes:

Where this is a question of activities clearly directed to this end, we can speak of masculinising and feminising practices. In ruling-class boys' schools the project of 'making men of them' has historically been quite explicit; and much can be learned from an examination of their most visible masculinising practice—sport, and especially football.

---

8   Poofter or homosexual, once a member of a persecuted minority group. Also known as 'gay'.

He goes on to give two hypothetical examples of youths brought up within the system and relays their individual responses to the process of indoctrination:

Bruce Anderson, son of a company manager, is being trained as a competitor by his family and by his school. There is fierce pressure behind his involvement in football. Unfortunately, he is still physically slight and consequently has endured a series of injuries culminating in concussion. Only through the intercession of an anxious teacher was Bruce, to his great disappointment, put into a lower grade playing with smaller boys. When asked what he would most like to improve about himself, his answer was 'to grow bigger physically'.

He strongly identifies with his father who regards prowess in the game as indicative of masculinity. 'I hate football,' says Mrs Anderson. Mr Anderson is intensely competitive on his son's behalf and regularly attends all his training sessions and Saturday matches.

Bradley Lamb is even more pressured. Mr and Mrs Lamb both follow all their sons' matches, yell from the sidelines, praise good play, but, more often than not, abuse bad. Mr Lamb gives up his Saturday golf, and Mrs Lamb attends every sports day:

'Wild horses wouldn't drag me away,' she is reported as saying. Alluding to the school's sports colour, she said: 'The three of them are very much blue men—we are all blue men.'

Small wonder, then, that men reared in such an environment endured crises of sexual identity or that football clubs of the time saw fit to engage the services of team psychologists. Our authority concluded his survey with some observations about both Bruce and Bradley:

A dose of old-fashioned school spirit, rather overdone? We think not. Something systematic and important is going on here. Competitive sport, and particularly football, is important as a means for the production of a particular kind of masculinity linked to the class situation these boys are moving towards and the work they will later engage in. Why football? It's rarely played by women, therefore

unambiguously male. It's rough, competitive, highly ritualised, and
confrontative in a way that other competitive sports are not. In the
course of play the boy is constantly running up against someone and
has to overcome him in a test of personal superiority.

The game, concludes this educationist, 'is well suited to the emotional
focus of the masculinising practices of the school'.

Let us acknowledge, then, that we seek for more in the letters of the
artist than such narrow and mundane observation as educational pundits
are wont to supply. We are certainly not disappointed by the enthusiasm
of the painter's response to a series of weekend games confided in a letter
to his friend, the poet:

A typical Oz autumn morning in the footy season as I write, the replays of
yesterday's round being show. I watch, sound off. The commentaries, however
informed, distract from the visual. Detail is obscured with the intruding
voice... so Schubert's 'D Major Sonata' assists the Darth Vader/Roger Merrett
clone take a screamer over a passle of Eagles... Assyrian-like, coming down
like the wolf on the fold with the cohorts this time gleaming in blue and gold...
with the sheen of their spears like stars on the sea... from whence rolls the dark
wave yet again. I'm not sure, but it certainly is rolling on. Galilee-bound
or not... come to think of it, despite the marvellous legend from Hawthorn
playing Jesus Christ at full forward and moving Hudson out to half forward,
it's about time Jerusalem produced another full forward. Arafat, a dinosaur
from the mould of coaches like Devine, Baldock, Malthouse should really by
reaction have provoked the Israeli reserves to come up with a promising heir
apparent in the line of Coleman, Hudson...

The poet replies by sending a poem called 'Weather Report' and asking
that her friend explain the political and religious references. 'I don't give
a damn whether Hawthorn wins or not,' she writes. 'I really wanted to
know whether or not you liked those bottled plums.'

The painter's reply contains no reference to the plums. Undaunted by the
unintelligible poem, he continues to explore the national football scene:

Yesterday's round showed yet again that the top sides have
subconsciously understood the von Moltke/Schlieffen strategy

of war without mercy. Not for them the impromptu desperation of the proud larrikin,[9] beyond discipline. Relentless unnerving endless pressure on all fronts permitting precise surgery at the correct moment when eye and nerve are aligned.[10] Thus Essendon and the Eagles yesterday... the winner was determined only by the full-time signal as they both took turns leading. The Brisbane Bears, taking over the experiment begun several years ago by the San Diego Chargers[11]... putting together desperadoes from all clubs and asylums into something that redefined the concept of TEAM: individuals hitherto known as show ponies suddenly developed a stomach for the game never suspected by their previous clubs...

After a good deal more of this, and in spite of an anguished note from his friend begging respite and asking him to get her a ticket for the ballet the following week, he instructs her on the necessity for giving up smoking, concluding with the following paragraph:

The nationwide footy spectacle is really taking some sorting out because nobody, NOT NOBODY knows the form... I even imagined Baldock could find something in St Kilda... hope springs... disillusioned yet again after round 2 they show bloody nothing worth a pinch of shit. Just wasting honest folks' time and using up good oxygen into the bargain. God, if they were horses they'd have been put down seasons ago. Christ we're forgiving. The Rugby[12] people both in Sydney and Brisbane have shown again that they can't cope with the onslaught of Oz Rules... they've made some really infantile decisions both domestically and regionally. They are testimonies to Tuchman's proposition of the March of Folly.[13]

---

9   Larrikin, (O. Aust.), young street rowdy, hooligan.

10 Further corroboration of the expression 'to axe', p. 1.

11 San Diego Chargers, an American football team that played according to patterns of offensive and defensive action far more rigidly determined than the comparatively anarchic possibilities of Australian Rules. Heavy padded clothing, face masks, shin guards, etc., made it impossible for players to rise more than a few inches from the ground.

12 Rugby, a rival game played with an oval ball that could be kicked or carried. Again, rugby players were too solidly built for leaping, but sufficiently weighty to withstand the smothering heap of bodies covering the ball known as a 'scrum'.

13 Barbara Tuchman, a contemporary historian of moralistic propensities.

We may feel inclined to discern in such letters an excess of hyperbole and violent antipathies that strain plausibility on the subject of *le sport australien*. How, we ask, is it possible that such intense passions should have been generated by *rien qu'un divertissement* among a people so little inclined to passionate utterance? How are we to credit the fact that such attitudes prevailed in past eras on a 'continent void of speech'?[14]

In the interests of truth, my guiding principle has been to leave the texts uncorrected wherever possible, to maintain barbarisms in their entirety. I am aware that, in the rendering of technical terms relating to the ancient sport as once played in the states of Victoria[15] and Western Australia,[16] I may have laid myself open to criticism on the score of inconsistency. Let me defend myself in advance by saying that, if consistency were the *nom de jeu*, one would not attempt translation at all.

I have tried to follow Australian vernacular usage wherever possible in order to preserve the nuances of prevalent regional antipathies; for example, 'Start with the good old SCG itself. It isn't a footy oval at all. It's round.'[17] A more sinister reminder of interstate rivalry is to be found in the following caption beneath a blurred photograph: 'West Coast Eagles wingman Chris Mainwaring is the meat in this St Kilda sandwich.' Not only were players killed but also, it would appear, eaten.

Comments and footnotes have been interspersed to provide explanation of local allusions wherever possible. It is clear, for example, that punishment for infringement of rules differed from region to region. In an article headed 'Hit 'em in the pocket—or just ban 'em?' the writer, native of Melbourne, intimates the presence of an unequal division of wealth within the states, and also attributes a degree of moral corruption to Western Australia that is seemingly non-existent in Victoria. From this we deduce that no agreement between the states on what constituted 'maximum punishment' had been reached in the winter of 1987:

---

14 D.H. Lawrence, a disappointed English visitor to the Antipodes, unable to find good conversation.
15 The place of origin of the game known as Australian Rules.
16 The state known between the years 1965-75 as 'The State of Excitement' (see Ch. 9).
17 From a report by a Melbourne visitor attending a match at the Sydney Cricket Ground between the Melbourne Hawks and the Sydney Swans.

For many years the ultimate punishment in Melbourne was a suspension.[18] Nothing is more painful to a Victorian than to miss his game on Sat'day arvo,[19] whether as a player or a spectator. In Perth, money is the religion, and a wealth of millionaires are its profitable prophets. So it was not surprising David Rhys-Jones was fined rather than suspended after his misdemeanour against the West Coast Eagles last Friday night.

If we are to fully understand the demoralised condition of a nation, the general state of unpreparedness, the inability to marshal consensus on any one issue subsequent to our unhappy projectile mishap, we might do worse than study the moral confusion revealed in the extract cited above, not only in relation to sport but also as a symptom of broader social malaise. Whether football as played according to Australian Rules is seen as the embodiment of an archaic ethos or as a last-ditch stand of waning masculinity, I hope that the following pages will help unlock some of the game's hidden mysteries.

I am indebted to Drs Grimble and Macnutt, and to Messieurs Thomas Canard and Bruno Coquatrix of l'Institut Noé for their respective encouragements and criticisms of my translations used in this study.

Théophile Fourrage
Paris, 2285

---

18 Suspension, banishment of a player for a fixed period of time following misbehaviour during a game. Penalties could be incurred for cursing the umpire, gouging out an eye/eyes; breaking cheekbone/nose/jaw, etc. Damage to knees and elbows seems to have been largely exempt from punitive action. For example, a Carlton player has been quoted as saying, 'Someone once told me before we played Geelong that the way to beat their full back, D—, was to get him round the knees because he had bad knees and you could finish him off easily that way.'
19 Vernacular rendering of the phrase, 'Saturday afternoon'.

VIN MASKELL

The Sherrin

Vin Maskell writes personal essays about sport, music, family and life. His work has appeared in such publications as *The Big Issue*, *The Age*, *Best Australian Essays* (2008), *The Footy Almanac* and on various websites. He co-edits scoreboardpressure.com and stereostories.com. Vin assisted Syd Sherrin in preparing his book *The Family Behind the Football* (Melbourne Books, 2010). 'The Sherrin' appears for the first time in this collection.

It is nearly time to play. On Sunday mornings before kick-to-kick and circle work with a few mates I sit on the back step with my football, a brush, and a tin of Joseph Lyddy Dubbin ('for waterproofing, softening and preserving of footwear, boots, jackets and sports goods').

I prise open the Joseph Lyddy lid. I place the ball in my lap. It is five years old, made by a neighbour from up the street. The ball has lost most of its red colouring and its unique lettering is faint, but there is still much to see in the faded leather.

There are cracks and scratches and scars, lines that are like veins and roads and creeks, lines that are tributaries to memories, lines that are maps of stories. Stories of childhood and adulthood, of generations, of grass and grounds, of kicks and kinship.

When you look at the wrinkles and creases of an old football you might just see wear and tear but you might also see the veins and the skin on the back of your hands, those hands that mark and fumble and handball and drop the ball to your feet, those hands that work and feed the family, those hands that polish old leather on a Sunday morning.

In 1879 a saddler's hands in Collingwood grew tired of repairing the English-made rugby balls that were then used for Australian rules.

The saddler designed and made a ball specifically suited to the rigours of the indigenous football game. A year later T.W.Sherrin Pty Ltd was established at 32-34 Wellington Street, Collingwood.

When you look at the markings of an old ball you might see the roads and the streets of your home town, roads and streets full of backyard games and local footy grounds. In my childhood I ran with a football under my arm from 6 Cremona Street to the Mentone football ground in Venice Street, to play kick-to-kick after school with mates and brothers.

The only football I remember from those days was one my father repaired at the kitchen table. I don't remember if it was a Sherrin or a Faulkner or even a Burley but I remember watching my father struggling with the lacing and the bladder and then finally saying, 'There, I think that's better.'

I gave him a clumsy hug of gratitude, clumsy because although we were a large and lively family, we were not physical in our affections. I held a football in my hands more than I held my father or my mother in my arms. A football couldn't feed me or love me but it didn't tell me to wash my hands or eat my peas or feed the dog.

Thomas William Sherrin died in 1912, leaving the family business in the hands of a nephew, John Sydney Sherrin. Three years later the National Football Council of Australia cited the size and the shape of the Sherrin football as the standard for the game. By 1927 the small factory at the Victoria Parade end of Wellington Street was making about 20,000 footballs per year, as well as cricket, boxing and other sporting goods.

I dab the brush into the boot polish, the Lyddy liniment, and imagine some of the lines on my football to be the footpaths of my teenage years, the footpaths that ran from 165 Minerva Road, around the corner to Elderslie Terrace and up to the Newtown and Chilwell football ground, an oval almost in the shadow of the old cement works.

Newtown wore bright shorts for at least one season in the mid-1970s and during one game I called out several times 'Carn the red shorts!' until the resting ruckman in the back pocket turned around and said 'I'll give you a red nose if you keep saying that.' At quarter-time he headed off to hear Hughie Strachan's instructions, while my mate and I kicked and handballed and passed our footy, a ball that seemed to convey the teenage friendship between us.

When John Sydney Sherrin died in 1942 his son Tom, aged twenty-five, took over the business, much later juggling the responsibilities of the growing family business with the pressures, and the joys, of being president of the Collingwood Football Club.

I begin to polish my football, noting the instructions printed inside the lid of the Dubbin tin: 'Rub in evenly with brush or soft cloth giving special attention to stitching and welts. Allow to penetrate.' My football has 220 stitches, each five millimetres apart, and it's hard work, its maker told me, pulling the waxed string through the leather over and over and over again. The stitches remind me of railway sleepers, of train tracks that take you to old suburban grounds. Collingwood, Footscray, Glenferrie, Moorabbin, take your pick. Box Hill, Preston, Coburg, Williamstown.

Massaging the Dubbin into the leather my mind wanders and thinks of rivers and streams and creeks, of the water that flows from them and feeds the footy ovals I only know through reading the sports results before I sit on my back step: Lake Boga, Lakes Entrance, Lake Wendouree, Stony Creek, Campbells Creek, Olinda, Ferny Creek, Fish Creek.

On wet Sundays the footy becomes as slippery as a fish, as heavy and tough as, say, a carp. Then, through the week, it dries and hardens, and you've really got to work the Dubbin into the leather. The scratches look raw, the leather looks bare. It gets me thinking of rock hard grounds I've never seen: Gunbalanya, Titjikala, and Papunya up north, Queenstown down south in Tasmania, and the gravel rash grounds in Western Australia. The footballs in those places must take a hell of a hiding. They must age quickly, before their time.

An old football wouldn't be an old football if it didn't have some welts, or scars. You could imagine those scars to be the gouges in the grass—or dust or gravel—that you see after a game, where boots have twisted and turned and churned across the surface. In a way, these markings on the oval map the story of a game, of players being tackled, or changing directions, or accelerating with the ball in their hands with their eyes looking upfield.

Or you might see a scar on your footy and think of one thing and one thing only. A tree.

When one of my Sunday morning mates kicked a football high into a boundary line cypress tree at Fearon Reserve, Williamstown, the ball stayed there for a week. Our warm-up the next Sunday saw us lobbing fist-sized rocks up into the tree where the ball was lodged goalpost high in a cluster of branches. After several attempts the ball fell from its nest, with a new scar, like a badge of honour.

At least that ball eventually came down. About ten years ago a mate tried to roost a torpedo goalward at the other end of the Fearon. The ball went up and up and up and disappeared into a tree bordering the local botanic gardens. It was the most spectacular behind I'd ever seen scored. And it was the last I saw of that football. It might still be up there.

Of course, getting a footy stuck in a tree, and then trying to get it down, is a rite of passage for all football lovers. It's a moment when you realise that sometimes there are forces beyond your control.

Tom Sherrin made a very tough rite-of-passage decision in 1969. The business could no longer keep up with demand for its footballs. He decided to sell the ninety-year-old family business to the Spalding sporting goods company. The balls would still be made in the Collingwood factory for another thirteen years but the Sherrin brand was now part of a much, much larger company. By 1975 Spalding was producing about 35,000 Sherrins a year.

The Wellington Street factory is an art gallery now, exhibiting Indigenous art. Tom Sherrin's son Sydney Stewart Sherrin closed the doors at Wellington Street for the last time in December 1982, with Spalding now producing footballs at its Sunshine factory.

Still polishing my footy, I imagine Syd Sherrin making his way from Wellington Street, then turning right up Victoria Parade and heading west to Elizabeth Street, then Flemington Road and Smithfield Road, all the way to the Spalding factory in Ballarat Road.

I polish the top two panels of the football. I can still read some of the lettering: 'Inflate to 69 kpa' is printed beside the six lines of lacing and the valve. But you wouldn't know the words 'Kick to Kick' and 'The Genuine Article' are printed onto the leather if you hadn't requested such wording when you put in an order with your neighbour to make a hand-made football. Those words are but a ghostly outline now. I turn the ball over on my lap and finish polishing my once new and red and bright football, made by my neighbour from up the street, a fourth-generation football maker.

Syd Sherrin left Spalding in 1985 and became a real-estate agent. He still lived and breathed football and footballs but T.W.Sherrin Pty Ltd, created by his great-grand uncle all those years ago, was out of his hands.

More than a decade later a mate, a fellow real estate agent, asked Syd Sherrin to hand-make a football for him. Syd picked up the tools of his forebears—of T.W., of his grandfather John Sydney, of his father Tom, and set to work in his garage. He made his mate a football and then, enthused, three more, one for each of his daughters.

The Sherrin brand of football is now made by the Russell Athletic company, which took over Spalding in 2003. Russell Athletic has football factories in Scoresby, in Melbourne's outer east, and also in India. Each year Russell Athletic sell about 500,000 new footballs.

A new football is hope, I ponder, as I put away the Dubbin and the brush, but an old football is history.

A new football is the future, an old football is the past, I think as I pump up the footy a little. Not 69 kpa. Not too hard for these ageing feet.

A new football is a new lover, an old football is a long-time partner, I muse as I pick up my footy boots.

A new football is another chance. An old football might be your last dance.

My Sunday morning mates are making their way to the Fearon Reserve. I tuck my footy under my arm, just like I did when I was a boy in Mentone and when I was a teenager in Newtown. It is time to play.

BILL CANNON

The One-gamer

Bill Cannon began his journalistic career with the Melbourne *Herald* in 1974 as a cadet. He moved to London and covered the 1979 British Open Golf Championship and Wimbledon Championships before returning to Melbourne in 1981. He worked in the sports department of *The Herald* for five years, covering football, golf, tennis and boxing. Between 1987 and 2000 he was the sports producer for Seven Nightly News (Melbourne) then moved to Fox Footy in 2002, where he produces *On The Couch* and *After The Bounce*. He played one game for St Kilda in 1975. More than 12,000 men have played VFL/AFL football—and more than a thousand have played just one game. This essay first appeared in *Australian Football Quarterly*, April 2005.

I lived for footy from the time I was old enough to pick up a ball. Just one of tens of thousands of young Melbourne boys. Kick to kick at the local park; trying to take hangers every lunchtime on the primary school oval; fierce competition with my younger brother as I pretended to be Darrel Baldock. I shared the dream.

But the difference for me was that I was given a chance to use my talent; the door opened. Then it shut. I've just turned forty-nine. I had my big chance thirty years ago. So what does that sort of missed opportunity do to someone? How does it feel to be a 'one-game wonder'? Walk with me...

I was in the St Kilda medical room on 31 July 1975 when I received some stunning good news. Club physio Adrian Wright, who was treating me for fluid on the knee, confided that quite a few players looked like being out with injury. He suggested I get out onto the track and have a crack at impressing 'Yabby'—coach Allan Jeans. I slid off the medical table and charged down the race. I was nineteen. I'd joined the club in late 1974 and, like any red-blooded young VFL wannabe, was desperate to make my debut. It was the opportunity I'd been waiting for.

The session was competitive. The youngsters were out to seize a rare opportunity and the experienced players were showing very clearly that they weren't going to be replaced without a fight. I was pitted against the rugged Allan Davis, who had played in St Kilda's one and only premiership in 1966 as a skinny seventeen year-old. On this July night, the mature Davis wasn't about to let a teenager take his spot. Every time we went for the ball he made sure he drove his elbows and knees into as many parts of my anatomy as he could. Brighton Grammar circle work, circa 1973, this was not! After training, Kevin 'Cowboy' Neale and Russell Reynolds puffed on their fags and Jeansy went about his business of trying to get someone to 'rassle' (Jeans-speak for wrestling). I headed home with no great expectations.

Dad woke me at about 10.30pm *Sun* sports writer Scot Palmer was on the phone and wanted to talk to me about being selected for my first game. Wright had lived up to his name. 'Scotty' (who I vaguely knew because I was a cadet journalist at the *Herald*, where my uncle Jack was sports editor) asked a few questions about being named at full-forward. The next day the headline read: 'Cannon shot into seniors'.

I went to work as usual the next day, but it was not a normal day. Tony Homfray, who sat two desks in front of me and would be covering the Round 18 St Kilda-Geelong match the next day, joked that he would give me a mention in his match report. Chief-of-staff Max Grant told me to take it easy, so I wandered over to the milk bar and bought the glossy VFL magazine, *Football Life*. The cover headline read, 'The VFL's toughest backmen' and the story described Geelong full-back John Scarlett as one of the League's most feared players. He was to be my opponent the next day!

St Kilda secretary Ian Drake rang mid-morning to congratulate me on my promotion and suggested I visit a particular chemist in the city to pick up some pills that would help me sleep that night. *Herald* photographer Peter Ward took a picture of me, my dad Keith and younger brother Ian. He got Dad to toss a coin because he and Mum had to decide who they would watch the next day—me at VFL Park (Waverley) or Ian as he tried to help Brighton Grammar win its first premiership against Haileybury College. They decided to watch the first half of my match and the second half of Ian's.

I slept well that night (maybe the pills helped) and had a special breakfast—a huge rump steak, compliments of our local butcher. A mate, Richard Salter, picked me up at about 10.30 and we chatted idly on the way to Waverley. I vividly remember how luxurious the rooms were, with plenty of rubdown tables, a huge shower and bath area and a full-sized kicking net. No question, this was the big-time. I found it hard to fill in the time until the team arrived and that's when I started to get really nervous. It was hard to believe I was about to run out onto the ground with some of my footy idols, players like Brownlow Medallist Ross Smith, Barry Lawrence, Jeff Sarau, Barry Breen, Paul Callery, George Young and Glenn Elliott. My two best mates at the club— Trevor 'Barks' Barker and Colin 'Carts' Carter—were also in the side.

The Saints were just inside the five (it was a final five in those days), while the Cats were near the bottom. With only five rounds remaining, a win for us was critical. Jeansy told me to make sure I gave myself plenty of room to lead into; to stay deep in the 10-yard square. (He would say later it was the first time he had used a decoy full-forward!) I floated down the race onto the ground feeling fantastic.

I vividly remember everything about the game. Doesn't everyone? Walking down to full-forward with big Cowboy, who was in the pocket next to me, was reassuring. He introduced me to Scarlett and told him I was playing my first game. Scarlett and I had a bit of a natter; he asked me what school I had played at, whether I'd played at Waverley, gave me some advice about the camber of the ground—though what a camber was, I had no idea then. He said that field umpire Kevin Smith was one of the best going around. I couldn't believe how chatty he was. The ogre I had been reading about the previous day seemed like a ripper bloke... until the opening bounce. That's when he 'welcomed' me to the big league with a punch to the side of the head. 'Cowboy' yelled out to Scarlett—something about putting his head into the fence if he touched me again. Geelong got off to a great start; I remember seeing their left-footed centre half-forward taking plenty of marks, although from where I stood, I could only see him from his waist up. I was starting to understand what camber meant! I got to know this player better the following year when he came to Moorabbin. His name was Rex Hunt.

My first touch of the nut came when Carts charged around the outer side of the ground and bombed a torpedo in the direction of yours truly with Scarlett breathing down my neck. We both arrived at the ball at the same time, but somehow the ball stuck in my arms and an angry Scarlett slung me to the ground. Umpire Smith awarded me a fifteen-yard penalty. I remember thinking I would have preferred not to have been brought to within forty-five yards of goal because now I was expected to become the next player to nail a major with his first kick in League football. I pulled the kick slightly and it went through for a behind.

At the start of the second quarter, Scarlett didn't come down to fullback. I learnt later he had tweaked a hamstring and gone into the forward line. (Homfray said in his *Herald* match report that my pace had forced the move!) Unfortunately, Scarlett was replaced by Phil 'Snake' Baker, whose oiled arms and protruding veins still give me nightmares. He was built like a bodybuilder, but with the spring of a high jumper. Just ask former Hawthorn full-back Kel Moore, who played on 'Snake' (by then a 'Roo) in the 1978 Grand Final and watched six goals sail over his head.

I fancied taking some hangers, but every time I went to leap, it seemed Baker already had his knee on my shoulder. I started moving around more. I distinctly remember charging towards the members' half-forward flank and launching myself towards a beautifully weighted drop punt. I was propelled skywards and just failed to bring the ball to ground. It was the ride of a lifetime, but I came down to earth in more ways than one when I saw 'Barks' crawling to his feet holding his back and with a scowl on his face!

At half-time, we were down by twenty-one points. Jeansy asked me how I felt; I was afraid he might take me off. I was pretty drained—probably more emotionally than physically—but it was hard to believe we had already played for nearly an hour. The time had flown. In the third quarter, we had plenty of the ball and I got a few touches, but we managed only 3.8. We should have led at three-quarter time, but trailed by eight points. There were some anxious players in the huddle, but the experienced blokes were reassuring. They insisted we had the momentum.

The last quarter was a real arm wrestle as we continued to pepper the perpendiculars. I still regret not following my instincts when Barry Breen had a set shot at goal late in the game from about forty yards with the game in the balance. He was holding the ball on an angle for a torp and I knew that if he hit the ball sweetly, it would easily clear the goal-line where about a dozen players—including me—had congregated. But often Breeney's attempted torps turned into mongrel punts and dropped short. I momentarily contemplated standing ten yards in front of the pack in case he produced a 'mongrel'. That's exactly where the ball went and, after a scramble, the Cats cleared it. If I'd followed my instincts, I would have marked the ball, slotted the goal and sealed the match. My poor decision—or was I playing it safe because I didn't really want to put myself under the pump?—remains with me.

I had no idea of the score when the siren sounded, but tears welled up in my eyes when I saw we'd snuck home by four points. I bumped into two girls as I trotted off the ground—my sister Sue and her friend Rosalie. I can tell you it's pretty embarrassing to be caught crying by your fifteen-year-old sister.

It was heady stuff after the game—a few beers with my 'chauffeur' Richard and mates 'Barks' and 'Carts' then to the social club at Linton Street where we were greeted like rock stars. It also turned out to be dangerous. I hadn't eaten after the game and after a few more 'neck oils', found myself in the toilets vomiting. The highs and lows for a young League footballer!

In Monday's *Sun*, sports journo Rex Pullen gave me three out of ten for my performance. Whenever I passed him in the office after that I'd shoot him a dirty look. I don't think it worried him though, because I'm sure he didn't know who I was!

Five days later, I was spewing again. I'd been dropped. There had been no inkling this was going to happen, though in the back of my mind I knew some senior players were due back and, because we were still a chance for the finals, they were obviously going to be preferred to me. I had been pretty happy with my performance against the Cats and, at nineteen, was confident a permanent spot in the side was around the corner.

You can imagine the reception I received from the Footscray reserves players at the Western Oval the following week! I copped a punch in the groin area in the first five minutes, and then my opponent kept giving it to me about 'getting the arse after one game'. Worse was to come, however, once the seniors started. 'My' place at full-forward had been taken by brilliant left-footer George Young, who normally played on a forward flank. He had a day out. I think he kicked nine goals on Gary 'Chook' Merrington, who had an absolute 'Barry Crocker'. Every time Chook attacked the ball, it would bounce over his head to an unattended 'Youngy'; in fact, I'm sure the cherry bounced between Chook's legs at one stage to give George another 'sausage roll'. Suffice to say that while all my reserves teammates and Saints fans in general were in raptures about George's efforts, I knew each goal represented a nail in my immediate football coffin. The seniors flogged the Dogs by eleven goals, but lost the final three games of the year and missed the finals. I played out the season in the 'magoos'.

But my appetite had been whetted and I trained with Jeansy right through summer, doing weights, hill sprints, 400s, boxing and Jeansy's favourite, rasslin. He loved pinning you and letting a little bit of spit hang from his lips as you tried to squirm away from the dangling object. 'The trouble with you kids from Brighton is that you've all got Labradors,' he'd say. 'I want players here who've got Alsatians and Rottweilers.' By the following March, I was stronger and fitter than I'd ever been.

Going into a practice match at Moorabbin, rugged Carlton backman Vin Waite no longer frightened me. For years I'd watched him belt rovers—and not just the little blokes in the red, white and black. So when Waite tried to execute a blind turn out of a pack, I put my elbows and knees up thinking that would hurt him. I was about twelve stone two pounds (77 kilograms) and he would have been about sixteen stone seven (105 kilograms). It was like throwing marshmallows at a locomotive. Waite ran straight through me, spinning my body like a top. Unfortunately, my right leg was anchored to the ground. I crumpled. There wasn't a lot of pain, but I couldn't run, so I came off.

The following Wednesday, the club surgeon pushed, pulled and prodded my swollen knee and casually said my football days were over. I struggled to comprehend his words. Before the appointment, I had no perception of how serious my injury was. I stumbled down the hospital driveway, my head spinning. Out on the street, I slumped onto the footpath and started bawling. At nineteen, my VFL career should have been ready to take off, but here I was being told it was *finito*. I got a second opinion from another surgeon, John Grant, who pioneered knee reconstructions a decade earlier when he successfully operated on Peter Steward, a gun centre half-back from North Melbourne. He told me he could operate, but that I would miss the whole of the 1976 season. Fine by me; I had time on my side and the Saints were an ageing team. They'd be looking for some young blood in a year or so.

During the rehab, I spent a lot of time with Jeansy. I'd often train with him in the police gym in Russell Street playing volleyball with a medicine ball. He left at the end of 1976, replaced by Ross Smith. I don't know whether it was the long rehab, or whether I'd lost a yard, but some of my enthusiasm was gone. I'd also had a strong relationship with Jeansy. I still loved the game, but I wasn't obsessed by it any more. I played some reasonable games in the backline for the reserves and had the thrill of playing on Collingwood superstar Peter McKenna, who was now with Carlton. In fact, 'Macca' now reckons he knew his career was over when I beat him at Moorabbin one day while we were kicking up the dew.

Smith was replaced as coach after one year by Mike Patterson and he seemed like a terrific bloke. I was looking forward to getting stuck into pre-season and re-establishing myself at the club under his coaching. My hopes were abruptly short-circuited. One night in March, I arrived home to be met at the door by my concerned father.

'Why didn't you tell me you'd retired?' Dad asked.

'I haven't,' I replied.

'Well, this afternoon on *World of Sport*, they put up the St Kilda senior list and your name was under 'Retired'.'

I thought he'd either had too many beers or had misread Channel Seven's graphics. I was filthy. I found it hard to believe that no one at the club had contacted me before the news was made public. I then knew I'd missed my opportunity. In the following years, it hurt every time I watched Barks star in the seniors because I believe we were on a par when we both started.

So there you have it, retired at twenty with one senior game to my name.

Through the next week, my phone at the *Herald*'s police rounds bureau rang non-stop with offers from clubs from every state in Australia. The offers ranged from $100 to $400 a game, which was big money considering I was earning about $85 a week as a cadet journo. (I got $45 for my one and only senior game). I decided to play for the Frankston Bombers in the Mornington Peninsula Football League. St Kilda premiership player Travis Payze, who I'd known for a while, was president and the club was only a short drive down Nepean Highway. I was to receive $100 after each game. The Bombers had recruited heavily and, under coach Pat Flaherty—the crafty former Dandenong star—aimed to win the flag in 1978. My knee was still giving me trouble; I played about ten games and came off second best in the semi when I tried to clean up a guy by the name of Richard Keddie—the brother of Bob Keddie who had sunk the Saints in the 1971 VFL Grand Final. Keddie's knee caught me on the inside of the thigh. The club decided it was better that I be right for our expected grand final appearance, so I missed the preliminary against Edithvale-Aspendale, a young side that included one Gerard Healy. But all those plans went awry when Edi-Aspendale knocked us out of the flag race. I never played another game of footy.

At the start of 1979, I went to London to work and stayed there for eighteen months. I kept in touch with the VFL results, but didn't touch a ball the whole time I was away. In fact, I didn't kick a footy again for about fifteen years—and that was a tiny ball with my young son, Jack. He's now almost sixteen and, out on the street, I entertain him and my other boy, Harry, by doing dropkicks. They may be able to perform tricks on their skateboards and rollerblades, but however hard they try, they just can't nail droppies! I love watching them both play and wonder how football will treat them. Will it give them the same rush then crush that it gave me? Will they have the commitment to endure the training and the injuries with so many more distractions? I know one thing: they will position themselves two or three metres in front of the pack when a teammate has a set shot for goal from within range. The mongrel punt is alive and well in under-age footy. If I'd done the same for Breeney's kick on 2 August 1975, I may have played more than one game!

JACK CLANCY

The Game That Never Was

Jack Clancy was born in 1934 and grew up in the Melbourne suburb of Brighton. He founded the Royal Melbourne Institute of Technology's Media Studies course and retired from that institution as Associate Professor of Communications. He's been called the ultimate Coodabeen Champion—the bloke who played league football without actually playing league football. But he's there in the record books: J.Clancy, Fitzroy, 1 game. It's the briefest but most talked about aspect of a long and notable football career spent mainly in the VAFA—as player, coach, selector, administrator and long-time supporter. He was named in the University Reds' team of the century. Jack also played cricket until well into his fifties—in the Victorian Junior Cricket Association (now the Victorian Turf Cricket Association), with the Parkville People's XI and in Melbourne's traditional *Meanjin* v *Overland* and Writers v Artists matches. He wrote this essay for *The Greatest Game* by Ross Fitzgerald and Ken Spillman (eds., 1988).

The first approach was from Footscray. A letter with the impressive red, white and blue letterhead at the top, and at the bottom the signature of the great Charlie Sutton.

It was immensely flattering, but Footscray was on the wrong side of town for me, geographically that is, and anyway I didn't really believe it. I'd only just started to develop the habit of getting a kick with the local church side, and for someone who had only begun playing competition football at the age of nineteen and a half, dreams of League glory seemed a long way from reality.

I'd always been obsessed by football and cricket. There were no other sports, no other activities even worth thinking about. They were the

242

reality; except that they existed in a world of unreality, of daydream. I did all those things that kids did in pre-television, pre-rock days. There was the paper footy (newspaper rolled up tightly to a catchable size and bound with a tough bootlace), the sock footy (an old sock stuffed with other old socks and bound with garter elastic), sometimes the rare joy of a real footy—which, unlike those two primitive imitations, had the enormous advantage of bouncing, so that if you didn't grab the mark in the endless duels of kick-to-kick, you could run and chase it, and pick up a kick when more skilled playmates couldn't be bothered.

But childhood footy was also a solitary pastime. If you had no one to play with, you created a game in your own imagination, kicking the footy (imitation or real) up in the air far enough away to force yourself to run for it, often to fall sprawling—at the cost of dirty or cut knees and elbows and grubbied clothes, which won you no credit from a harassed mother of nine.

An important part of this solitary performance was the structure of the world of the real 'big league' you superimposed on it. As you ran, you gave a running commentary, using the jargon picked up from radio broadcasters like Mel Morris. It is still possible to hear kids do this, for it has the great advantage of allowing you to live in a fantasy world and a reality world at the same time.

There were other versions of fantasy. There were 'pickup' matches with teams of anything from four to five to twelve a side, where each player would take the identity of a hero from the real world, such identities carefully bestowed according to the status of the individual in the group, and his ability as a player. The cricket versions were more elaborate. The solitary performance consisted of throwing a ball against the wall and then batting to it, with specific points in the backyard having specific scoring value; team versions could be any variation on this. The common factor was the fantasy element, with Australian and England test teams set down rigorously in batting order. Sir Don would have been surprised at the number of low scores he was credited with, and parents expressed puzzled irritation that the work on these meticulously kept scoresheets was always of finer quality than the hastily done homework that followed them.

Fantasy recedes as we age, and stern reality is supposed to preoccupy us. In my case, the fantasies of religion were receding by the age of nineteen and a half and being replaced with important matters such as books and Beethoven and films. And a delayed adolescence meant that I now found myself, greatly to my own and everyone else's surprise, to be almost six feet three inches tall. I'd always been too small and too slow to even fantasise about being in the school side. Reality was too close to allow thoughts of participating in a formidable team that included at least six members later to play League football.

So a season in the local church team was an introduction to the excitements, joys and disappointments of competition football. Regular training on Tuesdays and Thursdays, the furniture van converted to football bus for away games, the steady learning of the skills of ruckwork, the banalities and clichés of the coach's speech, similar to a hundred such speeches delivered by a hundred coaches at the same hour early on Saturday afternoon, the happy cameraderie of after-game beer drinking where conventions of mutual flattery and consolation cast a rosy glow on the afternoon's proceedings, the recovery Catholic Hour session at the club rooms after Sunday Mass, where the often hungover heroes of Saturday had special status among the young ladies of the parish; all these were part of the innocent ockerism of those fifties days, which doesn't meet the standards of today's changed values. Even the frequent impromptu singing sessions late on Saturday nights ('We were rough and ready guys, but, oh, how we could harmonise... ') were joyful male celebrations among a group of twenty-five, almost everyone a bachelor, and with ages ranging from seventeen to thirty-four. It was only the following year that I found that 'wedding bells were breaking up that old gang of mine' and reality remorselessly imposed itself on nostalgic fantasy.

But, by then, after losing the Grand Final by five points, I had made a decision to move up. It was only during the inevitable ritual of the drowning of the sorrows on that Grand Final night that one of my teammates broke to me the story of the coach's instruction about me. The coach, in most respects neither a brilliant tactician nor an outstanding psychologist, had observed that I started very slowly 'as if he's daydreaming' and that my daydreaming trance had been broken early in one game by an opponent's smartly delivered whack on the left earhole. He decided that if the opposition couldn't supply this salutary summons to reality, my team must do so. One player was therefore deputed to join in a ruck duel and make me, rather than the ball, his object. The player so deputed was the one now telling me the story; he was apologetic, even troubled, as he said, 'I didn't whack you too hard, and you've got to admit it worked.'

Now in my last year as a student, I would try the amateurs. Melbourne University had two clubs in the top grade, University Blacks and University Blues, and new players were allocated according to the needs of the two teams. After some fierce argument, I was later informed, I was allocated to the Blacks, since I had apparently impressed the trainers during practice games, and I looked forward to the first game against Old Melburnians. I knew nothing about them except that they were all old boys of Melbourne Grammar School. I therefore felt quite justified in an attitude of total hostility towards them, despite the contradictory fact that, of the Blacks side, of which I was a part, at least half were former public school boys.

Before selection on Thursday night, and throughout Friday and even into Saturday morning, my head was filled with anticipatory fantasies of great and glorious deeds. I would be the best ruckman on the ground, take soaring marks, and kick several goals.

Reality was somewhat different. I found it hard to get a touch, let alone a kick, and learned more in that one afternoon about the noble art of ruckwork than I had picked up in all the previous season. The teacher was a bald veteran with years of experience who anticipated and overcame my every effort, and who also had the good grace to tell me after the game that I had a lot of potential, but a lot of learning to do.

The difference in standard was a shock. I realised that very few players from my previous team would have survived at this level, and that I had some work to do if I were to stay alive in it. If I think about what motivated me at that time, I realise that every young player's dream of becoming a VFL star had nothing to do with it. The fun, the challenge, the feeling of physical well-being and developing athletic skill, the friendship—mateship if you like—all these were part of it. Most of all—and I suspect this is part of every athletic endeavour—there was the double bonus to be gained from a good performance. Part of this was the sense of satisfaction that comes from the self, derived from pushing oneself hard and succeeding, and this is particularly strong in a game as physically exhilarating as Australian football. The other element of the reward was praise—from one's fellow-players, from supporters, even perhaps from umpires and, very rarely, from a loving but sceptical father.

Two intensely enjoyable years with the Blacks brought developing skills and confidence, even some minor honours, and, at the age of twenty-two, another invitation, this time from Fitzroy. The pangs of departure were, if anything, stronger than before, but the extraordinary prospect of League football was irresistible.

In 1957 VFL players were subjected to only a fraction of the training regimen demanded today. A couple of months sufficed for pre-season preparation, although there were a number of players who had done their own fitness work before that, so that their practice match form would be ahead of their competitors, and they would win a spot in that all-important first game. Still, the training presented a different dimension from anything I'd ever encountered.

The coach was Bill Stephen, a fine player, admired and respected as a man, and one of the last playing coaches in the League. On the night when 'real' training began—which was, for me, when the footballs were brought out—he began his address to the sixty or so veterans and hopefuls by holding a brand new football in the air. 'This,' he said, 'is a football,' and then exhorted us to do as he had done. 'Handle it every day, pass it from left hand to right, go to bed with it, wake up with it. Let it be the first thing you handle in the morning.' The occasional sniggers from the experienced or the insensitive died away in the solemnity of the occasion.

And it was at this point, I believe, that my sense of reality clashed with the world I was now in the middle of. All this seemed obsessive, slightly absurd; the rational mind started to have its doubts. The element of competitiveness was now something to come to terms with. It had a depth and fierceness that shouldn't have been a surprise, but for someone going on twenty-three, young in football knowledge, and aware only that the game was essentially enjoyment and fun, it was a new reality.

Two incidents during the practice match period brought it home to me. One was a flare-up between two established players, Brian Pert and Vin Williams, during one intra-club match; punches were willingly exchanged in front of the grandstand before teammates and trainers separated them. They were competing for a wing position, with two other keen competitors, Ian Aston and Leo Smythe going just as hard on the other side of the ground.

Even more enlightening was a revelation by the great Alan Gale—barely an inch over six feet tall, but possibly the best ruckman in the League at the time. Over a post-match drink, Butch claimed that he regarded me, and anyone around six feet three or over, as a threat to his position. The very idea was as much a shock as seeing two teammates exchange punches in a practice match. It should have taught me something about the realities of football at the top competitive level.

For all that, my form in the practice games, all intra-club, was good enough to win some encouraging forecasts in the club and in the press, although in the second last of those games, it was helped in an unusual way. I'd had barely a touch by late in the first quarter, and the umpire (Harry Beitzel, I seem to recall, and bless him if it was) asked as I trotted back to the centre after a goal was scored, 'How's it going, son?'

'Can't get a touch,' I replied.

'Well stand back from the centre at the next bounce,' he said.

I did so, whereupon he bounced the footy, beautifully angling it so that it lobbed over the contending ruckmen's heads and into my arms. I turned, ran a few paces and thumped the ball forward for a clear goal. As I trotted back to the centre, he said, 'Good effort, son! From here on, you're on your own.'

It was a generous gesture, harmless in an intra-club match, and it set me on the road to a good performance in the game and probable selection in the first game of the season.

Perhaps I wouldn't have been the most popular choice. I was still coming to terms with the quite different culture of the dressing rooms and the club, from communal baths, with their opportunities for broad sexual humour, to the presence of the press doting on the stars—Gale, Murray, Abrahams, Ongarello. There was the close-knit camaraderie of the youngsters up from Len Smith's Under 19s and the political tensions that exist in any football club, complicated by vestiges of the absurd old Catholics versus Masons bitterness.

I had received my jumper, Number 38, after the final training list was announced, and the reality of League football was coming closer. Speculation about the composition of the first team continued throughout the week, with plenty of supporters and trainers assuring me that I would be in the eighteen to play mighty Melbourne, premiers for the last two years. As it turned out, selection in the first game was assured, so I was later told, until a new element appeared late on the scene in the person of one John 'Mulga' Shelton. Mulga was a country boy from Gippsland, tough as his nickname, and guaranteed, or so I heard, the first three games.

But I made the twenty, just. I was twentieth man, not interchange, for there was no such thing then. You had to hope for injuries. There was still the extraordinary thrill of seeing your name there in the paper on Friday morning underlined as one of the League's new players. There was the immense excitement of Friday and Saturday morning, and the even greater excitement among my family. Such glorious possibilities had never really been considered; it was as sudden for them as for me. It seemed like reality.

Then there was Saturday afternoon, and the game itself. Brunswick Street was packed, which meant perhaps 25,000 people, and the atmosphere, unfamiliar to me, of a League game was dizzying. The coach's address didn't reach me, although in my limited football experience so far I'd often been stirred by emotional appeals. I seem to remember the appeal to class from Bill Stephen, who painted Melbourne as the silvertails, Fitzroy as the honest working class battlers. As one of nine children whose father was still a labourer on the basic wage, but also as an honours graduate from Melbourne University, I probably found that appeal left me somewhere in between.

Did I run out with the eighteen? I don't think so. I remember them charging down the race, while the two reserves, Graham Gotch and I, followed at a walk. We were in dressing gowns, for tracksuits, like interchange rules, hadn't arrived in 1957. There was one injury, and Graham went on, and the game was close, and there was no chance for even that last minute call to action.

Then it was over, and we'd beaten mighty Melbourne—with, I have to say, a lot of help from 'Mulga', who played like a man inspired or demented. I don't remember feeling particularly deprived or disappointed. We had won, and the world was in front of me, and of the club. One friendly trainer, at the rub-down on the following Tuesday, told me what I knew then. 'Well, son, you haven't quite played League football yet, but you're going to. You can be sure of that.'

But I didn't.

Six weeks in the seconds, most of them with a mention in the best six players, was almost reward enough. Played on the opposite ground to the seniors then, before a bare handful of spectators, it was still a learning experience, and the Big Time was never as close as it seemed. I became aware, as naivety started to drop away, how fierce was the desire of my teammates. I got to know the levels of cynicism, desperation and idealism that were part of those earnest strivers.

Perhaps it was just at the time I was ready that the worst possibility became the reality. A knee injury against Collingwood (another reason for disliking them) came at the same time as a disastrous loss for the seniors. I would have been in next week. I could have been a contender.

There was the cartilage operation early the following year, a quick (for those days) return to football, some hopes that I might yet make it— then the end, with brutal abruptness, when the secretary came out to the training track, pulled me aside and said, 'You'll train Mondays and Wednesdays from now on.'

League football surely has a thousand stories like that. Some players make it; some don't. Perhaps I never really believed it. But there it is in

Fitzroy Football Club's centenary history, 'Clancy, John—1 game.'

The game that never was.

The postscript is the 200 games at various junior levels. I'd have played forever if I could have because I loved it. League football is great, but it isn't everything.

Footy is.

FRANK HARDY

Footy Fever in Chinkapook

Frank Hardy (1917–1994) left school at fourteen but went on to become a successful writer of short fiction, novels and plays. His best known novel is *Power Without Glory* (1950), controversially based on the life of Melbourne businessman John Wren and set in the fictitious Melbourne suburb of Carringbush (Collingwood). *Power Without Glory* found a new audience with its screening as a miniseries by ABC TV in 1976. A lifelong political activist, Hardy assisted the Gurindji people in the Gurindji strike in the mid to late 1960s and brought the plight of Aboriginal Australians to international attention with his book *The Unlucky Australians* (1968). 'Footy Fever in Chinkapook' first appeared in *Hardy's People* (1987).

I'm an Aussie Rules man myself. There I was at the Fitzroy–St Kilda match early in the season thinking, What's happened to the Lions? At half-time, they looked like losing to St Kilda.

Before I go any further I must let you in on one of the dark secrets of my life: I don't barrack for Carringbush (for that read Collingwood). I became a Fitzroy supporter when I was four, for reasons I can't remember. I tried to switch to Collingwood in 1951, after I'd immortalised it in *Power Without Glory*, but found that football is like religion: you can't change from the church you're brought up in.

And who should interrupt my thoughts that day at the football? You've guessed it! Truthful Jones himself!

Truthful sat down beside me, complete with Esky, a woollen cap, the *Football Record* and all the other paraphernalia appropriate to the occasion.

'Goodday,' said Truthful.

'What are you doin' here?' I replied. 'Thought you were a Rugby man.'

'I'm a supporter of all codes—Aussies Rules, soccer, League and Union. Can't wear that Yankee Gridiron they bung on Channel Nine... no skill in it—the brainless against the muscle-bound, if you ask me.'

Truthful gave me a sly look, and asked, 'What are you doin' here? Thought you were a Collingwood barracker.'

After I'd explained it was a question of religion, Truthful bought me a drink for the first time in his life! He pulled two tinnies out of his Esky, opened them and gave me one. 'Get that into your black guts,' he demanded.

And I said, 'What? Are you sick or something?'

'No, you need a drink. You spend a lot of time in Collingwood— pardon, Carringbush—and barrack for Fitzroy. You're not only Frank and Hardy but foolish as well. You need a beer.'

I took a sip, and Truthful continued, 'Those Carringbush supporters are a mad lot. Did I ever tell you about the Collingwood barracker who went to see his team in a semi-final—on his wedding anniversary?'

'No, did he take his wife?'

'No, she supported a women's hockey team—wasn't interested in football. But she was a great celebrator. She made a big affair out of birthdays, Mothers' Days, Fathers' Days, Christmases and New Years. But her specialty was their wedding anniversary. Always turned it on— roast dinner by candlelight, champagne, and a bit of nooky chucked in—without fail.'

'Must have been quite a lady...'

'Was she ever—would have been a feminist except for her love of the old tossle which grew between the legs of her football fanatic husband. 'Celebration Clara' was her name. Anyway, this day she gave her husband—he was called 'Fanatical Fred'—a big kiss before he left for the footie and made all sorts of sexual suggestions: a tiger in the sack was the old Clara! Fred went off rubbing his hands with glee, saying: 'Collingwood will win, no worries—and I'm on a promise from Clara!"

'Would have been quite a night,' I commented.

'Clara was really ready to celebrate in a low-cut negligee. But when Fanatical Fred came home he refused a drink; he even refused to respond to her kisses. He went to bed without eating a mouthful, pulled the covers over his head and went straight to sleep. Collingwood had got beaten by ten goals!'

'Yes,' I said. 'They take their football seriously in Carringbush, all right.'

'Not as seriously as in Chinkapook.'

'Where?'

'Chinkapook! A town in the Mallee. Did I ever tell you about the violinist from Chinkapook who wanted to be a League footballer? Funny thing about Victoria, young fellas don't want to be doctors or musicians or engine drivers; they want to be League footballers.'

At that moment, the Roys ran out on to the field followed by the St Kilda team, and I managed to shut Truthful up.

After Fitzroy got beaten by some miracle, Truthful managed to drag me to a nearby pub. He went back to his yarn.

'This bloke from Chinkapook could play the fiddle nearly as good as Yehudi Menuhin, but he didn't practise much because he wanted to be a League footballer. Lanky fella he was. Worst footballer in the district but a real good kick. Trouble was, he couldn't get the ball to kick it. Played a few games in the local team but never got a kick, so they dropped him. But he kept comin' to practice Tuesdays and Thursdays. Well, one day the captain of the Chinkapook Football Club got a brainwave. He said to the selection committee, 'Give this bloke another trial. Put him in the goals. Full back. He'll kick to the centre every time the other team scores a behind.' Selection committee put him in as full back.

'The violinist never touched the ball until the last quarter. The other team kicked sixteen goals straight without a behind, and Chinkapook were fourteen goals, seven behinds. Needed a goal to win with a few minutes to go. Well, this violinist bloke is standing on his own in the goals. Someone kicks the ball, and it hits him in the face. He grabs it and runs for his life around the wing, where there's no players, his legs flailing like a windmill in a high wind. Bouncing the ball every few metres, he was. Frightened as a sparrow locked in a barn.

'Well, he ran like a cartwheel without a rim, right up to the forward line, about fifty metres out. Easy for him from there. He was just going to kick one of his mighty punts on the run when the final bell rang. He never got another game after that.'

At this point, I asked Truthful, 'I suppose he went back to the fiddle and became a world famous violinist?'

'No,' Truthful replied. 'Last I heard of him he had sold his violin and was running an SP book in Mildura.'

ROGER FRANKLIN

Sons of the 'Scray

Roger Franklin was wrapped in the red, white and blue as an infant and neither time nor distance has diminished his faith in the Bulldog breed. The author of *The Defender: The Story of General Dynamics*, a celebrated expose of waste, fraud and abuse in the Pentagon, he returned to Australia after 25 years in the US, where he was a senior editor at *The New York Post*, *Time* and *BusinessWeek*. His Australian books include *Inferno: The Day Victoria Burned* and, most recently, *Fev Unauthorised*, a biography of the AFL's very own answer to Lord Byron (as in a genius that's 'bad, mad and dangerous to know'). Franklin now edits *Quadrant Online* and is completing his next book, a political history of Victoria's High Country that will detail the ongoing clash between environmental theorists and the practical wisdom of Indigenous land-management techniques and generations of mountain cattlemen. It will be released by The Slattery Media Group in 2014. When not tickling the keyboard, Franklin is an object of ridicule among High Country trout. This essay first appeared in *Grand Finals Volume II: 1939-1978* (The Slattery Media Group, 2012).

S ure, 1954 was the big one, the year everything came together, but what happened at the MCG on that last Saturday in September was only the half of it. If you want to know why Footscray's first, and still its only, flag was such a big deal, why a thinning cadre of old timers still talk about it in tones not far removed from awe, you need to go even further back—to 1924, when a suburb at the wrong end of Dynon Road was feeling its oats.

The Great Depression: who saw it coming? Certainly not Footscray's city fathers, who were just starting to think their municipality's luck had changed, and finally for the better. If one of the early notions of Melbourne had come to pass, the CBD would have been just down the road at Williamstown, making Footscray an inner suburb. Instead, the West's ambitions were paved over with abattoirs, glue factories and industries so on-the-nose that calling them noxious would have been to pay a compliment. Instead of the stately terraces and public gardens of the inner city, Footscray's lot was mean cottages and tall chimneys. Sure, the same could be said of Richmond and Collingwood, but those equally malodorous locales at least boasted the distinction of being on the road to somewhere nicer. Beyond Footscray there was what? Scotch thistles, salt pans and the Werribee sewerage farm.

It wasn't that things were bad in Footscray, just that they had never been terribly good, so the relative prosperity of the mid-1920s struck many as something worth celebrating. Footscray should assert itself, letters to the local rags insisted, demonstrate that there was a bit more to the place than stink and struggle. It was nothing short of a disgrace, one councillor thundered, to see the municipality make do with a town hall which should have been 'condemned and demolished' long ago: he wondered what impression the dilapidated pile made on visitors 'from the other side'. It was a rhetorical question, as all of Footscray knew what the rest of Melbourne thought and it wasn't much, not much at all. By unanimous consent the council voted to commission plans for a new town hall. When the work was done, visitors welcomed by a vista of municipal progress would know not only that they had arrived, so had their destination.

Public buildings? Terrific! But this being Melbourne, there was never any question that an up-and-coming suburb also deserved a football team of the first rank, and the Bulldogs had been repeatedly denied that status. In the Victorian Football Association they were without peer, romping premiers in each of the previous five years. But that was VFA, and sentiment held that the club, like its suburb, could get no respect. Three times the Bulldogs petitioned the VFL to let them in, and three times those pleas were rejected. Uppity? If that was the impression, it was perhaps understandable. Some still remembered when the old queen was on her throne and the club swapped its team name for something fancier. Taking the field as the Prince Imperials, however, didn't quite cut it. The club went broke and had to be bailed out by the council, and reverted to being known as the Tricolours. Another dream come to nought beside the Maribyrnong.

Dogged persistence, though, was the dominant streak at Western Reserve, as Whitten Oval was then known. Every year after the VFA Grand Final, the Association would call on the League to pit its premier against theirs, but the only result was an annual clash of frustration with contempt. As the *Argus* commented, the League 'made aloofness its policy' and would probably have continued in this vein had it not been for a most unlikely catalyst: Dame Nellie Melba. In 1924, when the League once again rejected a post-season game to determine 'the champion of Victoria', the diva was moved to protest. How could able-bodied men refuse to stage a spectacle whose proceeds might do so much to help limbless Diggers, she wondered? The League shrugged, Melba raised the volume and in less than forty-eight hours it was agreed that Footscray would play Essendon the following week at the MCG, a game both the Dons and League previewed as an imposition, a curiosity and, of course, a mere formality. Who could doubt the boys from the more refined precincts of Windy Hill would remind both Footscray and the Association that it was folly to harbour ambitions above one's station?

Footscray took the field with more than its own hopes riding on the result. North Melbourne and Hawthorn were equally keen to step up to the League, their many overtures having also met with curt dismissals. If the Tricolours—the Bulldogs name was not officially adopted until 1938—could pull it off, the case for admission would be impossible to deny. 'Never before has there been such interest in the respective merits of the rival premiers,' the *Argus* noted, 'and though the latest swing of the League pendulum seems to be in the direction of the non-inclusion of Footscray, there is still a keen desire to see how they will fare against the League premiers.'

A crowd just shy of 50,000 turned out to witness not just a game but one of those exquisite football moments, the kind when scoreboard and siren confirm that Divine justice can still order the affairs of men. On that day, 4 October 1924, the Great Umpire's throne was draped in the red, white and blue of the team that the morning papers gave no chance at all. Turn out to admire Bulldog pluck and support a worthy charity, the pundits advised, but do not expect a contest. The *Argus'* correspondent 'Old Boy' was blunt: 'No one, I think, really expects them to win save their own special supporters.' By the final change, such predictions had been rendered laughable, and something akin to shock 'settled over observers whose sympathies were writ in black and red'. Footscray had started slowly and trailed at quarter-time, but carried the day by twenty-eight points, almost doubling the Dons' score.

In Footscray, Yarraville, Tottenham, Spotswood, right throughout the west, a delirium began to spread, one that would last the best part of a month before the eruption of dinners and public meetings began to subside. The first to make it home from Jolimont were met at their stations by friends and families demanding accounts of the wonderful feat. At midnight a vast and jubilant throng still surged at Western Reserve, every sighting of a player prompting knots of hand-shakers and backslappers and demands to hear once again how Essendon's 'mosquito fleet' was swatted.

At Windy Hill the mood was poisonous at every level. In the change room and later in pubs, there were punches as teammates accused teammates of taking bribes to throw the game. There was even a whisper, quickly denied, of one Don whose reward for lying down was a new car waiting in the driveway. Officially, Essendon's attitude was dismissive. It was a charity game signifying nothing. We didn't win—big deal.

But it *was* a big deal, a very big deal. That 'swing of the League pendulum' against Footscray's inclusion was stopped cold, seized by public opinion, editorial writers, even members of parliament, and flung back very hard at the League, which heard all its former excuses for rejecting Association applicants howled down. Association grounds not up to snuff? They could be fixed. Recruiting boundaries too hard to adjust? Nonsense! What was so difficult about drawing fresh lines on a map? The clamour for reform grew louder, potentially threatening the League's dominance of the game. Why shouldn't football adopt a system akin to English soccer's, with divisions, promotions and relegations?

Why not a unified governing body with the League, Association and bush clubs all having an equal say? Throughout the week that followed Footscray's triumph, talk of reform and rebellion filled the papers. It was stopped cold by a strategic leak on Friday. The invitation to Footscray was in the mail, the League let it be known, likewise to North Melbourne and Hawthorn. A cynic might have discerned a defensive strategy. If so, it worked. Calls for a unified, multi-tiered competition subsided as talk switched to anticipation of the next season's twelve team competition. The League had given a little in order not to lose a lot.

In Footscray perhaps only the Second Coming could have generated a greater rapture. Every night for weeks, public meetings in rented cinemas and halls acclaimed the winners, who were awarded commemorative medals and substantial cash gifts underwritten by local businessmen. A local paper joked that no Footscray player would ever again need to buy shoes, as they were carried everywhere shoulder-high. The only regret to be heard above the cheers was the sad state of the town hall, too small to accommodate such crowds and joy. But that would change, as everything would change, when the council had a town hall worthy of its dignity and a premiership flag flew above the home team's ground. As something like a quarter of the councillors were also committee men, the nexus of football and civic pride was a given. Who could doubt the Champions of Victoria were poised to add a VFL premiership to their laurels? Who could doubt it would be another milestone in the rise of the West.

Now turn the clock forward through three decades not of triumph and acclaim but of crushing disappointment. Those hopes that Footscray would be the League's new broom? They were ground down through years of frustration. It was not until 1938 that the Bulldogs made the top four for the first time, and the club's fortunes mirrored its location. No sooner had the council ordered work to begin on its fine, new town hall than the Great Depression scoured the west of jobs and hope. Come the war, the Bulldogs would not even keep their own ground. Western Oval was requisitioned as an army camp and the club was booted down Williamstown Road to Yarraville, an Association ground so down-at-heel that many spectators dispensed with the need for tickets and slipped through holes in the fence. That the host team went by name of the Villains did little to lift the ambience.

After the war, hope of the long-awaited redemption flared again. Between 1945 and 1954, the Bulldogs made the finals five times, only to see their form evaporate at the deep end of the season. Take 1953, when round five saw them come within ten minutes of becoming the first club to keep an opponent scoreless, finally denying a hapless Fitzroy all but a single goal. Credit for that went to what was widely regarded as the best and toughest defence in the League. It was also the year the Dogs finally broke their September drought, chalking up a first semi-final win after a hard-fought clash with Essendon. Then they met Geelong in the preliminary final and led convincingly until half-time, only to collapse in a shambles of missed passes and blown goals.

Barracking for the Bulldogs has always demanded a certain unique perspective. A good clubman will look into a room packed with manure and know, just know, that there must be a lovely pony in there somewhere. And so it was at the conclusion of the 1953 season, when auspicious omens tempered September's disappointment. The team was one of the youngest in the competition, average age just twenty-two. There was so much promise—the young Ted Whitten for starters, plus a full-forward in Jack Collins whom true believers saw as a rising rival to Essendon's John Coleman. The appraisal was truer than they knew. Coleman would suffer a career-ending injury in 1954, ceding the top scorer's spot to Collins. Then there was Peter Box, a future Brownlow winner; the dashing Roger Duffy; the rock-like Ron Stockman across half-forward; and captain-coach Charlie Sutton. Finishing third didn't earn commemorative medals or shoulder rides down Hopkins Street, but the leap from 1952's tenth place was some sort of consolation. Sutton was shaping his kids into contenders. Next year, insisted that obligatory Footscray optimism, they would give it a hell of a shake.

It didn't start that way, not at all. The opening round saw the Dogs go down to St Kilda in a comedy of errors. It wasn't that the Saints played well, just that Footscray was worse. There were no surprises about St Kilda's ineptitude—it had won only five games in the previous season and would take 1954's wooden spoon—but the Bulldogs? They were a rabble. Next Saturday, when the Dogs were done by Richmond to the tune of eighteen points, the talk was of a season's hopes already dashed. But then, in the third week, something clicked. The Dogs thrashed South Melbourne, pulled off a squeaker against Carlton and rolled North Melbourne, Essendon, Hawthorn and Fitzroy. Overall, it was by no means a great season—eleven wins and a draw at the end of eighteen rounds—and the slumps said little that was good about consistency. Still, the tally was enough to secure second place on percentage over the Kangaroos. Geelong was six points clear and undisputed flag favourite, while Melbourne slipped into the final berth.

Punters and pundits, everyone liked Geelong. As it turned out, everyone was wrong. But the Cats had cruelled Footscray's hopes in the 1953 series and came within an ace of doing so again in the second semi-final. As usual, it was the Bulldogs' inconsistency that cast the matter into doubt. They floundered in the first quarter, surged ahead in the second, managed only three points in the third to tie the score at the last change, and then caught fire once again in the fourth. All through the season, barrackers had never been sure which Footscray team would turn up, the well-oiled machine or the duffers who were easy work, even for the lowly Saints. The following weekend an increasingly cocky Melbourne, fresh from dispatching North Melbourne, sent the Cats home to Corio. So it came down to the Demons and Dogs, the big question being Charlie Sutton's fitness. He had missed the Geelong game with a knee injury and remained a dubious proposition right up to Thursday, when the teams were announced. At the final training session, watched by a crowd of 7000, Sutton seemed to be hanging back. And what to make of the backman's decision to play in the forward pocket? Did it have something to do with his crook knee or was there a deeper motive? In and around Footscray the only certainty was that Melbourne needed to be watched. It was common knowledge, an old-timer commented years later and still with undiminished venom, that many doctors played for Melbourne and knew just how and where to hurt a bloke.

What Melbourne thought of Footscray, there was no secret about that, not after coach Norm Smith—coaching in his first finals series—laid out his logic. His team had beaten Geelong in the wet by seventeen points while the Dogs managed only a 23-point victory against the same team under ideal conditions. If the Dogs could not see the statistical inevitability of their coming defeat, he told the press, his boys would explain it on Saturday. That was the first of Smith's offensives in the psychological war he waged right up until the teams took the field under a peerless spring sky. As the Bulldogs cooled their heels on the ground and the umpires waited, Smith kept his charges in their rooms for a full five minutes after the scheduled first bounce—which Melbourne tapped, booted, marked and put straight through the goal posts. After three decades of dreams and disappointment, surely it would take more than Smith's petty gamesmanship to count the Bulldogs out?

The answer came within seconds. Galvanised by Melbourne's opening blitz, the Dogs came to life. There would be no quarter for Melbourne after that. With a sustained and overpowering brilliance seen fleetingly throughout the checkered home and away season, the young Bulldogs played the game of their lives. Nothing Smith tried could foil the massacre. When Ron Barassi and John Beckwith each took a shot at Sutton, both Melbourne players came off second best.

The strategy behind Sutton's move to the forward zone also became apparent. The Dogs had demonstrated a tendency to clump and bunch, hampering their own movements and generating large packs rising for long kicks. Sutton realised he needed to be there, a roving, bellowing field marshal to keep the forward line open and fluid. Full-forward Collins had the speed to outpace opponent Lance Arnold—an opinion voiced often by fullback Herb Henderson, who played against him in Mildura, their hometown. If Sutton and Henderson were calling it right, Collins would be out in front, setting up leads and snapping up low, fast, grass-burning stab passes from the likes of Roger Duffy and, indeed, Sutton himself. There was another advantage: infamous for his muscular temper, Collins would be less likely to give away free kicks if Sutton could steer him clear of packs. Keep the game open, keep it fast, smother every nascent Demon drive before it could reach the centre line—that was Sutton's playbook, and it worked to perfection. At the first change, the Dogs were 6.3 to 1.4.

Nothing Smith tried could turn the tide. Against North Melbourne and Geelong, his boys had surged in the second term to sweep their opponents aside with speed and muscle. Sutton was ready for that tack; so, too, Whitten and the entire Dogs backline. The scoreboard said Melbourne won the quarter, having added three goals to the Dogs' two. At the centre bounces, ruckman Denis Cordner dominated, while wingman Ian McLean and captain Geoff Collins launched repeated drives, but most of Melbourne's heroics came to nothing and they could not sustain such a frenzied, all-out assault. Observers noted that the team looked weary, almost spent, as it left field at half-time, and their spirits would have been no less bruised by an inexplicable lapse of judgment by Arnold, who took a fine saving mark in the goal square with just minutes on the clock and decided, against all logic, to play on. A lurking Sutton ploughed him into the turf with a tackle that left the defender visibly wobbly, and then nailed the first of what would be three goals by day's end.

After that, Melbourne's lost cause was apparent to all but Smith, who tried a slather of positional changes to no avail. Ruckman Cordner repeatedly saw Dogs midfielders, especially rover John Kerr, make off with the fruits of his hard work. By three-quarter time, the Bulldogs led by thirty-eight points, and in the final quarter they did pretty much as they pleased, subject only to Sutton's shouted orders.

Sutton had warned his team at every change not to respond in kind to Melbourne's frequent provocations. Half-back flanker Alan Martin copped a punch that broke his nose, and Box was dropped behind the play in what a local rag termed 'a very cowardly way'. The umpires missed both these incidents and numerous others, but the omniscient Sutton, who would follow the ball for brief periods to visit and adjust his defenders, continued to stress that the best response was more goals. The lower Melbourne stooped, Collins would recall Sutton shouting, the more certain a Footscray triumph.

Triumph, though, is probably not the right word. Slaughter, dismemberment, humiliation—these come closer, but still cannot capture what the scoreboard proclaimed as the final siren sent the crowd surging onto the field:

FOOTSCRAY:	15.12 (102)
MELBOURNE:	7.9 (51)

Sutton had been telling his men they were twice as good as Melbourne, and the scoreboard confirmed it to the last digit.

These days, getting on for sixty years after the Bulldogs finally wrapped a flag about Footscray's long-thwarted hopes, there is much in the brittle and yellowing newspaper clippings that can only strike followers of the modern game as strange, almost like news from a parallel universe. Then and now, the local papers brought out special editions with adulatory profiles of all the day's stars, but what surprises the modern reader is the Dogs' deep connections to the suburb whose honour they championed. A market gardener, plumbers, a couple of carpenters, storemen and a butcher—the Bulldogs of '54 were blokes that people on the spectators' side of the fence saw often and many knew personally. Today, when the League's guns complain of being hassled and provoked at nightclubs and bars, who can imagine an AFL player doing anything but playing footy? The marketers and business managers swear it is the way football had to go. A billion-dollar business cannot be left to tradies playing for nothing more than love and a few notes a week.

Much as you might detest it, there is no point arguing with progress because it will never listen. That said, there is a modern deficit no balance sheet can show—a loss in the vanished sense of place and identity that filled Footscray's streets on that night of wonder. One supporter, heavy with child, drifted with her mum and sister into the throng from their home near Yarraville station, not quite knowing where they were going, revelling in the celebrations and many shouted choruses of 'Sons of the 'Scray'. Eventually they found themselves outside Footscray's elegant new town hall, built at last and just as imposing a building as those ambitious councillors of 1924 had intended. There was no reason to be there, not really. No celebrations were in progress, nor had any been planned. But they were not alone, not by a long shot. Scores of others were there as well, none quite knowing why but also feeling no need to explain themselves.

As that mum-to-be put it many decades later, while rummaging in a cupboard for the treasure trove of premiership mementos she had promised to let this writer study, it was much, much more than a splendid victory. 'It was about us, about all of Footscray—the Depression, the war, everything we had been through... In all my life I have never been so happy. That night, we all just glowed. There was nothing that wasn't possible.' Three months afterward, she gave birth to her first child, named Roger in honour of that dashing Doggie hero, Roger Duffy.

Thanks, Mum, for raising me a Bulldog. We'll see our second flag soon. Don't lose the faith.

BASIL ZEMPILAS

Saturdays with Uncle Paull

Basil Zempilas was born in 1971 and attended schools in Perth before graduating from Murdoch University with a degree in media and mass communications. He played for West Perth in the WAFL before the blossoming of a career as a television and radio presenter. In 1996 Zempilas was named 'Best Television Personality' at the West Australian Football Commission media awards, and from 1996 to 2001 he was weekend sports anchor for *Seven News*. The following year, he hosted *Basil's Footy Show* and the Seven Network's coverage of the World Aquatic Championships. Since then he has been part of Australia's media team at both summer and winter Olympics, famously calling Steven Bradbury's speed skating gold medal in 2002, and has hosted Seven's telecast of the Australian Open tennis. Since 2012, Zempilas has also been a key part of Seven's AFL coverage. He wrote 'Saturdays with Uncle Paull' especially for this collection.

I t was always the best, most exciting part of my week. And how I looked forward to it. At 12.30 on a Saturday afternoon, the horn would beep. Like clockwork, he was. My Uncle Paull Zempilas idling out the front, ready to take me to the footy. 'See you mum, Uncle Paull's here, I'm off'.

I felt like a king being driven through the gates at Leederville Oval. Membership had its privileges and my Uncle Paull's gold membership carried with it the *ultimate* privileges. A car park inside the ground, a seat on the Golden Cardinals terrace, and for this Cardinals-loving nephew, access to pretty much anywhere I wanted to go.

It was 1981. I was nine turning 10 and I lived, breathed and idolised the West Perth Football Club. If only *Mastermind* was there to ask me my chosen subject, 'The West Perth Football Club from 1978 to today'. I would have brained them.

Q. What was West Perth's winning margin over East Perth in Round 21 1980? A. Thirty points. *Correct.*

Q. How many goals did Alan Watling kick against East Fremantle in his 250th game? A. Seven goals. *Correct.*

Q. What was West Perth's record score against East Fremantle in Round 10 1981? A. 37.17 (239). *Correct.*

I could have gone all day. What Ben Cousins was to midfield gut running I would have been to quiz minefield brain busting. Because this was my team. I loved and lived the red and the blue. The Mighty Cardies, later to become the Falcons. Like our famous song—borrowed from Melbourne of course—said, 'my heart beat true'.

I didn't know it then but looking back, these were the most uncomplicated and most fantastic days of my life. So simple—so special.

When a brash television youngster by the name of Dennis Cometti (who could have guessed we'd later work and share so many great times together?) was appointed coach in 1982, my unrestricted access all areas privilege seemed to dry up. Uncle Paull, a long-time sponsor, wasn't happy that the new coach had put a stop to his nephew (and most others) from entering the change rooms after matches. Uncle Paull was a man of principle. The Golden Cardinals were by then Golden Falcons. His protest? Farewell Golden Falcons, hello grass bank on the Leederville Oval outer.

It hardly mattered. We were watching West Perth! The way I saw it, it was a bit like a ticket to a U2 concert—there was no such thing as a bad seat. And whereas the dignified surrounds of the Golden Falcons terrace brought with it a certain subdued barracking, out on the grass it was go for your life.

I reckon I watched the Falcons play (and barracked my red and blue heart out) from the bank at Leederville Oval every weekend until the end of the 1998 season. The next year, I was sitting in the players' area. My schoolboy footy had been good enough to earn me a spot in the

West Perth colts. The year after that, as an eighteen year-old, I went from dreaming the dream to living it. I made my league debut for West Perth in the ruck against Swan Districts at Bassendean Oval. It was a split round, Easter 1990, and twenty-seven members of the extended Zempilas family were there to watch me play.

My dad Tony even gave away the races. Just as they had done as young men in the 1940s and 1950s, the Zempilas boys—Tony, Paull and younger brother Con—stood together again to watch West Perth. This Zempilas wore No. 1 that day. The same number the great Polly Farmer wore in his 392nd and last game of football, when he captain-coached West Perth to the premiership in 1971—the year I was born. The same Polly Farmer, incidentally, who had sold my mum and dad their first car many years earlier.

Like Mum and Dad's car, my league career quickly ran out of gas. Injury and opportunity elsewhere—with Channel 7 as it turned out—meant I couldn't and didn't give it my all. Twenty four games in a bit over four years was a measly return for someone it meant so much to.

But that first league game, the day I became a West Perth player, the day I brought my family together on the banks of Bassendean Oval, remains one of the proudest, most satisfying days of my life. From supporter and dreamer to player, a young man's goal had been ticked off. I no longer had to worry about Dennis Cometti's doorman because, for a time there, I actually *belonged* in the hallowed rooms of the West Perth Football Club.

Fast forward over twenty years and my Saturday afternoons are spent broadcasting AFL footy for Channel 7. Routinely it's the MCG one Saturday, Etihad Stadium the next. It's the best job in the world. And every week when I leave home in Perth for the airport, often sharing the plane ride with Cometti, I remind myself how privileged I am.

Professionalism demands impartiality and in the AFL, at least, I no longer barrack for a team. But as I file in or file out of Etihad or the 'G', I'll spot a young nephew with *their* Uncle Paull. I see the passion in their eyes. I hear the excitement in their voices. Their club colours are wrapped around them, and *I* get wrapped up in their enthusiasm.

And I think how lucky *they* are. For them, football is not a job. Football is everything. In another seven days the car horn will beep and they'll shout back through a screen door, somewhere out in the suburbs, 'See you mum, Uncle Paull's here, I'm off to the footy!'

ALAN HOPGOOD

The Manangatang Mystery Man

Alan Hopgood is a playwright and screenwriter, with credits including *And the Big Men Fly*, *The Carer* and *Alvin Purple*. He is also a successful actor, with ten years as part of the Melbourne Theatre Company and many high-profile TV roles including Dr Reed in *Bellbird*, Wally in *Prisoner* and Jack Lassiter in *Neighbours*. In 1998, his personal story *Surviving Prostate Cancer—One Man's Journey* was published and adapted into a play and video for the Cancer Council. He has since become the 'health playwright', writing plays about diabetes, widows, palliative care, geriatric sex, depression and dementia. In 2005, Hopgood was made a member of the Order of Australia for service to the performing arts and the community. The year 2013 is the 50th anniversary of the first production of *And the Big Men Fly*, which has sold more than 200,000 copies and which remains a popular text in schools. 'The Manangatang Mystery Man' is an excerpt from this successful play.

'And The Big Men Fly' follows the fortunes of Achilles Jones, a simple country boy with extraordinary—if raw—football talent. Acky and his girlfriend, Lil, have been brought to the city by J.J. Forbes, the president of the East Melbourne Football Club, otherwise known as the Crows. Although Acky has never previously played football, he can drop-kick a bag of wheat ten metres. The Crows have not won a premiership for thirty years; Acky is their only hope.

[COMMENTATOR, HARRY HEAD, talks directly to the audience as if into a television camera. Short introduction theme, for example, 'World of Sport' type]

COMMENTATOR: *[crisp, intelligent style]* With the 1963 season only one week away, the biggest query on the East Melbourne front is their mystery recruit, Achilles Jones.

To this moment, the Crows have not been prepared to furnish any information about their Manangatang mystery man, save this... that he is the greatest football potential ever seen... that he has the longest kick on record... that he can ruck all day, non-stop... and that through the agency of Achilles Jones, the Crows will win their first premiership in thirty years.

They're pretty sweeping statements, even from East Melbourne president, J.J. Forbes, who has been known, in the past, to make some rather rash promises. And, to me, it seems unwise, to throw such a load of responsibility on the shoulders of a green recruit from somewhere up in the Mulga, who—from what I can make out—has never even *seen* a game of football let alone *played* one.

Wobbly Coates, our football roundsman, asks *(reads)*, 'If all this is true about Achilles Jones, why haven't we seen something by way of proof? Why have I been banned from watching him train? Why hasn't this mystery man been allowed to play in the practice matches? Is there any truth in the rumour, currently sweeping the football world, that J.J. Forbes... now acting in dual capacity as president *and* coach of the club... has used Achilles Jones as a means of averting a major revolution that could have swept Forbes out of office and ruined his chances in politics?'

Coates asks, 'If this is not true, JJ, you owe us all some proof to the contrary.'

[In his office JJ switches off the TV set; as he does so, blackout on COMMENTATOR. LIL, dressed in her fur coat, has been watching with him]

JJ: *[pacing angrily]* Bah! Wobbly Coates—he's just a highly paid sniper. He's never played a game in his life! Malice, that's all it is, Lil. Sheer unadulterated malice!

LIL: Doesn't he think Acky's any good, JJ?

JJ: No, of course, he doesn't. Because they don't know what we know, Lil. Once they see Achilles, they'll eat every single one of those slanderous remarks. And if they don't... I'll *sue* 'em.

LIL: But, shouldn't you let 'em see Acky? He'd be awful hurt if he knew people were saying such nasty things about him.

JJ: Lil, like I told Achilles only last night. This is psychology. This puts the fear of the devil into the opposition before Acky even takes the field. What they don't know, they fear. What they haven't seen, they can't plan to counteract. They'll tremble at the sight of that tall timber before he puts his boot to the ball. Besides, you know as well as I do that we can't afford to play Achilles in a practice match until he gets some idea of the rules.

LIL: Well, I s'pose you know what you're doing.

JJ: Every inch of the way, Lil. Now, how about you? Enjoying everything?

LIL: Oh, yes.

JJ: Do you like coming down in the helicopter?

LIL: Aw, yeah. It's so exciting, JJ. The first time it picked us up, I was so scared. Then, we just seemed to go sailing up in the air, and there was our place, right way down below us, like a little bit of fly-dirt on the window.

JJ: High time you had experiences like that. Er, you don't reckon you could get Acky to stay down here permanently, do you?

LIL: Oh, he'd fret if he didn't get back to Milly every night.

JJ: I could hire an overseer to look after the place.

LIL: No, JJ, Acky wouldn't stand for that. You just believe me. Why the first time we left to come down, Acky was so worried about Milly, he wanted to bring her with us.

JJ: Well, it's not really important. Achilles is great. He's been training like a steam engine. All we gotta do is get him to understand the rules! *[laughs uncertainly; takes a pill]* Yeah... the rules...

LIL: What's the matter, JJ? You look worried.

JJ: Worried? You gotta be joking. I guess I just feel like a bloke who's got the electricity put on for the first time. Here's this wonderful power, capable of so much, that you can just flick on and flick off... but what if that power got out of control? What would happen if you suddenly couldn't control it... flick, flick. It'd burn the place down.

LIL: Don't you worry about Acky. He's just a great big kid. Some kids never get scared of anything. That's Acky. Some kids never know what it means to get tired. That's Acky too. And some kids'll sit in a corner all day and sulk. And that's Acky. *[sighs]* I dunno, JJ. I can only tell ya what I reckon.

JJ: Believe me, Lil. I want to know what you reckon. 'Cause you know something? Achilles can win us the flag. Just that one big hunk of humanity is capable of making all my wild promises come true. *But*... without you, Lil, we wouldn't have him at all. He'd still be up on that farm kicking wheat-bags around and cleaning Milly's teeth.

LIL: *[a little disgruntled]* Aw, Milly...

JJ: What's the matter? *[panics]* What did I say wrong?

LIL: Aw, it's just I get a bit sick of Milly, Milly, Milly. All the time Milly.

JJ: I was only giving an example...

LIL: Oh, it's not you. It's Acky, really. He's the one I mean. He's all the time worrying about her, looking after her... honest, I reckon he thinks more about Milly than he does me. I know I'll never get a kiss goodnight, until I grow four legs and a tail. It's that bad sometimes.

JJ: You got a problem, Lil?

LIL: Aw, it's private, really. We'll be right. We'll leave it private.

JJ: You don't reckon it'll affect his football?

LIL: Acky will stick at football for you. I know he will. I've just

273

got my own little problem, that's all.

JJ: Well, just so long as everything stays rosy, Lil. As the old saying goes, behind every great man there's a woman... what's it matter if it's a woman and a horse!

[WALLY, in trainer's sweater, etc., comes in followed by ACHILLES, in football gear and carrying a football. WALLY is practically crying with exasperation]

WALLY: JJ... could you... please, just tell Achilles, once... for me...

JJ: Take it easy, Wally. What's the matter?

WALLY: Just tell him again, about the ten metre rule.

LIL: Aren't you behaving, Acky?

ACHILLES: Aw, Lil... it don't make sense.

WALLY: Acky reckons if he can run the length of the ground with the ball, why shouldn't he?

ACHILLES: It's only like chasing Milly once around the paddock.

[WALLY slumps, head in hands]

That's true, ain't it, Lil. You tell 'em.

LIL: Yeah, that's true. When Milly doesn't want to pull the plough, Acky's gotta chase her. And that can happen twenty times before arvo tea.

ACHILLES: Yeah.

JJ: *[gently]* I know, Achilles, boy. We're not questioning the fact that you can run forty laps of the ground without raising a sweat. But, there are rules to this game. And one of them is that you can only take the ball ten metres, then you've got to bounce it or kick it.

[JJ goes to take the ball, but ACHILLES won't give it up]

Otherwise, the umpire will take the ball off you, and it'll be kicked the other way... and we don't want that, do we?

ACHILLES: I s'pose not. It just seems silly, that's all.

WALLY: And would ya tell him, JJ... just for me... that he's got to learn to wear boots.

LIL: But Acky's never worn boots in his life.

[JJ looks at ACHILLES's bare feet]

JJ: Oh, you've got to wear boots, Achilles.

ACHILLES: I ain't gonna wear 'em. They hurt me feet.

LIL: Why's he gotta wear boots?

[WALLY crumples again]

JJ: Because all the other players wear boots... and because their
          boots have stops, lumps of metal on them... and those lumps
          of metal are stuck in with nails. And I don't care how hard
          Acky's feet are, those nails will tear them to pieces. Right,
          Wally?

WALLY: *[defeated]* Right JJ.

JJ: So you wear boots, Achilles, you get used to 'em. Wear 'em
          round the farm. Wear 'em to bed. But get used to 'em. Now
          go and have your rub-down before you get cold.

[Goes to desk to take another pill]

ACHILLES: Hmmph! I don't get it. All the things I can do, nobody'll let
          me do 'em.

JJ: All we want you to do is keep kicking that ball ninety
          metres every time. There's no rule to stop you doing that.

ACHILLES: I won't be long, Lil. I wanna get back and see how Milly's
          going. She was off her tucker again this mornin'.

LIL: Couldn't we stay down one night and watch a bit of telly?
          There's a movie on tonight, with Mae West in it.

ACHILLES: Not when Milly's off her tucker.

LIL: *[annoyed]* Oh, all right.

[ACHILLES goes. WALLY hangs back at the door]

WALLY: JJ?

JJ: What.

WALLY: Do I have to give him a rub-down?

JJ: Of course you do. What's wrong with giving him a rub-down?

WALLY: I'll tell ya what's wrong with it... he's ticklish, that's what.

LIL: Use a brick, Wally. That's what I always do.

WALLY: A brick?

LIL: You heard me, didn't ya? A brick! A brick!

[She storms off]

DAVID BEST

I Think, Therefore I Am—a Footy Fan!

David Best was one of England's most distinguished practitioners in the philosophy of the arts and a prolific author and lecturer noted for his work in the performing arts. Among other academic posts, he was Professor of Philosophy at the University of Central England. His books include *Expression in Movement and the Arts* (1974); *Philosophy and Human Movement*, (1978); *Reason and Feeling in the Arts* (1985); and *The Rationality of Feeling: Understanding the Arts in Education* (1992). He wrote this article while Senior Research Fellow in Philosophy at the University of Wales, and it appeared in Melbourne's *The Herald* in 1988.

B efore leaving Britain, I received a letter from Dr Ged Martin, of Cork University, who had been in Canberra for five years. Among other sage counsels, he strongly urged me, when in Melbourne, not to miss the chance of seeing the essence of Ockerism—a footy match—and to be sure not to eat any Australian meat pies. He explained the former injunction but not the latter. The roughest, toughest sport he'd ever seen.

I asked Australians, in various States, about the game. Ged's impression was confirmed: fights among the players; list of injuries given at the beginning of newspaper reports; fiercely partisan barracking by supporters; if you're among the barrackers for one team be careful never to praise the play of the other; abusive invective shouted at the umpires, who are escorted off the ground by mounted police; beer cans thrown— or on amiable days merely fizzed over the crowd in front, &c.

Alarming. But also confusing. What are the rules? This question, from a naïve Pom, always provoked derisory but hardly explanatory replies: 'We've played and watched the game for years without asking such an irrelevant question'; 'if you find out, let us know—you might even write the first rule book'; 'quite simple—there aren't any'; 'the umpires make them up during the game' &c.

I was lucky. Typical of the remarkable Australian hospitality I met, a ticket was obtained for me to go to watch a game between Carlton and Geelong. Lucky? Ambivalent. Yes, because they were top teams and the excitement and barracking was expected to reach fever-pitch. Yet not so sure, because surely there would be a correlative sharp rise in the hazards—proliferation of punch-ups, storms of stubbies, fountains of fizz.

So the innocent eye went to the footy, at a *sanctum sanctorum*. My role was that of an objective observer, although, discovering I was surrounded by a throng of Blues barrackers, I refrained from overt enthusiasm for any Cat's performance.

But was objective appraisal of this unknown game possible, in view of my previous enthusiastic participation in sporting activities such as rugby union and soccer? Immanuel Kant wrote: 'Thoughts without content are empty. Intuitions without concepts are blind.' Part of what he meant was that it is impossible to receive 'bare' or 'ideally neutral' perceptions, which are not brought within the realm of our understanding by being subsumed under concepts we already have; understanding depends on those concepts.

As a philosopher I am emotionally attached to rationality. One of my major concerns is an examination of the concept of objectivity—for instance, I argue that aesthetic judgements are as fully objective as scientific judgements. Nevertheless, since I have been the target for many good natured Pommy barbs, I am delighted at the opportunity to poke sacrilegious fun at the Ockers by satirising their national religion—footy.

Yet, as I watched, my purpose was increasingly thwarted. It really was a very good game, and it interestingly exemplified the philosophical issue. The capacity for objective critical appreciation of this unknown game was not limited or prejudiced by my knowledge of other games. On the contrary, such objective appraisal *depended* on the reference points of games I did understand.

The accuracy and length of the kicking was remarkable for someone brought up on rugby union. There was a commendable fluency about the play, partly because, with no off-side law, there were not the frequent stoppages which so often mar other football codes.

The high scoring is an advantage over many games for two reasons. First, it is more exciting for both players and spectators that there should be numerous goals. Tediously often in soccer, for instance, there are games which end without any score, or in which there is only one goal. And second, with high scores, it is far more likely that the better team will win.

There are enchanting idiosyncrasies. I succumbed totally to the superb dramatic timing of the goal umpires. In cases of doubt the whole vast crowd was kept in a cauldron of suspense until, with decisive histrionics, the umpire delivered his verdict, inciting a maelstrom of approval and abuse. What a supreme feeling of power that must be! A goal umpire is the conductor of an orchestra of 90,000 vivid emotions, which explode at the mere, if dramatic, gesture of a finger or two. And, as an encore, he gives a peacock-semaphore display with flags.

Most of all I was enthralled by the exquisite aestheticism of the high-marking. Big men soared elegantly into flight to pluck the ball from mid-air, spraying below them a pyramid of lesser mortals. But not only high marks. Players also flew at or even below the horizontal fractionally in time to take thrilling and apparently impossible marks. I froze such moments mentally, and can still recall them. Beautiful, graceful, balletic.

Balletic? But this is the religion of the Ockers!

There was one minor skirmish among the players. There was volatile barracking, and some abuse of the umpires. Yet, on the whole, it was very good-natured, with good sportsmanship from players and spectators. Far better, I regret to say, than the behaviour at many British soccer matches.

So, unfortunately for my mischievous intent, I can certainly offer an objective judgement—an objectivity not prejudiced, but conferred, by my understanding and enjoyment of British games. Thwarted! I wanted to poke fun at you Aussies through your national sport of footy, and I can't—it's a splendid game. Vigorous, good-natured, fluent, exciting and aesthetic.

Next time, I'll try the meat pies.

JACK HIBBERD

Lemon Time

Jack Hibberd was born in 1940 in Warracknabeal, Victoria. He studied medicine at the University of Melbourne and is an immunologist, as well as one of Australia's best-known playwrights. Hibberd has around forty plays to his credit including the ever-popular *Dimboola*, *A Stretch of the Imagination* and the more recent *Guantanamo Bay*. He co-founded the Australian Performing Group in 1970, founded the Melbourne Writers Theatre in 1983 and has served on the Theatre Board and Literature Board of the Australia Council. 'Lemon Time' first appeared in the *Times on Sunday*, 7 June 1987.

As a young lad I followed Sandhurst, the 'Maroon-and-Blues', in the Bendigo Football League. Sandhurst had for its home the city's main sporting oval, the Upper Reserve, which was changed sycophantically to the Queen Elizabeth II Oval during the 1950s in anticipation of a visit by the monarch.

Sandhurst shared the Upper Reserve with South Bendigo, its arch rival, whose players competed in the colours of South Melbourne. Our matches against South Bendigo were invariably unpleasant encounters, both off and on the field. The southerners and their supporters epitomised iniquity.

Whenever Sandhurst lost to its co-tenants, I took it terribly to heart. Tears of grief and outrage would tumble down my cheeks. We were robbed by the white maggots or undetected foul play. I refused to eat and apply myself to homework. Bed-wetting recommenced.

Our favourite possie for watching a clash was on the stone steps of a rather elegant old grandstand. We preferred the grandstand itself, but to get there required darting past a white-coated attendant. I've forgotten this argus-eyed bloke's name. He had the most thankless task: we scaled the stairs and walls ceaselessly, like monkeys.

I think I must then have physically resembled a monkey, of the baboon kind. I had a large head, bulbous cheeks, adenoidal voice, misshapen torso, and twig-thin legs. I was not considered mascot material. How I detested those show ponies and pampered twerps who trotted down the race before the real men.

The Upper Reserve rejoiced in a strange and possibly unique feature. Around some of its perimeter stood an elongated, roofed, but otherwise open, structure. It could have been a huge semi-circular veranda detached from the apse of a bush cathedral. On wet days barrackers would assemble underneath in the hope that the wind-whipped horizontal rain would do the unexpected: fall directly from above.

I remember with great pleasure running out onto the ground at lemon time and listening to the coach's address as the players sucked sullenly or contentedly on quarters of orange. Country coaches of the 1940s and 1950s were mercifully not over-familiar with modern psychological cant. They tended to foam at the mouth like demagogues. It was startling stuff.

An even greater pleasure was to sneak into the rooms before the first bounce. Most players sat silently around the walls. Some lay on tables and were ministered to by trainers. The salient sounds were the taps of the boot-studder's hammer and the slaps like butter-pats on glistening calves, thighs, and buttocks. The dominant odours were those of liniment, resin, Penetrene, and sweat.

Bendigo is thick with gullies—California Gully, Sailers Gully, Maiden Gully—where alluvial gold had been won. In my day a San Francisco tram rocked and rolled over many of these gullies to the Borough of Eaglehawk some miles north. I knew of no finer adventure than to take that tram with a motley crew of mates and do battle with the Borough boys. The latter were fanatical. We had to move in packs around their ground. Should an Eaglehawk gang shanghai one of our number, the victim was likely to end up at the bottom of a disused mine shaft.

Eaglehawk fostered some crack footballers: from Geelong's Peter

Pianto to Carlton's Rodney Ashman. They were the Footscray of the BFL. When they snared a flag, the relevant hotels brimmed with jubilant customers: the trams were choked and barnacled with thrashing human figures and seemed drunken as they careened around the first of many tight corners on the track to Eaglehawk.

One of my childhood heroes was Sandhurst's Ray Shearer, a player possessed of all those natural attributes that are beyond inculcation or 'motivation': balance, ball sense, anticipation, and nous. Ray also seemed a heartthrob with the ladies, who frequently spoke of him being blessed with 'a wonderful pair of hands'.

They were reasonably flourishing days for Sandhurst. The club took out at least one premiership and produced footballers of the calibre of Brendan Edwards and Graham Arthur, who both played illustrious roles in Hawthorn's snaring their first pennant.

Sandhurst players seemed then to go to Hawthorn, as later they streamed to Carlton. Some did the reverse trip, such as Hawthorn's gnarled and craggy Kevin Curran. It was probably no coincidence that the first game I saw in Melbourne featured Hawthorn against Essendon. I stood behind the goals at the Glenferrie Road end, my mouth open like that of a cod fish, and watched John Coleman take extra-terrestrial marks, take a heap of punishment, and score a swag of goals.

Still, it was all a bit impersonal. The Maroon-and-Blues were an integral part of my physiology. I couldn't throb to John Coleman the way I could to a bantamweight Sandhurst winger called 'Todder' when he nipped between the parted legs of an opponent, executed two dummies and a blind turn, handballed over the head of the full back, scooted around him, scooped up the pill with one hand and drove it through the hi-diddle-diddle for the winning major. We kids on the steps went berserk.

I swapped allegiances to VFL teams a lot. I fancied Fitzroy first, because of their colours and my mother's fondness for them. Then I followed Richmond for a while, because an uncle had had some games with them. Next I admired Melbourne, since my father felt their sides of the fifties and sixties were the greatest imaginable.

Despite the radio, newspapers, and swap cards, it seemed all rather remote down there in Melbourne. Football for me then was personal and physically immediate (the sounds, smells, and colours, the weather). It was social (crowds at play) and distinctly Australian, not a mere vehicle for the accumulation of wealth, image-making, and Americanisation.

My last reminiscence is an indirect one. I heard it as a story retailed at family gatherings. My father had arrived at Spring Gully oval for a social match and found he'd forgotten to bring his clobber. He went to his mother's house up the road and commandeered a pair of her capacious pink satin bloomers. He donned these and ran onto the ground bootless and topless. According to aunties and uncles, my father played a tearaway game on the half-forward flank.

ANDREA STRETTON

Swans and Tigers

Andrea Stretton was born in Melbourne and made a significant contribution to Australia's literary culture as an arts journalist, television presenter, author and critic. A widely loved public figure, she presented SBS Television's *The Book Show* and *Masterpiece*, and ABC TV's *Sunday Afternoon*. She was also creative director of the 1998 and 1999 Olympic arts festivals. Awarded the *Ordre des Arts et des Lettres* by the government of France in 2002, Stretton died from cancer at the age of 55 in 2007. 'Swans and Tigers' first appeared in *The Bulletin*, 6 July 1982.

Young boys' arms were stacked with *Heralds*. Holding pieces of plastic over their newspapers to keep the rain out, they were calling, 'Ear ore out it!' in high voices. And it was not yet half-time. I had heard all about it and there I was, with images of Roman chariot races, fighting feathered cocks, bleeding bulls and matadors at my first encounter with Australian Rules. Taut male bodies, coloured socks collapsed on thick calves, tendons in arms, stretching and pumping, shorts and jumpers fuming with damp air and sweat.

At first I was uninvolved. I saw only a kaleidoscope pattern of bodies arching, running, backward trotting, pirouetting. When the play, and the ball, moved away from a player, there was a sudden falling motion of torso to knees, muscle-bound arms swinging, and lungs deep breathing. Large rag dolls with mist pouring from their mouths. Colour in the movement: black and yellow streamers grabbing at the wind from the end of sticks, red and white banners held high by overcoated arms, black and yellow hair ribbons, signs, badges, scarves, striped wool on wet hair.

On the other side of the field, a tiger roaring on the swollen skin of a balloon and, nearer, a swan flapping its head and rippling its long neck at the end of a high pole. Tigers and Swans filled the jungle, the lake; but the sound was black crows screeching in a swamp paddock.

'Car'n the Swans!'

'Car'n the Tigers. Car'n! Car'n! Car'n!'

The thirty-six players lusted for the ball; they chased it, grabbed it, kicked it parallel with the ground, threw it into other men's stomachs, hit it long and fast at eye level, and then high in an arc through the pale sky so you could watch it, slow motion, escaping into low cloud before a final spinning fall onto the tip of another boot or into grasping outstretched arms. When it reached the tall white goalposts at either end of the field, there was a hush in the enormous stands of people watching, and the players went quiet and stared anxiously as if the moon were about to fall. The player with the ball ran slowly backwards for twenty or thirty metres, lined up his kick, and then ran methodically forwards and aimed high through the posts. When he achieved a goal, a massive cheering and roaring broke through the stands, and the player would smile bashfully as he was banged on the broad back by fellow team members and whistled to by his coach from the sidelines of the field.

The bitter wind made my eyes water and my nipples harden beneath my clothes. We were in the outer stand, without cover or seats, and I had to stand on tiptoe most of the time, to see over the backs of heads. I stopped waiting for apologies from people who pushed me in the sides in their tunnel-vision excitement and began to shove back with my elbows.

At half-time a siren enveloped the ground with an ancient call, and small boys ran on the field carrying bags of orange quarters. There was a sudden surge of the crowd behind me, and I went down over the concrete step to a concerto of a siren toll, beer cans clanging, and the crowd bellowing to some dispirited players lying on their backs, 'Stand up like men, ya mugs!'

I didn't want to take it personally. Elbow of my jumper ripped through to the flesh, I lay face down inside the passionate pressure of feet, and then a man's arm made a helping motion to me at ground level. He did it ceremoniously, pulling with the swaying weight of his massive stomach and left arm, and balancing a stubbie in the other. The beer spilled over the edge of the tin, on his slip-on leather shoes, and into the parting of my hair. It trickled down my scalp and on my nose like putrid rain water. As I wiped it and other debris from my face, he bowed slowly and with attempted grace. He tried to close his eyes as he did this, mimicking humility ('I am a man retrieving a lady's glove from a puddle'), but the control was missing, his narrow brown eyes went cross-eyed, and he stumbled.

'Don't go gettin' yerself too (burp) excited-able now, sweetheart,' he said, straightening himself up. The 'sweetheart' was said slowly, and the syllables were drawn out as though he was singing them. He sauntered back to his mates who were all smirking at him. 'Bewdy, Mick,' said one, with a flushed, leering face. He had tins of beer zipped into the front of his parka jacket, resting on his fat stomach, to save the inconvenience of the long bend to the ground. I thought how cold his stomach must be, but maybe the tins were just getting hot from the flesh.

'That's the historical ock,' said my friend Samantha, grimacing. She put her umbrella up, which was a grey as soft as the silken sky stretched high above the oval. The rain was falling in a fine mist, but gathering a thicker force slowly. She wore jeans and a man's black parka; her only concession to loyalties was a yellow and black pompom on the top of her woollen cap. Sam called herself a 'footy-ite'.

'I suppose we're all ocks here, one way or another,' I said.

'Don't be absurd,' she said. 'There's a time and place for altruism, and it ain't here. This is a stamping ground for approved intolerance.'

I shrugged. 'Those kinds of men are probably okay underneath. They just show off,' I said stubbornly.

'Yeh?' she said sarcastically. 'But "underneath" all that, they can't see out, and don't want to.'

The stench of beer going stale on the concrete, and in my hair, curled my nose in the cold air. At least we were not in a covered stand, where all the odours of a wet Saturday at the football would be trapped in a belljar of hot chips, hot dogs, and the yelling of hot mouths. The people in the outer were mostly men, standing in groups, eyes glazed from trying to listen to the horseracing broadcast on transistors, held to their ears, while they watched the game; or, when the game was in full heat, standing in seagull rows on the concrete steps, with one hand cupped against their mouths as they squawked and yelled, and hair ruffling around intent eyes watering from the sea cold air coming up from St Kilda Beach.

The siren blew to signal the beginning of the second half. The ground hushed and watched the players bolt through their respective slip gates into the arena, heaving their haunches and looking around. Thousands of people waited expectantly. Then the umpire blew his trill whistle. A haemorrhage of yelling spurted violently onto the ground again. Everything speeded up, and the sky began to throw heavy layers of rain stones upon the earth. Players grappled for the ball in the mud and did flying leaps that ended in head-first skids along the balding ground. The stops on the soles of their boots left scars in their tracks. Mick (alias 'Newk') and his mates were swollen faced from yelling. Every time the ball reached within fifty metres of the Swans' goalposts, the Tigers diverted it back up the field.

'Car'm on!' bellowed Mick. 'What d'ya think you are? Ya broken necked idiots!'

'Ya lettin' the Tigers lick ya arses,' echoed the fat friend with the tin babies in his parka.

'Ah, ya bloody birds. Ya sheilas!' Mick curled his top lip and looked away from the field. Then he spat. The phlegm landed on the lid of his Esky, and he turned back to the field, snarling.

I felt uncomfortable; a small stone of concern withdrew my participation for a few minutes. Everyone was delving into their vocabulary for the worst abuse they could muster. My friend was yelling out names: Kravencko, Brownie, Palouski, Miro. Every nationality of name, except Oriental. The players with European names were considered more Australian than anyone else in this battlefield, and they were granted a sporting respect. The insults were reserved for: 'Jesus, what d'ya reckon. Yer bleedin' women or somethin'?'

I was menstruating too. No, I did not like this at all. There was a scuffle over the ball involving five or six players. Galliboli went down on his back in muddied yellow and black stripes and lay rocking from side to side on the ground with his powerful arms crossed over his stomach. The umpire in white sped across the field on his short legs and blew his whistle loudly. All the players in the scuffle stopped and looked at him with defiant condescension. A little white bull trotting into a paddock of mad herefords. He waved his small hands about and presented the ball with a bow to Galliboli, who stood up immediately and began circling his shoulders in a canoe rowing movement. There was some critical anger around us.

'What are ya, blind or something? Got ya blinkers on, ya stupid woman, ya white turd!' said Mick, with a loud nasty growl. He and his mates all stood jeering and shaking their heads, and showing their anger by punching at the air. Every section of the stands had yellow and black patterns of streamers and balloons waving through the rain that was falling across the field in a diagonal veil. In a concentrated patch of this in the stand far over on the other side of the oval, chanting began amid the boos:

> *One, two, three, four,*
> *Who do you think we barrack for?*
> *Five, six, seven, eight,*
> *Who do you think we appreciate?*
> *T-I-G-E-R-S, Hooray!*

Streamers rippled across the lake of faces at the finale of the chant. Umbrellas were popping up in front of us with exasperated movements against the rain. Sections of the view were completely hidden by the smooth taut surfaces, and a new tension was stirred up. Empty cans and screwed up food papers began to bounce off the umbrella tops, clattering on to the concrete.

'Get em down, ya mugs! How's a man supposed to see?' said a woman.

'Yeah, get em down.'

'Ah, shut up,' said an old woman in a check raincoat who turned around and did a thumbs up with her thermos flask. She put her umbrella down though and held her hands over her head instead. Mick was staring at Sam and me, waiting for something to happen. After a minute or two of this, I narrowed my eyes at him and glared.

'What's with him?' I said to Samantha.

'Maybe he's going to ask you for a dance,' she said, and turned away.

'What do you want, a camera or something?' I said loudly in his direction.

He was suddenly pleased and read an invitation to stroll over, nodding his head knowingly and squeezing his lips. I lifted the collar of my wet grey pullover up around my neck and crossed my arms defensively.

'YOU,' he said, addressing me, 'can tell your friend here, that it's not good form to go to the football and block the views of these geysers behind you with a bloody umbrella. If ya wanna stay nice and dry and cute, you stay at home with the little box, see?'

'Sor-ry mate,' said Sam. She put her umbrella down and turned her head away from us.

'That's better,' said Mick, condescendingly. Sam flicked her eyebrows above her topaz gold eyes, and she sniffed.

'Who are you backing?' Mick said to me.

'Not sure,' I said.

'Well, that's one way to win, I guess,' he said. 'Ya wanna put your money on the Tigers this arvo; South's playing like a pack of poofs. Should be home with their toeshoes on, doin' their knitting, the fucking women.'

'Hey, watch your language when you're talking to a lady, mate,' said a man behind us.

'Yeah,' said Mick, belching and wavering forwards. 'Very so-rry, sweetheart.'

He repelled me with his beer breath and leering face, but I thought I saw him laughing at himself, inside his bloodshot eyes, as if he only needed a little prod to enable him to break through his football match self. Maybe a little friendly logic would do the trick.

'How come whenever the game gets rough and everyone starts to get nasty, they start to call the players women?'

'What are you on about?' he said aggressively.

Sam dug my ribs with her elbow.

'You know,' I said, 'as if it's the lowest possible insult, the dregs.'

'Yeah,' he said, frowning. 'What's it to you?' He pulled the cap off a beer tin that was on the step behind us.

'Well, I am a woman, I think...'

'What's this, bloody charity week?' interjected the owner of the can behind us.

'Don't get your balls in a knot,' said Mick, in a friendly voice. He guffawed loudly, and his friends heard and smirked. 'Oh, Mick, you naughty boy,' he said, to himself. 'Excuse ME.'

I just stared at him. A cold glare would win the day, if logic did not.

Sam glanced at Mick and me. 'Don't worry about her,' she said dismissively, 'she's doing a thesis on terms of abuse in the Antipodes.' She grinned, in her wry way.

'Oh well, oh well,' said Mick, flustered and nasty again, 'now that really clears things up.' And he added, without looking at Sam's face, 'Smart arse.'

'Rubbish,' I said, annoyed with Sam. 'I just don't like you calling out 'bloody women' all the time as if it crystallised your worst feelings. How do you think I feel?'

'Ah, cr-ystall-ised,' he droned sarcastically, closing his eyes in a swoon. 'Lovely word. Is it worth a kiss if I change the lines?'

'Come off it,' I said, appealing to him.

'Go on, let's see how serious you are; no more 'women' calls, and I get a kiss. Mate.'

It must have been either the unfamiliar injection of abandonment in my veins, received from the spike of the match, or that I felt tentatively close to some desperation operating at a deeper level beneath his drunkenness (or because of it), that determined my decision. Maybe I just wanted to get rid of the bastard, and was sure I would that way because I was confident of winning; but anyway I agreed to the deal. He sauntered back to his friends, and they splattered with laughter at what he said to them. He rocked back and forth on his feet a bit, wiping his hands on the thighs of his wet jeans.

'You're mad,' said Sam, blinking raindrops from her eyelashes. 'You'll end up with a pie in your pretty face.'

'But how do you think all the other women here feel about the abuse?'

'Take a look,' she said, waving her arm. 'They don't even notice. It doesn't mean anything. The words have no literal sense. It's just the footy, you know, the *footy*.'

A couple of Mick's friends turned and raised their tins at us. The fat one was not impressed. He rested his three chins on the edge of his can and slurred loudly, 'Probably just bloody dykes.'

Mick glanced at him, and the skin over his prominent cheekbones flushed.

'Come off it,' he said to the fat one. But he sent nervous darts of his eyes in our direction. Don't tell me I've made a deal with one of those, I could hear him thinking. I stifled a grin. The hands of the big red clock on the opposite side of the field were nearly at the three-quarter sign. A scuffle broke out at the Richmond goalposts, and a tremendous roar of voices hurtled five men three metres off the ground stretching out their arms and hands for the ball like muscular seals. Three of them were knocked down and thudded backwards onto the ground. The other two players came down wrestling for the ball that was squashed between their torsos.

The player in yellow and black thumped the other one in the stomach, grabbed the ball where it had dropped and started running sturdily backwards to line up a kick at the white posts. His thick body and legs swelled and breathed like the flanks of a pacing horse. The player in red and white made signals of abuse with his arms, and the umpire jogged up and told him to clear off by waving his hands and flicking the chest of the player's jumper; scolding a cattle dog who'd broken up the sheep.

'Since when's punching been allowed!' yelled the man behind us.

Thousands of people began to scream in every stand except the Tigers' grandstand, which gave out an aura of smug satisfaction. The Tiger lined up his kick, just thirty metres from the posts. The ground was having a heart attack around his closed intensity.

'That's not fair is it?' I said to Sam.

'The Swans player is really winded.'

'No,' I said loudly.

The South player was still lying on his back in a pale ray of sun. A man in a white uniform carrying a black doctor's kit was running in a cowering motion onto the field towards him.

'Car'n the Swans!' I yelled, as the Tiger player kicked the ball dead centre between the goalposts.

The Swans' disciples were divided now between outrage at the decision and fury that their team would accept such humiliation. They either abused their players or flapped their hands dismissively at the entire field.

Mick suddenly turned to me and called, 'This one's for you, sweetheart.'

I looked at him as he cupped both hands to his mouth and yelled, 'What do ya think this is? Bloody Abo Week?'

He grinned.

'Jesus wept,' I said.

The anger passed, leaving an undercurrent of agitation. The ball was being bounced on the ground in the centre of the players. It flew high in the air. Mick stepped over the radios transmitting the 3.30 race at Flemington racetrack.

'Well,' he said to me, grinning expectantly like a boy waiting for the surprise at the end of the pumpkin. 'I've kept my side of the bargain.'

'You've got to be kidding,' I said.

'Hang on there, what's this? You're not going to come with the backout trick, I hope. Even though you're a woman, you do know what a deal is, I suppose?'

'Christ, first it's women and then it's Aborigines. How would you like it?'

'Like *what*, for gossake?' he said, flicking his large red hand in front of my nose.

I looked at Sam for support.

'Don't look at me, I'm not the umpire,' she said, crossing her black quilted arms.

The play had started again.

'You owe me a kiss, honey; it's as simple as that,' said Mick, leering now and holding his tin with a clenched hand.

'No,' I said. 'It was a stupid idea anyway,' I added angrily.

'Jesus,' he said. 'Fucking women, you give them an inch and they take a bloody mile. Every time.'

As he turned, I murmured, 'Well, you didn't even think about it.' It sounded like the voice of a spoilt child.

'You're lucky he let you off so easily,' said Samantha, without looking at my face. 'You are kind of disturbing his day at the pictures.'

'I know that. And he's disturbing mine.'

'Ah, you're both just having your own match inside the main one. It's an old Australian game, as old as Rules... older probably.'

'Well,' I said. 'I'll get through to him. There must be something I could say to wake him up.'

Sam just pursed her lips and shook her head, very slowly.

'But what if I called him a brainless fool?' I persisted. 'What if I called him a fascist, an idiot, a cultural dodo?'

She snorted quietly through her nose.

'Or I could tell him that women invented overarm bowling in cricket...' I went on.

At that Sam screwed up her face and gazed at me as if she'd just spotted a real loony.

'Well, it's true,' I said. 'There's lots of...'

'For God's sake, forget it, will you?' she said impatiently. 'He's only interested in two things: winning the game and advancing his reputation for manhood... and the two things are intertwined... you know? The virility of the *balls*.'

Virility? Balls? Maybe attack could win the day yet.

'I see,' I said emphatically.

Sam raised her eyebrows, glancing my way.

The game was flowing towards the end. Galliboli was pacing around the edge of the field, lining up the movement of the ball. A last flood of adrenalin was sharpening the game. Mick resumed his abuse. It looked like the Tigers would get another goal. The Swans players were struggling and speeding, but their boots kept skidding over the surface of the earth. A couple of their players just lay there where they landed, with their hands across their faces, while the Tigers manoeuvred the ball away.

'What is this, Women's Week?' came from behind us.

'Come on, Galliboli!' yelled Sam.

'One minute to go.'

'Come on, the Swans,' I yelled, opposing her.

'Get ya bloody dresses off, you sheilas!' yelled Mick, blood-faced.

Everyone was shouting. My heart thumped from the pressure. There was a sudden visual clarity from strong squares of sunlight brightening the ground where the players made their final burst.

'What do you think you are, Tigers?' I screamed. 'You making up for being impotent Australian male beer guts, or something?' I quickly placed the back of my hand over my mouth.

The siren went; a long magnetic call like a ship's horn as it leaves dock, and the people on the wharf are left, looking at the sea. Mick spun round at me. His fat friend looked at me, appalled. So did a few others, and some tittered. I felt as though I had just taken my clothes off.

Sam put her hand to her forehead and made a groaning noise. Mick looked me straight in the eye as he placed his tin firmly on the step. People were stamping their feet in a last burst before the drift away. He walked over to me, fists by his sides; a suddenly sober spokesman. His friends watched and waited behind him. He prodded me in the chest bone with his forefinger and leaned into my face. Streamers were waving all around his head as I looked up at him, and then I pointed my face at the ground.

'Listen,' he said, with enormous seriousness, over the siren. 'It's all a game. One big happy game. Right?'

I nodded.

'Yeah?' he said loudly.

I nodded again, and squeezed drips of water from the wool at the bottom of my pullover, disrespectfully.

'But there's something you gotta learn. There's one thing you just don't do. Not ever. You understand?'

'What's that?' I said, looking into his face.

'You can say whatever you like here. But you never, but never, get bloody personal,' said Mick. Then he bent his head, right at my breast level, and belched.

MAX PIGGOTT

Swansong

Max Piggott was born in South Melbourne and played football for Queenscliff and South Sydney while in NSW on military service. He served in commando units in New Guinea during World War II and, on his return, played in the VFL for South Melbourne, once kicking seven goals against a powerful Carlton combination. He retired prematurely for business reasons in 1947. Piggott farmed in Victoria and, from 1967, in the south of Western Australia. From the 1970s he became well known as a rural affairs writer. He was killed in a road accident in 2010, at the age of ninety. 'Swansong' first appeared in *Overland*, No. 102 (1986).

I fell in love with and married a woman who, on rare occasions, would use a little Eau de Cologne 4711 behind her ear. Later, I was to learn from her that 4711 soothed the pain of a bull-ant bite. But I'm digressing. I would like to have said that the attraction of her scent stays with me still, nearly forty years after I began wooing her, but it doesn't.

The fumes so readily conjured up come from a mix of sweat and liniment, a mingling from the dressing rooms of football clubs.

When I read that the Sydney Swans had irretrievably broken the umbilical cord that linked the football club to Melbourne and, more particularly, to South Melbourne, I was shattered, stunned. Here was one hundred years of endeavour and tradition going down the drain. Tradition and loyalty no longer count. No longer the sound of masseurs slapping shiny thighs, of coaches berating and urging, no longer the rat-a-tat-tat of studded boots as the players run down the race and on to the arena at the lakeside oval. I could weep.

You don't understand? Ian Turner would have. I wish he were here—a consoling Tiger licking the downcast neck of a despondent Swan. Swan? Swan? That's where the rot started.

As kids my generation knew them as the blood-stained angels, their red-and-white guernseys revered warriors' tabards. Listen to the old cry, 'Car'n, the Bloods', or better still, the call to arms, 'Up There, Cazaly', and you'll understand why old men are crying. Cazaly was typical of the Irish Catholics, the pro-Mannix, anti-conscriptionist working class of South Melbourne in the 1920s and 1930s. The suburb was not formerly known as Emerald Hill for nothing. From the window of the room I was born in, above a shop in busy tram-lined Clarendon Street, you can lean your head out and see the club's 1933 premiership pennant hanging dejectedly from the main grandstand flagpole.

I was inducted into the club at birth; there's no other reason for my devotion. Surely the sound of leather on leather must have drifted up from the arena on the June day long ago as my mother tensioned in the midwife's arms. The 1920s and 1930s were depressing years for South Melbourne's adults. Many of them were sustained only by their loyalty to family and their beloved football team.

At primary school it was quite useless of Miss O'Brien, or tottery 'Argie' Hargreaves, to try to drum the heroism of Horatio into the hearts and minds of their Dorcas Street state school pupils. We knew that down the road in our coliseum eighteen heroes battled it out every Saturday arvo.

While, bless her, Miss Sheehan hoped we saw beauty in 'wandering lonely as a cloud', we kids found it in the grace and balance of Brylcreemed Ron Hillis (an Australian ballroom dancing champion), as he cleared the ball down field. There was, for us, more elegance in the flight of a dropkick as it left the toe of waterside worker Peter Reville than in a host of nodding daffodils. We could touch *our* heroes, carry their bags from tram to turnstile and receive, if our hero was in a good mood, a pat on the head and an autograph.

Few of us could afford a football of our own. We tightly rolled a *Sun Pictorial*, tied it with string to the size of a 1920s sausage roll, and booted it in school grounds and carless streets. Like Christmas holidays, the start of the next season's football never seemed to come quickly enough. Over long summers our anticipation was kept below boiling point only by knowing that cricketing giants like Bill Woodfull, Lindsay Hassett, Keith Miller and Ian Johnson were wearing our beloved red and white.

You could sit beside old men who would recall South Melbourne sporting giants like Trott and Blackham and hear tales of how Belcher and Mark Tandy—'the greatest ruck combination ever'—thrashed their opposition. Maybe, in their excitement, forgetting Cazaly. At the height of the Great Depression I recall seeing a middle-aged woman, who had been standing quietly behind the goalposts, turn and begin belting a spectator over the head with her umbrella. On another occasion South Melbourne supporters, riled by the umpiring decisions of the then doyen of umpires, Jack McMurray, waited on him after the game, carried him to nearby Albert Park Lake and threw him in, clothes and all. No one could accuse South barrackers of being unsupportive.

The canker from which the club never recovered suppurated in 1934 and 1945, the only years in which the club might have won a premiership after its successful campaign in 1933. Red-hot favourites in both those years, yet falling unexpectedly to Richmond and Carlton. Rumours abounded, with accusations of bribery of leading players by Melbourne's baccarat fraternity.

The patient hung on for another forty years. War matures. In our youth we knew League football was for gods and heroes, and I was but an ungodly, gangling kid. My reputation as a schoolboy footballer rested solely on the relished accounts of the day I kicked the ball into the back of the head of the school's sports master. He never forgave those who laughed, or me, and promptly dropped me from ever again representing the school. I never forgave him.

Six years of wartime army life convinced me there were no gods, least of all football ones. Determined to get at least one game of senior Victorian League football, I turned up at South Melbourne for the opening of training in 1946. 'At twenty-six he's a bit old for a recruit,' they said. I would stick it out, one game, and the three quid would be useful too. On the sixth game of the new season I ran out on to St Kilda's

Junction Oval to play against the Saints.

'You're going to make it hard, I'm only a new chum,' I said to the Adonis who ran across to oppose me. He was national idol and Test cricketer, Keith Miller, the Saints' full back.

I had to wait until the opening of the 1947 season before I achieved the ambition I'd nursed unconsciously for so long: to run out on to the hallowed South Melbourne arena to the cheers of a South Melbourne crowd. (The arena and grandstands had been abused by US marines camped there during the war.) About 25,000 spectators jammed the ground, and they saw South Melbourne beat Carlton. It was a victorious homecoming; we were delirious.

You find it hard to understand such a display of emotion? Then you don't understand what life was like for two decades in places like Fitzroy, Collingwood and South Melbourne. Football made life bearable. On one day a week football broke down class barriers. Football developed a sense of loyalty among people who were questioning whether loyalty meant anything after the senseless slaughter of the Great War and the mindlessness brought about by industrialisation. Football gave hope, winning was possible.

Now the symbol of that hope has gone for those who remember it as it once was. I'm saddened to think the Lake Oval lies silent. Never again will 'Up there, Cazza' be heard in the homeland. Maybe if you listen hard enough the cry of 'Car'n, the Bloods' will be heard as the wind whistles through the grandstand's trusses. But even that is asking too much for someone who can't recall the scent his lover used.

I'm sorry you don't understand, but you see, you never grew up in South Melbourne.

PETER SCHWAB

Inside the Bubble

Peter Schwab was born in 1960. He trained as a teacher and at heart remains one. His passion for football developed on a Burwood street with his brother and mates, and he later graduated to Bennettswood and the powerful Hawthorn teams of the 1980s. Schwab played in three Hawks premierships (1983, 1986 and 1988) and notched 171 games before moving into other football roles, including coaching (as an assistant at Richmond, and as Hawthorn's senior coach in 2000-04), administration, coach education, umpires manager and AFL match review chairman. He has written for *The Age* and broadcast for ABC radio, and enjoys travel, reading and writing. 'Inside the Bubble' first appeared in *Australian Football Quarterly*, November 2004.

Saturday, 24 July 2004 would have been my daughter Emily's fifteenth birthday. It was also the last time I coached the Hawthorn Football Club. I understand perspective. I try to live it every day, but in a world called AFL football, it is sometimes hard.

The Tuesday before, I was told by Hawthorn that I was no longer required as coach. The message was delivered by representatives of the board—the president, Ian Dicker, who I had come to know over the previous five years; Dermott Brereton, who I first met when he was a precocious talent aged just eighteen; and Jason Dunstall, who arrived at Glenferrie at the start of 1985 as a goal kicker. Brereton and Dunstall are not only playing legends of the club, they were also my premiership teammates.

The dream was over.

When I awoke on that last Saturday morning as Hawthorn coach, I felt how someone feels when the person they love tells them the love will no longer be reciprocated. I'd known the Hawthorn Football Club since I was sixteen, and was then forty-five. In that time, I had always believed in Hawthorn, given my heart and soul to it, even loved it, if you can love something as intangible as a football club. My passion, drive, energy, optimism, enthusiasm and my working life… all collapsed when I was told I wasn't needed any more.

I followed Hawthorn from a young age. I watched with rapture from the top of the Northern Stand with my older brother Ken when the Hawks stormed home to win the 1971 flag. Did I know who coached them that day? Probably not. I probably never gave it a thought. For me—and I'd guess for most young football supporters—the game was not about the coach. It was always the players.

So when did I first notice coaches? It's difficult to know. When I look back to try to remember, I feel I am always clouded by the present. I'd guess that the first coach I knew was Ron Barassi. It was because he did something at half-time of the 1970 Grand Final that made a difference, or so I have come to believe. Did he? Did Barassi make a difference? Only the players who represented Carlton that day have the answer. In my experience as a player, the coach can make a critical difference, but not as often as people might believe. As a coach? I don't know, but I hope I did a little more for some players than attempt to change the outcome of a game.

My first coach in football was a man called Keith Dalgliesh or Mr D as we all referred to him. He became, and remains, a family friend. I was eight when my parents finally allowed me to play in the Bennettswood under-11s. We won the premiership and I played all year on the wing. Can I recall any particular instructions from Mr D? No, but I remember how much I loved going to training and playing and I am sure he encouraged me every step of the way. What was a coach to me when I was young? Someone who took me for training, told me where I was playing, how I was playing and how I played. Did I expect more? No; I just wanted to play.

In 1977, I arrived at Hawthorn. I played in the under-19s and, in the final game of the year, was promoted to the reserves. I have a clear recollection of my first reserves game and the coach—John O'Mahoney, a former Hawthorn player, a stalwart of the club. He was a thin man who spoke in an earnest and urgent manner. He was clear and definite in what he said, even if his words to me after that game seemed at the time to have a certain naïvety about them.

'Peter,' he said after he had looked around the room and found me, 'you've got to keep running in this game. You've got to learn to run and run.'

Run? I thought to myself. Didn't he watch me? Didn't he know I ran? What did he mean I've got to learn to run? But in time I knew he was telling me, in his way, that my chance of playing at the highest level would depend on my ability to run all day. He was telling me I wasn't quick.

David Parkin was my first senior coach. Enthusiasm oozed from his every pore. It was as though every word he spoke was vital, such was the effort he appeared to give when talking to you. I have never forgotten the most memorable piece of advice he gave me: 'Develop quick hands.' I credit that single piece of advice as the major development in my game, advice which, I believe, made me into an AFL player. I was starting to understand that a coach could make a difference.

It was under Allan Jeans that I started to realise what attributes I might need to become a successful coach. Allan will tell you that great players make great coaches, and that dictum is true, but great footballers, like ordinary footballers, respond to some basic principles of people management. Allan had those basics in bundles.

Just moments before I took the field in the second semi-final of 1983 against North Melbourne, on a cold and wet day at Waverley Park, Allan grabbed my arm and led me slightly to one side, away from the group as we milled at the doorway ready to head down the tunnel and onto the ground. He brought me in close, in a conspiratorial way, and I was drawn to lean towards him. He looked me in the eye. I saw the fire in them, felt his strength. He whispered to me in an urgent but measured voice: 'Don't forget son, you're not a real good player, just stick to what you're good at.' Why tell this story? Because he knew me. He knew I'd burn in my soul to show him, to prove to him, how good I was. He had me, I was motivated.

Allan Jeans knew footballers; he knew how to reach each player. He knew what motivated each individual to perform. In my opinion, it was his greatest gift as a coach. His greater gifts were beyond coaching—his human qualities. He cared for you as well, but as a coach, he needed to motivate every player, and he could.

In the end, did I fail as a coach because I couldn't master or grasp Allan's gift? Not necessarily. To me, AFL football is a journey that can be travelled in many ways, but the final destination that every person involved in the game wants to reach is a premiership. As a coach, I am just one of the many who couldn't reach that coveted final destination. Do I feel a failure because I couldn't do it? No, and maybe I can say 'no' without any sense of real loss because I was fortunate to get there as a player. Did I want to get there as a coach? Of course, but in all honesty, more for others. Maybe, in a strange way, that's why I never made it. Ultimately, motivation is always stronger when you want to succeed more for yourself than for someone else.

For me, the journey ended where it started—at Ian Dicker's private residence around his dining room table. A few of the faces had changed and so had the mood. When I first became a coach, I was so excited about getting a chance that I didn't really know, nor was I aware, of the responsibilities and the pressures that came with the dream job. As my father-in-law said when I was first appointed, 'You are like the taxi driver who gets the chance to drive in a Formula One race. If it doesn't work out, you can always go back to driving the taxi.' But I would always know the thrill of having driven in the big league.

At that time, I saw all the possibilities and very few, if any, of the obstacles in my way. I believed in the playing list, thought it was capable of rapid improvement from the previous season. Finals were expected. It was mentioned—but I wasn't fully aware—how much the club needed me to promote it in all areas. Corporate sponsorship, club supporter groups, membership promotions, functions and press conferences to name a selection of the ongoing commitments. I came to realise most of what I had to do wasn't coaching. I was expected to be Hawthorn's public face and I learnt very quickly that as the public face, I needed to be accessible to the media. They knew they had complete and public access to me at least twice a week. What I also learnt was they'd have access every day of the week if they decided to. I knew none of this initially; this was my first time in the job. All of a sudden, I started to wonder when I could do what I had got into this business to do: coach players, run a football team, make them play exciting football, make them winners. In addition to the players, I was responsible for the management of the coaching, fitness, medical, player welfare, statisticians, forward scouting and recruiting staff.

My ideas on football were essential—don't get me wrong—but I knew if I couldn't manage people, handle the media commitments and comment, promote the club, have public speaking ability or sell a vision to the members and supporters, then I wasn't doing the job the club expected of me. In the English Premier League, the head coach is called the manager. I learnt rapidly the same term should apply to the AFL. This is not to complain about the job, but to say how different it was from what I thought before I started. I discovered if I wanted to remain a pure football coach, then I would be called an assistant. By 'pure', I mean dealing only with footballers and teaching football.

For all that, it was in the first two years on the job that I believed I had the biggest impact on the team. That was natural because everything was new. My aim was to create a playing system based around players who could run the ball from the defence to forwards who could mark inside the forward fifty. Ultimately, I tried to create a team of players who would think for themselves, make decisions based on the situation at any given time in a game. I knew it required risk by coach and player, but I also knew it was the best way to achieve my aims. If both players and coach accepted the risk, progress could be swift and decisive. But the flipside was that some players required structure and rules for every facet of the game, and their game; they couldn't handle the responsibility I wanted to give them. In the end, I lost my nerve to proceed with the player-driven game plan and converted to a more structured system. But I left maintaining my view that the philosophy of player initiative based on decision-making is the better way to coach and to play.

In those first two years (2000 and 2001), things didn't always go to plan, but we made the finals in both seasons. In 2000, we won a final and in 2001, we made it to the preliminary final and almost to a Grand Final. We had our problems in 2001. After winning our first eight games of the season—a club record—we won just five more for the home and away season. Still, we recovered our form in the finals. In the week leading up to our semi-final against Port Adelaide in Adelaide, the world was changed by the events of September 11. One of our players, Daniel Chick, lost his brother-in-law in the attack on New York's World Trade Centre. At the MCG the next day, we gathered as a football team in the changing rooms of the southern stand before training, and spoke openly about what had happened. People spoke if they wanted about how they felt. Some could express their dismay, their shock, their sense of the situation, their sympathy for Daniel; some could not find the words, but nodded when others spoke. It remains one of the most special memories of my time as coach. We knew a game of football was not important in the context of September 11, but we also decided that a game of football was a chance to immerse ourselves in something for two hours. We could make sense of a game of football. So we went to Adelaide and, against the odds, beat Port Adelaide with a late surge. It remains the greatest victory and team moment I was involved in as a coach. I can still recall sitting in the players' dug-out with then chief executive officer Michael Brown about an hour after the game and looking out onto the empty ground. I look back on that time and think coaching was worth it—for that moment.

The next week we almost overcame Essendon to make the Grand Final. I remember saying to the players after the game that it was a lost opportunity; that in this business there is no guarantee we would get back to this position the next season. They knew how much hard work it took, even how much luck. Would we have the hunger to go back to the start and try again? Would we have the belief? Those who have not travelled so far think that because you finish so close, it is only natural you will get back to where you were without a problem. This is the beast called expectation. It is a dangerous animal. The media use it as a double-edged sword. Your club uses it as a selling pitch, but the greatest burden is carried by the players and the coach. Time has since shown that the group that got so close could not get back there. We either lost the hunger or the belief. Maybe both.

If I could go back and change one thing in my tenure, it would be to spend more concentrated time on who we recruited. This is not a criticism of our recruiting manager, John Turnbull, but an understanding by me—albeit too late—that the coach must know and approve every player he intends to recruit, regardless of what number in the draft that player is selected. As a coach, I set my own recruiting criteria, but on occasions I allowed players to be selected who didn't fit that criteria. This generally happened late in the draft when the talent was much thinner and the players selected had obvious deficiencies—deficiencies that were going to make it difficult for them to play at the elite level. I recall a meeting with Liverpool Football Club assistant manager Phil Thompson when I visited England on a personally funded education tour at the end of 2002. I asked Thompson how Liverpool dealt with players who had skill deficiencies. He looked at me with total bemusement then said rather bluntly: 'They don't get here.' Because of our participation levels, we must accept that a percentage of the players coming into our elite system lack all the talent that is required to play AFL football. As a result, we cannot be as selective as they are in English soccer, but we must still adhere to criteria that will lessen our error rate when it comes to recruiting.

In the end, the playing list of 2004 failed—as did the whole club. So what went wrong and who was ultimately to blame? Did I make an error in judgement about the player list? I felt at the end of 2003—when we stormed home and won nine games out of twelve and easily could have beaten both the eventual premier Brisbane and the minor premier Port Adelaide to make it eleven wins from those twelve games—that we should add experience to our list, go after a top-four position and have a realistic challenge over the next two seasons before we would need to rebuild. I knew the core group was ageing and had injury concerns, but I was confident we could hold together for two more seasons. We made the decision to add experience during the trading period and secured Trent Croad back from Fremantle, Simon Beaumont from Carlton and Danny Jacobs from Essendon. In addition, we were reasonably conservative in our training approach with some of our older and bigger players because of their history of injury. It was a calculated gamble that failed. We never balanced up after our great first-up win against Melbourne.

In addition, we lurched from one off-field problem to another. We drew the heat of the media for those issues and had the double-edged sword of losing matches with it. As coach, I was beginning to feel all was combining to run our football club onto the rocks and sink us. The media focus on off-field issues is a new beast to overcome. I can best sum up my personal views on this phenomenon by using the words of someone else. An article about sport in the United States stated: 'Sports, having somehow become the medium through which Americans derive their strongest sense of community, has become the stage where all the great moral issues have to be played out, often rough and ugly, right alongside the games.' I truly feel that this is what happened to the Hawthorn Football Club in 2004. As the leader, I felt enormous pressure. Did the club support me? I'd have to say not as much as I needed. I confided my concerns internally to my assistant coach, George Stone. Outside the club, I sought advice from my wife Jenny, my close friend and team manager Bill Tyson, and a mentor in George Norris. Jenny, who has been with me since I started with Hawthorn in 1977, wisely suggested I should spend more time talking with the players. It was a critical piece of advice I accepted and took on board. It led me to schedule weekly meetings with players in an attempt to gain a better understanding of 'where they were at' in their thinking and for them to know my true view of their personal situation.

Looking back on 2004, I felt we might have been able to resurrect our season if we had won two close games. I believe it would have changed the group's mindset and maybe got the media to focus elsewhere for a time. We lost to Richmond by one point in round six and to Sydney by one point in round nine. The game against Sydney was the big one. We had come off a good win against Fremantle in Launceston and if we had backed up and won two in a row, we would have gained some momentum and confidence. Alas, we did not, and we lurched to the 74-point Essendon debacle in round 11. Our season was lost.

Did I feel I was losing the players while all this was happening? No, but only the players themselves can answer that question. I know winning is the only answer in this game and I sensed the distance between the decision-makers and myself was widening. Any tacit support I felt was based purely around 'a contract for 2005'.

The end came swiftly. Was I caught by surprise? To a degree. Maybe the timing surprised me, but as Allan Jeans has always said: 'There are two types of coaches: those who get sacked and those who will get sacked.' Coaches are not pessimistic, just realistic. I went into coaching knowing that only continued success would allow me retain my position. Only a few, too few, reach that final destination.

I accept that a season like 2004 cost me the dream job, but I was true to myself and to the players and people I worked with. There were some circumstances we could never have planned for, and some we could have controlled better. I left knowing I did my best, and that is all I need to know.

STEPHEN ALOMES

Poachers, Gamekeepers and Coaches

Stephen Alomes played footy at lower levels from Huonville to Oatlands, Canberra to Young, and in the Japanese mountains; he has also umpired in Canberra and Helsinki. During the 'big trip' he enjoyed kick-to-kick on London's Muswell Hill green. He is an Adjunct Professor in RMIT's Globalism Research Centre and author/editor of ten books on nationalism, Australian studies, expatriates in the arts, popular culture and Australian comparisons with France and Japan. He paints portraits of footy people and other figures, from Dermott Brereton to Patrick White. He writes on footyalmanac.com.au and worldfootynews.com, and his book on footy's stories, footy as performance and our changing game, *Australian Football: The People's Game 1958-2058* is available from wallawallapress.com. This essay is a revised version of a paper first published in *Bulletin of Sport and Culture*, September 2010.

When I played amateur reserves football in Hobart and Canberra in the 1970s, the game was often scrambly. That was mainly due to muddy grounds and cricket pitch areas, and our poor kicking skills. The play-on skills, precise kicking and team plays that you see today in local football, and in snatches at AFL matches, were not to be found. Flat punts, torps off the side of the boot, wrong foot kicks which didn't go far were all common. It was also less physical footy, except when lighter Uni players got flattened by a Claremont 'tank' who trained on hard work, and maybe the gym and beer. Today it is different. Fitter and more skilled players produce classy football at local levels. Perhaps many grounds have better drainage as well.

Football has changed, often for the better though not always. In today's AFL you will see moments of great skill, as handballs and short passes take the ball from the defensive goal square to a kick for goal in under thirty seconds. However, much of the time, half the ground is empty as the defensive team seeks to block opponents from scoring, and the attackers try to stop the other team moving the ball out of defence. In the 2010 replay grand final between Collingwood and St Kilda I took photos in the third quarter in which all the players, bar two, were inside one of the fifty-metre lines; most were in one half of that semi-circle. At other times, as you can see on the crowded shots on TV screens, players cluster around a 'stoppage' anywhere on the ground. The usual result is a secondary or tertiary ball-up, unless a 'brave' umpire plucks a free kick out of a stacks-on-the-mill situation—either in the back for falling on the player with the ball, or holding the ball in, against the ball-holder. He is not the 'ball carrier' for, in what Robert Walls has called a 'rolling scrum' and others term a rugby 'maul', the ball sometimes moves over thirty metres without one effective kick or handpass.

At its worst the situation has become so dire that commentators chorus, 'It's starting to look like Auskick'. This is a comparison with half-time grid games, when a fleet of men and women in lab coats, all carrying flags, white poles, advertising banners and small digital cameras invade the ground. Close on their heels come an excited flood of youngsters, and soon they are all 'followers'—not rucks or rovers but followers of the ball up and down the small marked oval. At times, ten out of twelve players gather at one end. At other times, during a ball-up, up to seven boys and girls gather around two nominated ruck contestants. There is a difference, however. Auskickers chase the ball to try to get a kick for themselves; the senior AFL players are instead, in the jargon which they have been taught to mouth, 'playing to our structures' and 'following team rules'. They are actors, following the director's script—or puppets dancing to the puppet-master's tune.

The game has changed since the 1960s and 1970s. Scrambly play was common in top leagues on wet days, and intensified when teams desperately defended a lead during the last quarter. One result was the kicking out of bounds 'on the full' free kick rule in 1969, soon followed by the centre diamond (which became a square). Generally, however, footy remained a position game with a play-on aspect. You could confidently predict match-ups, as Alf Brown did in his Friday Melbourne *Herald* previews. Brian Dixon would be selected on the wing for Melbourne and, in his later years, was opposed by Dick Clay, the tall wingman for Richmond. Now, the positions schematically presented on an oval graphic in the papers and the *AFL Football Record* don't mean much. There are still forwards who play more forward, backs who play more back, and midfielders who go everywhere. But now, the wandering 'mids' are not just the rucks and rovers and the centreman—often they include the half-forwards and half-backs. When the 'forward press' or its predecessor the 'flood' is on, they use their full aerobic capacity to run and block up the other end of the ground.

The change has come about because of new training methods. In player profiles, AFL players are asked whether they prefer weights or running and the new game is based on both. Whereas once top league clubs had little gym equipment, aside from a few medicine balls, now they look like industrial scale torture chambers. One photo showed Collingwood cult star Dale 'Daisy' Thomas training in a gym with a heavy chain, worn as a weight necklace, around his neck, chest and shoulders. The results are obvious. The weights produce a new level of tackling which 'stops' players in ways unknown in the past. Running training produces the aerobic capacity to both run to the other end of the ground to block the opposition and to run forward creating goals in mad, exciting but previously rehearsed manoeuvres or 'plays'. Sports science now dominates footy, from blood tests, skinfolds and GPS measures, to hyperbaric chambers and blood products injections to treat hamstring injuries. As Collingwood coach, Mick Malthouse viewed his sports science guru David Buttifant as more important than his coaching assistants, and perhaps even some of his best players.

The coaches and the analysts (the chess players, would-be generals, aficionados of American football, and business strategists in the crowd) discern new strategies and tactics. They see this as advancing the game as it borrows roles, as well as jargon ('playmaker', 'sweeper', 'quarterback')—appropriately and cringingly *in*appropriately—from other sports. First a world of 'talls and smalls', it is now one of 'inside and outside' players. While even Ross Lyon and Mick Malthouse have creative as well as defensive moments, simpler people like me, and most footy followers, see something different. They see the result as what I call 'stoppageball' or 'tackleball', or often just a damn scrambly mess. Whatever it is, except on muddy days and in desperate last quarters, it does not seem like footy.

Optimists rightly point to some skill improvements, including the dribbled goal—pioneered earlier by the Macedonian Marvel, Collingwood's Peter Daicos—and elaborate midfield plays which move the ball faster than ever, often leading to a goal. Wrongly, they assume that creative coaches will sort it all out, checkmating the negative, 'stopping' ploys of a Paul Roos or Ross Lyon, or the boundary-line defensive game of Mick Malthouse. While teams have sometimes managed to cut through the forward press (the Roman box, the flood) with accurate long-passing, the game still has long periods of stoppageball and tackleball and there's no question that defence is the major focus. I don't see the trend as 'good for football'.

We should not blame the AFL's rules committee, the formal gamekeepers of footy. It has implemented changes to curb stoppageball—reduced wrestling at boundary ruck contests and ball-ups around the ground to speed up play and ideally produce more clearances. The AFL commission has not yet approved a cap on interchange totals, which have increased from 92 per team in 2009 to an average of 131 in 2012. A cap of around eighty interchanges per team would reduce the aerobic capacity which allows players to lock down the opposition forward line, not just in the first quarter (as in local football) but throughout the game. The rules committee is simply responding to the coaches' latest stratagems, coaches whose job description is not to orchestrate good and attractive football. To keep their jobs they need to win, at all costs, including 'winning ugly'.

The game has evolved significantly during the last decade, the second decade of fully professional AFL football. During the 2009 season, although slightly redeemed by the brilliance of Nick Riewoldt, Lenny Hayes and the irritatingly effective small forward, Stephen Milne, St Kilda kept its opponents to an average of 64 points. New jargon words described the social approach as well as the game-plan: the Saints players lived in 'a bubble', separate from their fans and their aim was to put a 'Lyon cage' or a 'blanket' over the opposition, particularly through zones and 'frontal pressure'. In the 2009 Grand Final, which Geelong won by resorting to the second verse of its club song, 'to stand up and fight', St Kilda laid 118 tackles, forcing Geelong to respond with 96—that is almost two tackles a minute—tackleball. Over a hundred hit outs for the day indicated a game which was also becoming 'umpireball', with new game-plans giving umpires more opportunity to exercise their skills. But as Ross Lyon's St Kilda found in two losing and one drawn Grand Final, a Somme-like game of winning ten yards at a time could fail; a game of inches could be lost as well as won by inches. While some fans love tackles and biffo and others celebrate close matches as 'enthralling contests' (the 2006 and 2010-12 AFL grand finals) they are not necessarily good football matches.

Similar tendencies are now ubiquitous in other sports: the defensive away game seeking a nil-all draw after a home win in European soccer, and the 2012 Bledisloe Cup rugby matches in which Australia scored no tries, only field goals and penalties. England's 2003 rugby World Cup victory was the ultimate, focusing its scoring plans not on tries, the original aim of the game in which you run with the ball, but on field goals kicked by Jonny Wilkinson.

In footy, statisticians measured the change. Dr Ken Norton's research for the AFL demonstrated that average player speed had increased from 6.46 to 7.48 km/h between 2006 and 2010. It was made possible by interchanges increasing from 46 to 116. An emerging correlation was increased numbers of games missed due to injury. As Adrian Anderson said while AFL Football Operations Manager, 'players are fresher and travelling at higher speeds, and the medical advice is telling us that there is an increased risk of injury from high-intensity collisions if we let the speed of the game continue increasing unchecked'.

In recent years, several 'change-agents' have moved from being poachers—coaches who bend the rules to maximise the team's advantage—to gamekeepers, or at least critics of the new forms of the game. Mick Malthouse and Leigh Matthews both recognise that the game is now harder and more physical. 'I don't care what some former players say, the intensity of the game has lifted dramatically,' Malthouse has said. 'There are more tackles than ever before, bodies are bigger and players are faster, leading to greater impacts'. Leigh Matthews, who would know, remarked that although 'the game was once dirtier it was now much tougher'.

Ted Hopkins, premiership goaling Carlton small forward, concrete poet and statistical guru, helped change the game through the resources collated by Champion Data. In 2010 he reflected in the *AFL Record* on the outcome by using the term 'Ugby', which he described as 'a style of play which looks more like a combination of rugby and ugly'. According to Hopkins, Ugby's features include 'all in mauling-scrimmages, with, at times, nearly all players positioned on the defensive side of the ball, too much backward ball movement, more handpasses than kicks, gang tackling, slam tackles, violent hit-ups and regular injuries. To boot, Ugby footy generally produces low-scoring affairs.' The change is also visually disfiguring. While at the match I can look over a half-empty MCG during a Grand Final, television screens also present a changing image. Leigh Matthews remarked recently that whereas in the 1981 Grand Final there were often ten players in most camera shots, now there could be over twenty.

Footy has nearly always been the most creative of field sports and invasion games. Lacking an offside and a send-off rule, its large playing spaces and the distance covered by a kicked football ensure a high-scoring game, unlike most soccer matches. Footy's interesting midfield game differs from its absence in basketball. Today, given hours of skills training, the perfect surfaces and even drier grounds in the era of global warming, it should be a classier game. Already a leader in sport's visual aesthetic, it should be an even better spectacle. Often it is—but it's not often enough. Sometimes, when I watch Aberfeldie play in the Essendon league at Clifton Park, an oval among the gum trees, I see that level of skill. However, whether at the SCG, the MCG, Kardinia Park or another AFL ground, I usually see only *moments* of brilliant skill, like the glint of gold specks in a game, which only glitters some of the time. Unless the gamekeepers can save us from those generals in the coaches' boxes—the poachers—or unless one coach can neutralise defensive play, we may all be waiting a long while.

MANNING CLARK

An Abiding Magic

Manning Clark AC (1915–1991) was the author of the best-known general history of Australia. His six-volume *A History of Australia* was a project of unprecedented ambition and scope, published between 1962 and 1987 and performed as a musical for Australia's Bicentennial (with a script by Don Watson, whose work also appears in this volume). A lifelong Carlton supporter, Clark attended Melbourne and Oxford universities and taught history at Geelong Grammar School before returning to study and embarking on a distinguished academic career at Melbourne University and the Australian National University. His last works, written with characteristic eloquence, were the autobiographical *The Puzzles of Childhood* (1989), *The Quest for Grace* (1990) and *A Historian's Apprenticeship* (1992). 'An Abiding Magic' first appeared in the *Times on Sunday*, 27 September 1987.

W hen I was young, I was told many things about life.

One was that some things were from eternity and would not change. One variation on that piece of wisdom was the Australian saying, 'Things are still the same as ever out on the Never Never.' Now, in the years of the sere and yellow leaf, I know that a Grand Final in Melbourne is not one of those things that never change.

The Grand Final has survived many threats to its existence. It has survived the threat from the advertisers—the ones who had the effrontery to attempt to degrade our one day of the year to a People's Day of Thanks for Foster's Lager. It has survived the threat from the moneychangers, those men who used the thirty pieces of silver to persuade some of our Wagnerian godlings to betray both club and local loyalty. It has survived the attempt to downgrade the game into a contest in 'keepings-off' by excessive use of handball. It has survived the disappearance of the place kick and the drop kick.

Grand Final day still has its magic, its sources of enchantment and delight. After taking communion once again at one of the few altar rails left to us in Australia—a sporting occasion attended by a huge crowd—at Waverley on 12 September 1987, when Carlton came back from the dead as it were, and defeated Hawthorn, I left the ground elated. It seemed to me that in such a moment of euphoria, in such a moment of charity and goodwill towards all human beings, it was even possible to forgive the smugness and complacency of the patricians of Yarraside, those men and women who look as though there will be reserved seats for them in the Members' Stand at the Melbourne Cricket Ground on the Resurrection morning.

So I think of Grand Final day as one of the gifts of the people of Melbourne to all of us in Australia. I know all those 'wintry sneers' that have been directed against the devotees of the cult by the self-appointed improvers of humanity. I know that we, the worshippers, are chastised for our wanton indulgence. We are all, it is said, timidly perverts enjoying the subterranean satisfactions of watching strong men do what we want to do, namely inflict pain on other human beings. I know we, the worshippers, are accused of indulging in petty pleasures and ignoring the great problems of life. I know we, the worshippers, are said by our accusers to be so depraved and corrupted by spectator sport that we would stay on at the Melbourne Cricket Ground till after the final siren even if we were told before half-time that a foreign power had invaded Australia, or that Christ was on trial again in the Supreme Court of Victoria. It is perhaps the beginning of wisdom to draw up a list of the things in life which one cannot stop doing.

So the question is: Why a game with a leather ball should arouse such powerful passions? There are the extraneous attractions. There are the elements of chance, the unpredictable bounce of the ball, the direction of the wind, the fickle Melbourne weather in springtime. There is that great roar of the crowd heralding such moments, the wild, desperate shout of 'the bounce!'; the anguish and the agony of 'the wind's changing!' or the never-ending question before the game starts: What if it starts to rain?

What if the great city of Melbourne becomes sodden, not with rectitude but with water from the skies? What then! How, for example, will that affect Justin Madden or Dermott Brereton?

There is the skill of the players. There are the ones like Craig Bradley or Warwick Capper who can defy the laws of gravity like some graceful bird held aloft by an upward flow of air. There is the magic of David Rhys-Jones, who looks as though he is walking when he is breaking further and further away from his opponent. There is a Stephen Silvagni dash from the back line, which dwarfs even the heroism of the men who took part in the Charge of the Light Brigade. There is a Stephen Kernahan mark, followed, one hopes, by one of his now famous drop punts that bisects the tall timber and can make even an aged professor, a doubter about everything, believe for one moment that if life brings such pleasures there must be some sort of meaning somewhere, or maybe such pleasures are so intense that for a moment one stops the search for a meaning.

I know there are things I could do without. I liked it more when an attendant opened the iron picket gate and the crowd roared louder and louder, 'Here comes Carlton!' But some changes have been very pleasing to those who believe as I do that we are Australians, we know no other country. At least we are now not asked, before the game, to sing of the glories of someone living thousands and thousands of miles away, but about Australia.

Happily the roar of the crowd still drowns out the last words of the anthem. Happily, despite the decline and fall of the old Outer, the crowd still rises to its feet and yells, 'Holding the ball!' or 'Holding the man!' when the scores are close and a man neatly dressed in white shirt and shorts has to tell those giants his decision.

It is like going to a play about the wilder passions of the human heart, or hearing the coda of the last movement of Sibelius's 'Fifth Symphony'. There is at least a chance we can learn a little about what goes on in the human heart. We can also know the ecstasy of victory or the despair of defeat. We Australians know a lot about failure.

PAUL KELLY

Sic Transit Gloria Mundi [1]

Paul Kelly was born in 1955 and grew up in South Australia. A Demons supporter, he is one of Australia's most successful and influential singer-songwriters, having recorded more than twenty albums and several film soundtracks in a career spanning more than thirty years. He was inducted into the ARIA Hall of Fame in 1997. Kelly's memoir *How To Make Gravy*, published by Penguin in 2010, was accompanied by a CD box set of live recordings and an audio book with readings from actors Cate Blanchett, Russell Crowe, Hugh Jackman, Judy Davis and Ben Mendelsohn. A feature-length documentary about his life and music, *Paul Kelly— Stories of Me,* premiered in 2012. This piece first appeared in Melbourne's *The Herald* in 1986.

S ometimes there are sights seen in mild benevolent sunshine that chill a man right through; everyday events become charged, ever so briefly, with tragedy. It may take only a few seconds, be over before the mind has grasped it and pass largely unnoticed by those present.

Around you the amiable crowd still murmurs, upon you the warm sun still pours and before you, before your disbelieving eyes, the ball has been taken upfield and the rhythm of the game restored. No one has seen. Nothing remarkable appears to have happened, only what normally happens in a game of football, the usual knots and ribbons.

You look around you, searching the faces of the crowd for signs of horror, for a sense of high drama taking place, and all they show is a reflection of the present desultory play—two middle order teams playing

---

1   *Sic Transit Gloria Mundi* is Latin for 'Thus passes the glory of the world'.

each other in warm sunshine on a Saturday afternoon at the MCG.

But you saw, you saw, you saw.

Picture this—Robbie Flower has received the ball just ahead of half-forward, only fifty metres from goal. He is totally in the clear. For some inexplicable reason he hesitates. Perhaps his options are too many. He could shoot for goal straight away, he could easily sidestep the opponents charging at him and then shoot, or he could pass to a team mate. The Flower repertoire is extensive. He lingers, seeming to think of all three things.

Then the unbelievable, the unthinkable happens.

Robbie Flower has always appeared to be playing in slow motion. He does this by slowing down time. He makes the players around him look even slower. This is his magic. Everything he does is seen so clearly because he gives you time to see it. He slows down the whole world.

But today something has gone wrong, terribly wrong with the magic. Sure, Flower has slowed himself down, hovering like a dragonfly in the sunshine, but the rest of the world is still hurtling at the same speed. Two North Melbourne players catch him, one from the side, one from the front, as Flower, suddenly human, tries to handpass at the last minute. Down he goes in a heap, collared, dumped, the humiliation total: the umpire's decision—holding the ball.

Now every champion player gets clobbered at one time or another. They are often subject to close checking and any player can be at the wrong end of a hospital handpass. But I had never seen Flower start in the clear and end in a tangle. Usually it was the reverse—conjured from the pack into space and the ball unerringly delivered to a red and blue jumper further downfield.

It was a weird, sickening feeling watching Flower become inevitable meat in a football sandwich—an other-worldly sensation, like watching rain fall upwards.

Flower, aged thirty, picked himself up. He dusted himself down and trotted nonchalantly back to his position. The sudden rent on reality closed over as quickly as it had appeared. The fabric of the afternoon remained unchanged—the basking crowd, the intermittent oohs and aahs at individual displays of skill and brutality or sudden lightning patterns of team play. Flower did many good things that day, directing traffic along his wing in statesmanlike fashion.

But somewhere, up in the stands, a man thought of time and age and death and diminishment while, on the fence, two young boys in red and blue scarves and beanies were cheering younger, fresher-faced heroes.

BARRY DICKINS

$\sim\!\sim\!\sim\!\sim\!\sim\!\sim$

Royboys

Barry Dickins was born in the Melbourne suburb of Reservoir in 1949. He is a prolific playwright, novelist, artist, columnist and teacher. He has also written short stories, biography and other non-fiction, and children's books. In 1995 Barry Dickins' play *Remember Ronald Ryan* won the 1995 Victoria Premier's Literary Award. In 2009, he released his powerful memoir *Unparalleled Sorrow*, which chronicles his writing and working career and his battle with depression. Recent books include *Barry and the Fairies of Dickins Street* (2012) and *Lessons in Humility: 40 Years of Teaching* (2013). He has won a Prime Minister's Medal for Literature and the International Amnesty Prize for Peace through Art. This is an extract from *Royboys*, which opened in Melbourne in March 1987.

Barry Dickins wrote of *Royboys*: 'This is a play for life-lovers... It's about the need for all of us to have a bit of victory in this iron world.' In *Royboys*, the Fitzroy Football Club is bought by Dr Rupert Myxomatosis, a psychiatrist and business tycoon who plans to transfer it to Tokyo and re-name it Fitzsaki. *Royboys*, through its central characters Ray and Berryl Noble—sixty-year-old alcoholic Fitzroy fanatics—yearns for the old Australia and bemoans the world of takeovers, commercialisation and media manipulation. According to Dickins, 'Although *Royboys* is about the fate of the Fitzroy Football Club, it is also about the fate of Australia, which, if it were a club, would be out of the finals forever.'

[A completely empty stage. RAY and BERRYL stand closely together, centre downstage. A chill and very mournful wind blows, then ceases. This duologue is acted in a dead real manner; quietly, intensely. On the bottle heap, the UMPY mimes goals, points, throw-ins, ball-ups, free kicks. A wonderful

barbecue smoke floats across the stage. It is the mid-winter footy season. Ghostly crowds are heard. The lighting is low grey/blue]

RAY: Well?

BERRYL: Whattaya mean, 'Well?' Well what, Ray? What?

[Faintly, the siren wails]

RAY: Go, Lions!

BERRYL: It's all going, isn't it?

RAY: What? The world?

BERRYL: Yep.

RAY: Our little world.

BERRYL: One big home-and-away-forever game. One left. Let's win it!

RAY: They could leave us something. The memory of a pie.

BERRYL: The masters wouldn't give you the steam of their urine.

RAY: God, I've had a uterus of a day.

BERRYL: Bernie's not in this week. Gary Pert's out too.

RAY: What's wrong with him? Head? Leg? Gut removed? Poor Gaz!

BERRYL: I don't know what we're gunna do about it.

RAY: The voice of the people is the voice of God.

BERRYL: Gary Pert is God.

RAY: I've always thought so.

BERRYL: I dreamt about El Salvador last night.

RAY: We beat them, didn't we? Or did they play Collingwood?

BERRYL: The voice of El Salvador is the voice of the Royboys.

RAY: Go, El Salvador. Go, Dipierdomenico. No, he's not in the side, is he?

BERRYL: I don't know what we can do about it.

RAY: The bosses have stolen the old world. Our world has gone. For good.

BERRYL: The voice of the boss is the voice of destruction.

RAY: Everyone's got Sandy Blight. Even Malcolm Blight.

BERRYL: There's no one to look up to. No-one to admire.

RAY: What can we do about it?

BERRYL: The little thermoses, the families as small as snails, the naked foot running through the paddock, love gets the tap-down.

RAY: To whom are we speaking? *To whom are we kicking God's ball?*

BERRYL: The vital questions, the vital answers.

RAY: Why do we run away from trouble? Do we get to beat the blues? We cry out for them to be brave. Why not be brave as well?

BERRYL: The worst umpire in the League is Ronald Reagan.

RAY: He wouldn't know a scoreboard from Star Wars.

BERRYL: It's time the world got a free kick.

RAY: Time for Gorbachev to go up in the ruck against Reagan.

BERRYL: Go, Gorbachev!

RAY: Put in the boot.

BERRYL: Sink the slipper.

RAY: Give 'em nuthin'.

BERRYL: Talk to each other.

RAY: Freedom from Hunger.

BERRYL: Save Chile.

RAY: Save South Africa.

BERRYL: Put a whale on the interchange bench.

RAY: Save the rainforests.

BERRYL: Go, Lions! Go, Roys! Go, Third World!

RAY: Go, Herman Hesse! Go, Jim Jess!

BERRYL: Go, Phar Lap! Go, Don Bradman! Send John Sellout to Brisbane.

RAY: Go, Cat! Put the cat on the ball.

BERRYL: Go, Snappy Tom! Go the people of Chile. Go tell it on the mountain.

RAY: Go, Peter, Paul and Mary!

BERRYL: Go with what you've got. Give the masters heaps. Beat the bastards.

RAY: Go, black land rights! Go, white land rights! Go,

Collingwood land rights.

BERRYL: Can you smell the dripping on the ball? Can you smell the rain?

RAY: The voice of the rain is the voice of the people.

BERRYL: Send the rain to Brisbane.

[RAY looks at her]

RAY: That's a bit of a curly one, love.

BERRYL: You always wanted a win. Well, you can win if you want to win.

RAY: Go, Winfield in the green packet!

BERRYL: Go, Extra Mild!

RAY: Go in for the ball. The ball of life. Smell it. Know it. Do it. Think of Gabbo.

BERRYL: Go, Gabbo!

RAY: Gabbo's run.

BERRYL: Ray Gabelich's now driving bickie trucks. I seen him the other night in Hoddle Street.

RAY: Go, Hoddle Street! Go, the big left-hand turn into Victoria Street!

BERRYL: Go, the ding-ding-ding tram up the Eye and Ear Hospital where blind, deaf and dumb people are the voice of God and barrack for a win over blind, deaf and dumbness.

RAY: Go, the big victory over blind, deaf and dumbness!

BERRYL: Go, the big win over any sort of sores and sickness!

RAY: Go, the big recovery from spina bifida!

BERRYL: Go, the speedy recovery from nerve deafness, cholera and cervical cancer!

RAY: God, I've had a uterus of a day.

BERRYL: Go, Royboys, go Bernie Quinlan, go, Micky Conlan!

RAY: Go to church and say you've never been sorry in your life.

BERRYL: Get up off your knees and jump the fence.

RAY: Stop getting beat.

BERRYL: Go Siren!

RAY: Go Siren!

BERRYL: Go Siren!

RAY: Go Siren!

BERRYL: Go Siren!

RAY: Go Siren!

[There is a deafening footy siren, mixed with thousands of screaming, cheerful people. It dissipates. RAY and BERRYL shuffle through beer cans as they head offstage]

       Not a bad sort of a win.

BERRYL: Who we up against next week?

RAY: I thought little Dwyer did well today.

BERRYL: Dwarfie Dwyer.

RAY: Oh, let's get in this pub, out of the rain, eh?

BERRYL: I love you, Dad.

RAY: Go, Mum Noble! Give 'em nuthin'. Eh, two pots thanks
       pal.

[The UMPY hands them a glass of ale each. Blackout. Pub atmosphere, then silence]